D1617201

NGOs and the United Nations

NGOs and the United Nations

Institutionalization, Professionalization and Adaptation

Kerstin Martens

First published in 2005 by
PALGRAVE MACMILLAN
Houndmills, Basingstoke, Hampshire RG21 6XS and
175 Fifth Avenue, New York, N.Y. 10010
Companies and representatives throughout the world.

PALGRAVE MACMILLAN is the global academic imprint of the Palgrave
Macmillan division of St. Martin's Press, LLC and of Palgrave Macmillan Ltd.
Macmillan® is a registered trademark in the United States, United Kingdom
and other countries. Palgrave is a registered trademark in the European
Union and other countries.

ISBN-13: 978–1–4039–9284–0 hardback
ISBN-10: 1–4039–9284–3 hardback

This book is printed on paper suitable for recycling and made from fully
managed and sustained forest sources.

A catalogue record for this book is available from the British Library.

Library of Congress Cataloging-in-Publication Data

Martens, Kerstin.
    NGOs and the United Nations : institutionalization,
    professionalization, and adaptation / Kerstin Martens.
        p. cm.
    Includes bibliographical references and index.
    ISBN 1–4039–9284–3 (cloth)
        1. Non-governmental organizations. 2. United Nations. I. Title:
    Non-governmental organizations and the United Nations. II. Title.

JZ4841.M37 2005
361.7'7—dc22   2005049201

10   9   8   7   6   5   4   3   2   1
14 13 12 11 10 09 08 07 06 05

Printed and bound in Great Britain by
Antony Rowe Ltd, Chippenham and Eastbourne

Contents

List of Tables   viii

List of Figures   ix

List of Abbreviations   x

Preface   xii

Foreword   xiv

1 NGOs, International Relations
   and the UN System – Introductory Observations   1
      NGO participation in global affairs   2
      Theoretical approaches to NGO–IGO relations   5
      Contributions of this study   7
      Organization of the book   10

2 NGO Institutionalization into
   the UN System – Theoretical Framework   12
      Current theoretical approaches to NGO–IGO relations   12
      Transnational relations   13
      Transsocietal approaches   15
      NGOs in the UN System   16
      NGO activities in the UN system   17
      Institutionalizing NGO–UN relations   20
      Categories of internationally operating NGOs   25
      Case selection   33
      Summary   43

3 Activities in the UN Context – Changing Patterns
   of Interaction   45
      NGO activities with the UN and new opportunities
      for interaction   45
      Policy initiating activities   46
      Policy developing processes   49
      Policy implementing practices   52

Exploring individual cases of NGOs and their activities
with the UN   54
  Amnesty International: shifting priorities in its UN activities   55
  FIDH: deepening established areas of activity   69
  CARE International: broadening the spectrum of interaction   73
  Oxfam International: acting individualistically with the UN   79
  Other NGOs   85
Summary   90

4 **Representation and Representatives to
   the UN – Institutionalization as an Internal Factor**   95
   General observations about NGO representation to the UN   95
     The image of NGOs at the UN in the past   96
     NGO representation at the UN today   96
     NGO representatives at the UN in total   98
   Exploring individual cases of NGO representation to the UN 99
     Amnesty International: mobilizing resources for its UN
       representation   99
     FIDH: using limited resources to its advantage   107
     CARE International: increasing investment in its UN
       representation   111
     Oxfam International: only few resources mobilized   115
     Other NGOs   118
   Summary   121

5 **Accreditation to the UN through Rules and
   Regulations – Institutionalization as an External Demand** 125
   General observations on consultative status of
     NGOs at the UN   125
     Previous resolutions on NGO–UN relations and current
       legal foundations   126
     NGOs and the consultative status today   128
     Selection process of NGOs   130
     Withdrawal of consultative status as a threat   132
     Consultative status – two sides of the same coin?   133
   Single cases and their consultative status at
     the UN under examination   135
     Amnesty International: consultative status as an
       entrance key   135
     FIDH: dependence on formal status as mouthpiece   138

CARE International: consultative status as lowering
  bureaucratic hurdles   144
Oxfam International: little significance of consultative
  status   146
Other NGOs   148
Summary   151

6 NGOs in the UN System and Beyond – Final Remarks   **155**
Conceptualization and theoretical frame   155
Adjustments in NGO patterns of activity with the UN   157
NGO representation and representatives   158
Rules and regulations for NGO accreditation at
  the UN level   160
Contribution of this study and future prospects   162

Notes   165
References   174
Index   195

List of Tables

1.1 Types of international organizations   10
2.1 Types of NGO activities in cooperation with the UN   19
3.1 Patterns of interaction between NGOs and the UN   91
4.1 Recruitment factors today   123
5.1 Status-specific privileges   128
5.2 Number of NGOs with consultative status   129
5.3 NGOs and their consultative status   152
5.4 Perceived value of consultative status today   154

List of Figures

1.1 NGO institutionalization in the UN system – simplified
    model   8
2.1 NGO institutionalization in the UN system – expanded
    model   18
2.2 NGOs by function and composition   34
4.1 Steps of representation at the UN   122
6.1 NGO institutionalization in the UN System – evaluated
    model   161

List of Abbreviations

AAA	Action Aid Alliance
AA UK	Action Aid United Kingdom
AI	Amnesty International
CARE	Cooperative for Assistance and Relief Everywhere
CAT	Committee Against Torture
CCPR	Human Rights Committee
CERD	Committee on the Elimination of Racial Discrimination
DESA	NGO Section of the Department of Economic and Social Affairs
DHA	Department of Humanitarian Affairs
DPI	Department of Public Information
ECOSOC	Economic and Social Council
FAO	Food and Agriculture Organization
FIDH	Fédération Internationale des Droits de l'Homme
GONGO	Government-organized Non-governmental Organization
HCHR	High Commissioner for Human Rights
HRIC	Human Rights in China
HRW	Human Rights Watch
IASC	Inter-Agency Standing Committee
IBRD	International Bank for Reconstruction and Development
ICC	International Criminal Court
ICRC	International Committee of the Red Cross
ICVA	International Council of Voluntary Associations
IFTDH	International Federation Terres des Hommes
IGO	Intergovernmental Organization
ILHR	International League for Human Rights
ILO	International Labour Organization
ISCA	International Save the Children Alliance
MSF	Médecins sans Frontières (Doctors without Borders)
NATO	North Atlantic Treaty Organization
NGLS	Non-Governmental Liaison Service
NGO	Non-governmental Organization
OAS	Organization of American States
OCHA	Office for the Coordination of Humanitarian Affairs
OSCE	Organization for Security and Cooperation in Europe
Oxfam	Oxford Committee for Famine Relief

Oxfam GB	Oxfam Great Britain
SCHR	Steering Committee for Humanitarian Response
UIA	Union of International Associations
UN	United Nations
UNDP	United Nations Development Programme
UNESCO	United Nations Educational, Scientific and Cultural Organization
UNFPA	United Nations Fund for Population Activities
UNHCR	United Nations High Commissioner for Refugees
UNICEF	United Nations Children's Fund
UNRWA	United Nations Relief and Work Agency
WFP	World Food Programme
WGSC	Working Group on the Security Council
WHO	World Health Organization
WTUC	World Trade Union Congress

Preface

There are many people and institutions I wish to thank for their help and support. I have benefited tremendously from my time as a researcher at the European University Institute (EUI) in Florence. Throughout those years, the institute has been an inspiring source; its people, the location and the openness of its academic staff made it a most enjoyable intellectual journey.

My greatest thanks go to Thomas Risse. His continuous encouragement and enthusiasm for my project has not only strengthened my will to pursue it, but also provided me with the necessary support whenever needed. Moreover, special thanks go to Donatella della Porta, Philip Alston and Volker Rittberger, whose challenging questions helped me to strengthen my argument. I am also indebted to Jean-Mary Dupuy and Philippe Schmitter for exchange of ideas and comments at different stages of the project. Moreover, the financial support of the EUI and of the German Academic Exchange Service during my time in Floence provided the monetary means to realize this project. The EUI was generous to award me a publication grant during preparations of the manuscript.

Various other persons inspired me during different stages of this work and I would like to thank them: Peter Willetts triggered my interest in NGO–UN relations during research at the University of Nottingham; David Jacobson became a challenging discussion partner during my 'field work' in New York; John Boli commented on a paper containing preliminary results of my research which I presented at the International Studies Association Meeting in New Orleans in March 2002; Mary Kaldor gave me the chance to discuss my research at the Centre on the Study of Global Governance of the London School of Economics and Political Science (LSE) in December 2001; Paul Opoku-Mensah invited me to the Center for Development Studies at the University of Bergen to present some of my research findings in November 2003; Helmut Anheier enabled me to join the European PhD Network on 'Non-Profit Organisations' in 2002 and provided me with the opportunity to visit the Center for Civil Society at UCLA in November 2004 during the phase of finalizing the manuscript; the 'Arbeitskreis Soziale Bewegungen' of the German Political Science Association (DVPW) invited me to present some of the findings of my study at the Wissenschaftszentrum Berlin in July 2004.

Of course, a very special 'thank you' goes to all my interview partners, without them having dedicated time to my questions, this work would have never been accomplished. Only their outspokenness and frankness made it possible to carry out this study. My apologies go to those I persistently und unendingly annoyed with my emails, phone calls and in person until they agreed to give me an interview. I know there are quite a few of them.

Access to research material was provided by various libraries. Library staff of the European University Institute, London School of Economics, New York University, United Nations Library and the British Library was tremendously helpful in finding many references. Moreover, I benefited from discussions with staff members during visits to the Union of International Associations in Brussels, especially those with Joel Fischer and Anthony Judge.

I would also like to thank some colleagues for comments, and friends and family for encouragement: my colleagues at the Research Centre 'Transformations of the State' at the University of Bremen Reinhold Sackmann, Ansgar Weymann, Carolin Balzer, and Silke Weinlich for comments during preparation of the manuscript; my research assistants Celia Enders, Jegapradepan Arumugarajah, and Lisa Zelljadt for proofreading the manuscript; the NGO researchers from the University of Münster Marcus Lenzen, Dirk Growe, and Christiane Frantz for inspirations; an anonymous reviewer for helpful comments and suggestions; and Rosa Lugos, Sanen Marshall, Anais Charles-Dominique, Jocasta Gardner, Lars Becker, Kim Dietzel, Becket McGrath, Teresa Missimi, Devrim Karahasan, Navraj Ghaleigh, Alexander Börsch, Fatima Hassan, Ulrike Mühlberger, Martin Zagler, Maike Klähr, Matthias Eickhoff, Andrea Ohídy, my parents, and in particular my sister Irmtraut. Special thanks to Detlef for his loving support throughout the last couple of years.

Kerstin Martens
Bremen, June 2005

Foreword

It is no longer disputed that Non-Governmental Organizations (NGOs) play a prominent role in world politics and that we cannot grasp important developments in the contemporary world system without looking at transnationally operating NGOs. And this even includes the United Nations (UN) system, the quintessential inter-governmental organization on the global level. Most studies so far have tried to successfully demonstrate that 'NGOs matter', i.e. that they influence policies, that they contribute to the evolution of international norms, and that they contribute to ensuring compliance with international regimes and regulations. This is also what you mostly learn in 'NGO 101'.

This book takes a different approach. It opens up a new research venue by asking how the growing NGO involvement in world politics affects these transnational actors themselves. What happens when transnational civil society actors become 'partners in governance'? Will they bureaucratize and professionalize? Will they start establishing hierarchical structures, i.e., will Michels' 'iron law of oligarchy' kick in? Will they start losing touch with their social base, e.g., social movements? These are important questions for which we do not know the answers yet.

This is where Kerstin Martens' book comes in. Using a sophisticated research design which builds on the social movement literature as well as on sociological institutionalism, she investigates how NGOs adjust their internal institutional structure and organization in order to be able to affect UN policies and procedures. She also asks under which circumstances NGOs seek to formalize their relationship with the UN through official recognition. But not all NGOs look alike. As a result, Kerstin Martens argues that we can observe very different patterns depending on whether we look at centrally organized NGOs (such as Amnesty International) as opposed to those with a more federative structure (such as, e.g., the Fédération Internationale des Droits de l'Homme). Moreover, it should make a difference whether we deal with advocacy NGOs (such as Human Rights Watch) as compared to more service-oriented groups (such as Oxfam).

The book's detailed and extremely well-researched empirical case studies show some very interesting findings. Two stick out in my view: First, as to the patterns of activities of NGOs in the UN system, we can observe an enormous broadening. Advocacy NGOs no longer restrict themselves to initiate policies and to consult with the UN, but they directly participate in the processes of policy-making and implementation. At the same time, service-oriented NGOs no longer restrict themselves to the implementation phase, but their activities now cover the whole range of the policy cycle. Second, internal organizational structures matter a lot concerning the ability of NGOs to effectively influence the United Nations. On average, centralist NGOs with some hierarchical internal structure are best suited to expand their activities with the UN. This is a terrific book. It is a 'must read' for NGOs and other policy practitioners as well as for academics and graduate students interested in how global governance works in practice and in detail. The book grew out of a dissertation at the European University Institute in Florence where Kerstin Martens received her PhD. I learned a lot from Kerstin's work which constitutes an eye-opener for a new research agenda.

Thomas Risse

Freie Universität Berlin, 1 June 2005

1
NGOs, International Relations and the UN System – Introductory Observations

Non-governmental organizations (NGOs) have become an integral part of the United Nations (UN). Since their increasing recognition as influential actors in global affairs, intergovernmental organizations (IGOs) like the UN realized the benefits of working with them. Over the course of the last decade, the UN opened up for more interaction with NGOs and created diverse ways of bringing them into its system. In this book I explore how NGOs reacted to this increase in opportunities for participation with the UN. Instead of concentrating on NGO influence on the UN – as most research has done so far – this work focuses on the NGOs themselves. It examines the following questions: how have NGOs responded to increasing possibilities for interaction with the UN since the mid-1990s? And what accounts for different NGO responses?

This study reveals that NGOs have changed their interaction with the UN over the last decade. NGOs responded to increasing options and prospects for interaction by adjusting their patterns of activity vis-à-vis the UN. Though the opening of the UN system to NGO participation constituted the precondition for a shift in their activities, different organizations adjusted their patterns to varying degrees. Several factors account for this variation. In this work I show that such differences can be explained by how NGOs organize their representation to the UN and by how their accreditation with the UN is perceived. These factors, in turn, are highly dependent on the characteristic features of NGOs, that is, their composition and their functions.

This book explores the relationship between NGOs and the UN through eight single cases. The NGOs analysed are some of the most renowned players on the international scene: Amnesty International (AI), Human Rights Watch (HRW), the Fédération Internationale des Droits de l'Homme (FIDH), the International League for Human Rights

1

(ILHR), CARE International, the International Save the Children Alliance (ISCA), Oxfam International and Action Aid Alliance (AAA). Their individual relationships with the UN are traced over time and contrasted to each other, paying particular attention to changes since the mid-1990s. Based on expert interviews conducted with NGO representatives and UN staff members, this work presents new and original information about NGOs and their activities in international relations.

In this introduction I lay out my argument regarding NGO adjustments in their patterns of activity to the UN system and set it into the context of current research on societal actors and their involvement in international relations. I first explore NGO participation in global affairs and their relationship with intergovernmental organizations. In this context, I also outline the focus of present studies on NGOs and their relationship with the UN. Then, I explore how current theoretical approaches present the NGO relationship with the UN and reveal the gaps in these studies, showing how the theoretical framework of my study fits into the body of academic work on societal actors and official institutions. I also explain the research design and the methodology and, finally, briefly outline the structure of the book.

NGO participation in global affairs

NGOs have become prominent players on the international scene over the last decade (Salamon 1994; Mathews 1997). Their growth has surpassed that of intergovernmental organizations, and made them a visible participant in global affairs. Since the early 1990s, the number of NGOs increased continuously and reached almost 6600 by the year 2004. The growth of IGOs, by contrast, decreased in recent years. Since the late 1980s, when IGO numbers peaked at 309, they have slowly dropped to 238 (Union of International Association 2004). In the 1980s, the ratio of NGOs to IGOs stood at 15 : 1, whereas today the relation is 28 : 1.

NGOs have grown not only in numbers, but also in reach: they have become increasingly transnational. Many organizations that initially worked within the domestic sphere gradually expanded beyond national boundaries. Some NGOs founded new branches of their organization in several other states (for example, Amnesty International, Greenpeace International or CARE International). Others gradually became international by merging with organizations with similar aims and goals. They founded an international federative body to coordinate and develop common strategies or expanded their international scope by integrating other national organizations into the international federation (like the

Fédération Internationale des Droits de l'Homme, Friends of the Earth International or Oxfam International).

Today, NGOs work in a variety of issue-areas and promote a wide range of aims and goals. Most prominent NGO involvement occurs in the fields of human rights, environment, women's rights, development assistance, humanitarian aid, peace, and family issues (Smith 1997: 47; Keck and Sikkink 1998a: 11; Boli and Thomas 1999b: 42). However, NGOs are also active in politically volatile arenas such as disarmament and military surveillance (Price 1998; Rutherford 2000; Fitzduff and Church 2004). Moreover, they also engage in what has often been called 'non-political matters' such as leisure activities, recreation clubs and sports associations (Rittberger and Boekle 1996; Kim 1999).

Many NGOs nowadays seek to shape the proceedings and outcomes of international negotiations. NGOs are most visibly active outside of the venues in which governmental representatives meet and discuss international treaties and agreements. The anti-globalization protests in Seattle and beyond attracted large numbers of nationally and internationally operating NGOs. These occasions clearly revealed their potential to affect international decision making processes. In addition, the extent and the intensity of participation on the part of NGOs in the events showed their capacity for mobility and networking across borders (Smith and Johnston 2002; Andretta *et al.* 2003; van Rooy 2004).

However, NGOs are also often directly involved in designing programmes and policies, and therefore shape political processes from inside the official arenas. In particular, NGOs contributed to the proceedings of the world conferences of the early 1990s (Messner and Nuscheler 1996; also Schechter 2001) not only as outside spectators but also as official participants. Around 1400 NGOs officially took part in the Rio Earth Summit of 1992 (Clark *et al.* 1998: 18), up to 150 nations had NGO representatives for the preparatory meetings or the actual conference on their governmental delegations (Princen and Finger 1994b: 4), and the island state of Vanuatu even placed its delegation in the hands of an NGO (Mathews 1997: 55).

Although NGO–IGO relations have become particularly intense over the last decade, they have a long tradition. Both types of organizations were already interlinked in several ways during the nineteenth century when they worked hand-in-hand on important issues during international congresses (Charnovitz 1997: 191). NGOs interacted with the League of Nations and gave presentations before committees, submitted reports and participated in discussions (Hüfner 1995: 15). NGOs were also involved in the early phases of the UN because the US delegation invited 42 NGOs to send representatives as consultants to the founding conference in San Francisco (Robins 1960; Charnovitz 1997: 251).

Today, it is especially international NGOs which aim at working together with intergovernmental organizations (Anheier *et al.* 2001: 5; Smith *et al.* 1998: 396–7). Of these, the UN has become a major target. In the aftermath of the conference series of the early 1990s, many NGOs sought to become formally accredited to the UN and applied for consultative status in order to stabilize their relations. As a result, the total number of NGOs registered at the UN has risen to a striking level: from the introduction of the status in the 1940s to mid-2005, the number of accredited NGOs has increased from 40 to 2614 (Department of Economic and Social Affairs 2005). In response, many other IGOs, such as the Organization for Security and Cooperation in Europe (OSCE) or the Council of Europe, followed the example of the UN and set up directives for cooperation with NGOs.

In reaction to the increasing significance of NGOs in international affairs, the UN began working more closely with them. As part of the reform process after the end of the Cold War (Taylor *et al.* 1997), UN institutions offered greater possibilities for interaction with NGOs. In fact, the IGO sought 'to be open to and work closely with civil society organizations that are active in their respective sectors, and to facilitate increased consultation and co-operation between the United Nations and such organizations' (UN Doc. A/51/950 §59). Today, even the main organs take into account the opinions and contributions of NGOs. Most strikingly, since 1997 Security Council members meet regularly with NGO representatives – often even on a weekly basis – to get briefed on current affairs.

In his Millennium report, Secretary-General Kofi Annan re-emphasized that strengthening the relations between the UN and private actors constitutes a priority of his mandate. He sought '[t]o give full opportunities to non-governmental organizations and other non-state actors to make their indispensable contribution to the Organization's work' (UN Doc. A/54/2000 §367). To review the relationship between the United Nations and civil society and offer practical recommendations for improved modalities and interaction, Annan appointed a 'Panel of Eminent Persons on United Nations–Civil Society Relations' (UN Doc. A/57/387). Chaired by former Brazilian President Fernando Cardoso, the panel examined existing guidelines, decisions and practices that affect NGO access to and participation in UN processes. Its report, released in June 2004, provides the basis for ongoing discussions about reforming the UN system for NGO activities (UN Doc. A/58/817).

Although the NGO–UN relationship has long been of interest to political scientists (Liang 1954; Bock 1955; Stosic 1964; Chiang 1981), most academic works on the subject were only written after the mid-1990s. In many of these studies, scholars explore the relationship between NGOs and the UN by focusing on particular issue-areas of NGO activity or on the relationship between NGOs and a relevant UN organization. The majority of these works are overview studies that intend to show NGO impact on UN processes. Most often, scholars seek to demonstrate how NGOs improve their chances to affect international affairs when cooperating with intergovernmental organizations. Collections of such studies herald NGOs as the 'conscience of the world' (Willetts 1996a) or the partners for a joint 'global governance' (Weiss and Gordenker 1996; Weiss 1998).

These works have been necessary in order to show the increasing significance of NGOs and their growing recognition by intergovernmental organizations. In particular, they provide empirical evidence and concrete examples of NGO–IGO relations. Nonetheless, knowledge about the interaction between the two types of international organizations is still rather one-dimensional, as many aspects have not been sufficiently explored yet: research has focused on NGO influence on the UN, while other spectra of the relationship have been neglected. Regarding the interaction with the UN and its implications for NGOs, many scholars have pointed to a variety of possible developments; however they remain only speculative as far as specific results are concerned. My study fills at least part of this knowledge gap by focusing on the NGOs themselves and how they have adjusted the pattern of their activities with the UN.

Theoretical approaches to NGO–IGO relations

The growing involvement of NGOs on the global stage has been recognized by the social sciences in theoretical terms. International relations theory was extended to societal actors when scholars acknowledged non-governmental activity by turning away from state-centric perspectives to society-dominated views on world politics. The 'new transnationalists' examined the conditions under which NGOs gain influence on state institutions and intergovernmental organizations (Risse-Kappen 1995a). Others identified a 'boomerang effect' by which advocacy networks, including NGOs, bypass state blockages (Keck and Sikkink 1998a). Still others translated NGO participation in transnational relations into the concept of 'world culture' in which NGOs play the dominant role (Boli and Thomas 1999a).

Moreover, conceptualizations of societal activism which had developed within the domestic sphere were lifted onto the international level. That is to say, studies of societal actors and their relationship to the state were applied to internationally operating NGOs and their activities in international affairs. Scholars drew analogies from works on the national level for the study of the activities of 'transnational' social movement organizations (Princen and Finger 1994a; Smith, Chatfield and Pagnucco 1997; della Porta *et al.* 1999; Khagram *et al.* 2002); others also considered the role and limits of the 'global' civil society (Lipschutz 1992; Wapner 1997; Uvin and Weiss 1998; Taylor 2004; Centre for the Study of Global Governance 2004) or studied the 'third sector' from an international comparative perspective (Salamon *et al.* 1999; Anheier and Kendall 2001; Priller and Zimmer 2001).

Such theoretical analyses account for the importance of NGOs in world politics. In particular, these approaches show that NGO–IGO relations increase the impact of NGOs on global affairs. From working with IGOs such as the UN, NGOs gain greater opportunities to advance their objectives and to shape political processes in the international sphere. These models concentrate on explaining the influence of NGOs in world affairs, but neglect to account for the repercussion for the NGOs themselves. The theoretical literature thus provides an important but not the only perspective on the issue at stake.

Social scientists have always taken an interest in exploring societal actors and their relations with official institutions. Disciplines like sociology, political science, and economics investigate social movements, interest groups, and NGOs and their interaction with state institutions. Indeed, relations between societal actors and state institutions are one of the oldest themes of modern political science (Tocqueville 1835/1997). Of particular interest have been the rise and fall of societal activism, the reasons for the emergence of pressure groups, and the way they express their dissatisfaction with governmental politics.

Scholars have also pointed out the conflicting dynamics underlying societal activism. Economists have argued that the logic of collective action lies in individual profit: an individual of a group acts out of self-interest and not the group's interest (Olson 1965/2000). In studies on corporatism, interest groups have been shown to be dependent on state recognition and support, and are therefore caught between the conflicting interests of influence and membership (Schmitter 1979; Schmitter and Streek 1991). The American approach to interest group research argues that voluntary associations emerge to stabilize the relations between various groups in society. Interaction with the institutional environment is inevitable if groups want to exercise political pressure through conventional lobbying of governmental institutions (Truman 1951/1971).

Of the various approaches to societal activism in relation to official institutions, works on social movement organizations capture particularly well the way NGOs interact with official institutions and its implications. Models used to analyse social movement organizations explain not only their emergence, but also the ways in which they expand and intensify their interactions with official institutions. Social movement theory is thus a dynamic theoretical construct since it focuses on the different stages of relations between societal actors and official institutions.

Studies of social movement organizations have developed into a great body of literature on the processes and dynamics of increased interaction between societal actors and the governmental environment. Scholars have explored and identified the reasons for and results of such relations, which are understood as 'institutionalization'. The argument goes that as societal actors increasingly interact with official institutions, their relationship becomes institutionalized and eventually leads them to adjust their pattern of activity. I will draw from the conclusions about this institutionalization of social movements in my study of NGO responses to extended opportunities for interacting with the UN.[1]

Two major tracks of institutionalization have been identified as reasons for these adjustments. First, classic approaches to societal activism (Michels 1911/1970) and resource mobilization theory (Zald and Ash 1987/1966) argue that links between societal actors and official institutions increase *internal* factors, such as professionalization and bureaucratization which lead societal actors to change their patterns of activity in relation to the governmental actor. Second, according to neo-institutionalist theories (DiMaggio and Powell 1983, 1991), adjustments in activities are due to perceived *external* factors. These have been described as 'institutional channelling' (McCarthy *et al.* 1991), and refer to the rules and regulations for relations between societal actors and official institutions. These scholars focus on the prospects for societal actors of official recognition and indirect legitimization, which in turn trigger their changed patterns of activity.

Contributions of this study

This book analyses the responses of NGOs to extended opportunities for interaction with the UN over the last decade. In principle, NGOs may participate in all processes of the UN today, however the NGOs examined in this study adjusted their patterns of activity to varying degrees. While some NGOs added new aspects to their spectrum of interaction with the UN or set different priorities, others expanded their involvement only to a limited extent. Following the theoretical approach, these differences are due to internal factors within the NGOs and external demands put on NGOs.

However, the analysis does not stop at this point, but even goes a step further and examines the reasons for such varying degrees of institutionalization. NGOs are categorized by their characteristic features, namely their transboundary composition (centralist versus federative) and their function (advocacy versus service). Applying such conceptualization of NGOs, the theoretical propositions about NGO adjustments resulting from institutionalized relations are specified and associated with these different types of NGOs. Since the NGOs selected for deeper study are representative of these characteristic features, the study accounts for the varying ways they have institutionalized their UN relations. Figure 1.1 presents the idea evaluated in this book in a simplistic way.

The argument of this book is that NGOs change their patterns of activity with the UN depending on how they have institutionalized their relations with the IGO; the degree of institutionalizing, however, depends on the NGO's characteristics. The empirical findings show that internal factors explain most of the differences in the adjustments of the NGO's patterns of activity with the UN; external demands, instead, account for less than the theoretical model suggested. That is to say, how NGOs organize their representation to the UN highly influences their patterns of activity with the UN, whereas rules and regulations for NGO consultation at the UN level are only perceived as formalities which grant access and have fewer implications than assumed. These internal and external factors, however, are themselves highly influenced by the characteristics of NGOs. Most notably, NGOs with a centralist composition, like Amnesty International and CARE International, are best capable of mobilizing resources for their UN relations, and, as a result, expanded their patterns of activity with the UN. An advocacy NGO with a federative

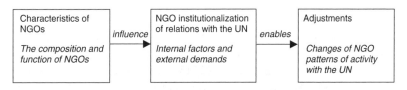

Figure 1.1 NGO institutionalization in the UN system – simplified model

structure like the Fédération Internationale des Droits de l'Homme, by contrast, is most dependent on formal recognition by the UN. My findings are the result of intensive qualitative research conducted for this book. Over the course of 16 months, 62 semi-standardized expert interviews (Merton and Kendall 1979; Meuser and Nagel 1991; Bogner *et al.* 2002) were conducted in order to gather the information needed for this study. The majority of interviews were conducted with current and former NGO representatives working for the respective NGOs. NGO staff members dealing with UN-related matters were also interviewed at headquarters level. In addition, information was derived from the analysis of documents (Scott 1990; Pole and Lampard 2002; Burnham *et al.* 2004). Most importantly, so-called quadrennial reports provided an excellent starting point for exploring NGO relations with the UN over time: since 1978, NGOs with the highest or second highest status at the UN are required to provide a short report on their activities within the UN system every four years.

The analysis covers changes in the relationship between the NGOs studied for this work and the UN from the mid-1990s until 2003. This time frame was chosen because the participation of NGOs at the series of conferences in the early 1990s has frequently been described as the 'turning point' in NGO–UN relations (French 1996: 254; Willetts 1996d: 59; Mathews 1997: 55). NGO involvement at these conferences became the impetus for more intense relations with the UN and triggered a review process of UN relations with NGOs (Hüfner 1996: 116; Otto 1996: 120). Thus, the information applies mainly to the last decade, but in order to portray the changes that have taken place over time, the NGO–UN relationship needs to be traced back to the 1980s and 1970s in some circumstances.

As far as terminology is concerned, in this work, 'NGOs' are the subject of analysis. The term was originally coined by the UN in Article 71 of the Charter to apply to international organizations which had links to the IGO but were not governmental; over the years, the term also found widespread application outside the UN context. Although it has been a subject of controversial and sometimes contradictory definitions, 'NGO' remains the most widely applied notion in academic works. Elsewhere, I have defined NGOs as *international, independent* and *formal societal actors* (Martens 2002). The notion of 'societal actors' should be understood as an umbrella term which encompasses the various expressions deriving from the different approaches to social activism, such as social movements, interest groups, NGOs and so on. The term 'societal actor' thus serves as a means to avoid permanent specification of divergent notions.

Table 1.1   Types of international organizations

	Membership	Criteria	NGO Status	Example
Intergovernmental Organization	Only governmental members	Links to NGO	NGO links not routine	North Atlantic Treaty Organization
	Only governmental members		NGO links routine	United Nations
	Governments and NGOs	NGO status in the international organization	Government dominant status	International Labour Organization
	Governments and NGOs		Equal status	International Committee of the Red Cross
	Governments and NGOs		NGOs dominant	Birdlife International
	Only NGO members	Governmental funding	Governmental funding welcome	International Planned Parent-hood Federation
Nongovernmental Organization	Only NGO members		Government funding not accepted	Amnesty International

Source: Willetts (1996b: 8) with own additions.

The term 'international organizations' encompasses all kinds of organizations (NGOs and IGOs) which operate across borders (see Table 1.1). 'Inter*governmental* organizations', by contrast, are those international organizations which are set up by agreement between at least two states and their governments (Bennett and Oliver 2002: 2; Rittberger and Zangl 2003: 26–7). 'UN system' is used as an umbrella expression for all bodies and agencies of the UN. This includes UN bodies mentioned in the Charter and the independent UN specialized agencies. NGO 'pattern of activity' refers to different types of interactions NGOs carry out in the UN system. NGO 'institutionalization' refers to a relationship between NGOs and the UN which changes the way that NGOs work with the UN. Such changes in the patterns of activity are called NGO 'adjustments' and explored in more detail in this book.

Organization of the book

Chapter 2 deals with theoretical approaches to the NGO–IGO relationship. First, I examine current accounts of NGOs as to why they seek interaction with the UN. Secondly, I develop the guiding theoretical approach for this research. Based on approaches to social movement organizations, the dimensions of the process of 'institutionalization' are explored in greater depth. I also introduce the two characteristic axes by which types of NGOs are distinguished: composition and function. I then briefly describe the cases chosen for deeper study in this work. The following three chapters present the empirical data. Each chapter contains a brief first section in which I explore general tendencies, followed by more specific parts for every individual NGO.

In Chapter 3, NGO adjustments in their patterns of activity within the UN context are the subject of deeper analysis. According to the operationalization of the dependent variable in the theoretical chapter, I examine NGO activities with the UN. I show how the NGOs responded to increasing interaction with the UN, and adjusted their pattern of activity with the IGO differently. In Chapter 4, I explore internal structures of NGOs in terms of their relations with the UN, examining NGO representation and representatives to the UN. In Chapter 5, I analyse external settings for NGO relations with the UN, exploring the NGOs' perception of rules and regulations for their accreditation to the UN system in detail. Moreover, in these two chapters I show how those two independent variables of internal structures and external settings are influenced by the characteristics of NGOs.

In the concluding Chapter 6, I summarize the findings of this study with reference to the theoretical assumptions about the causes of NGO adjustments in their patterns of activity with the UN. Their implications are embedded in the broader context of NGO studies and international relations. Finally, I indicate subjects for further research in response to the findings of my study.

2
NGO Institutionalization into the UN System – Theoretical Framework

Relations between societal actors and governmental institutions have been a regular topic of social scientific research and brought forward an extensive and rich body of empirical and theoretical literature. Through works on domestic societal activism, social scientists have gained knowledge about the dynamics of the relationship between societal actors and state actors. Such works assert that increased interaction between the two leads societal actors to adjust their patterns of activity. Differences in the extent to which they change their activities, however, are due to institutionalizing factors, which in turn can be internal (mobilization of resources) or external (rules and regulations for societal activism).

The first section of this chapter serves as the background for this study. By briefly exploring current theories of NGO–IGO linkages, I illustrate the reasons and motives for NGO relations with IGOs. I also reveal the limits of existing approaches and show why there is a need for a different frame capturing NGO adjustments in their pattern of activity. In the second section, I then develop that theoretical frame for institutionalizing NGOs into the UN system. As reasoned in the introductory part, the emphasis is on theoretical concepts deriving from approaches to the study of social movement organizations. These capture the diverse facets of the relationship between societal actors and official institutions particularly well. In the third section, I present the cases analysed in this book.

Current theoretical approaches to NGO–IGO relations

A variety of theoretical approaches has been developed over the course of the last decade for studying NGO–IGO relations. I distinguish between two tracks of NGO studies in international affairs. First, in models of international relations, NGOs attained more recognition through the various shifts from realist perspectives to pluralist images on world affairs. After the end of the Cold War, the *transnational approach* was revived and it inspired discussion and research on the impact of non-state actors in international relations. Second, models on societal activism which were initially developed in the context of domestic policy were increasingly applied to international studies. In such *transsocietal approaches*, scholars seek to explain the emergence and significance of organizations which have become increasingly active in global affairs.

Transnational relations

The 'new transnationalists' (Risse-Kappen 1995a) introduce an elaborate theoretical conceptualization of the conditions under which transnational actors like NGOs have an impact on international relations. In this view both NGOs and IGOs represent the highest form of institutionalized relations in their respective category. International NGOs (together with multinational companies) are the most highly institutionalized form of transnational relations because they possess administrative structures, and specific rules and functions for the organizational staff (Risse-Kappen 1995b: 10). Similarly, IGOs (together with international regimes) are the most institutionalized form of interstate relations.

IGOs as mediators for NGO activity

Two factors significantly affect the activity and sphere of influence of transnational actors: *domestic structures*, the normative and organiza-tional designs by which the respective states and societies are formed and interlinked, and *international institutionalization*, the degree by which international agreements, regimes or organizations regulate a specific issue-area (Risse-Kappen 1995b: 6). The domestic structure model explains why non-state actors have varying degrees of influence in different countries. It does not account, however, for the divergence of influence for different issue-areas in the same country because the different degree of international institutionalization varies by issue-area: the more a specific issue-area is determined by international cooperation, the more permeable state boundaries should become for transnational activity in that area (Risse-Kappen 1995b: 7).

Similarly, relations with intergovernmental organizations like the UN mediate the policy impact of transnational actors. First, they provide additional access points to the policy making processes of a state. In par-ticular, IGOs make it easier for NGOs to lobby governmental representa-tives. Hence, they open up channels for NGOs which would otherwise be limited by the domestic structures (Risse-Kappen 1995b: 31). Second, intergovernmental organizations reduce the resistance of states to transnational activity. As Risse-Kappen (1995b: 32) puts it,

> highly institutionalized inter-state relations tend to lower state boundaries thereby allowing for flourishing transnational relations. At the same time, these institutions also legitimize transnational activities in the 'target state'; actors are less and less treated as 'foreigners', but as almost indistinguishable from other domestic players.

Hence, linkages with IGOs are highly fruitful for NGOs because they increase their ability to influence political processes.

IGOs as allies to NGOs

The 'boomerang pattern' is a particularly precise model of how NGOs use IGOs as a means to influence a state. This approach is a conceptual frame which exposes how domestic societal actors form alliances with international groups and with IGOs in order to put pressure on a repressive state. Keck and Sikkink (1998a) studied *transnational advocacy networks* and discovered that domestic societal actors bypass the repressive state in order to find international allies who bring pressure on a state from outside. National groups, domestic NGOs, and social movements link up with international NGOs which then establish (or use already established) bonds with intergovernmental organizations or other states in order to put pressure on states that violate norms.

In the human rights arena, Risse, Ropp and Sikkink (1999) further elaborated the boomerang effect to a 'spiral model', which reveals the single consecutive steps of bringing about changes in the human rights field. The model presents the five different phases of institutionalizing international human rights ideas and norms into domestic arrangements (Risse and Sikkink 1999: 3). The adaptation to these norms follows in a socialization process, during which IGOs play a major role for societal actors. As in the boomerang model, societal actors link up with international institutions to put pressure on states violating human rights. IGOs are particularly important in this respect during the socialization process of norms, since they set the standards for rights (by passing the necessary resolutions), and most of the talk (the process of arguing over human rights violations) takes place within the framework of international governmental organizations. In these models, thus, intergovernmental organizations like the UN can function as allies for NGOs in the fulfilment of their objectives.

Transsocietal approaches

Transsocietal approaches were mainly developed in the 1990s in the study of human rights and environmental actors. In these approaches, the emergence and increasing importance of intergovernmental institutions is seen as the transposing of political processes from the national to the international level (Lipschutz 1992: 399; Finger 1994a: 59; Smith *et al.* 1994: 125). This implies that societal actors also increasingly concentrate in their activity on the international level (Passy 1999; Rucht 1999).[2] Not only has the content and organization of social activism become more and more global, the addressee of societal activism has also shifted towards intergovernmental organizations.

IGOs as the upholder of a global civil society

Global civil society is concerned with the interlinkages between different societal actors on the global scale and across borders. NGOs are perceived as a major component of global civil society, as they are its political organizations and seek to change and influence international political processes (Coate *et al.* 1996: 100; Wapner 1997: 66). Disregarding the principle of nationality, non-governmental organizations form the societal bonds which connect different national societies with each other on the individual level (Wapner 1995: 311). Moreover, they introduce issues of worldwide interest to the international agenda in order to raise and mobilize global public interest and awareness. In doing so, they enhance the transnational exchange of science, ideas, and culture, and contribute to the formation of international norms and values.

Relations between NGOs and IGOs are the most visible example of cooperation between societal actors and official actors in a global civil society (Turner 1998: 31). Interaction with IGOs is particularly rewarding for NGOs because IGOs support the establishment of a global civil society by offering a formal way to advance societal aims and goals. IGOs legitimize global civil society by consulting and honouring NGOs with a recognized status (Wapner 1997: 74). Moreover, they contribute to upholding global civil society by providing NGOs the opportunity to establish contact with each other. Particularly international conferences – often organized by IGOs – bring together diverse NGOs and enable them to build up and intensify their connections and networks (Schoener 1997: 562).

IGOs as the provider of transnational political opportunity structures

NGOs target intergovernmental organizations because they provide political opportunity structures which shape the impact of societal actors on the international level. Political opportunity structures are the 'consistent – but not necessarily formal or permanent – dimensions of the political environment that provide incentives for collective action' (Tarrow 1998: 77). In international studies, authors have increasingly employed this concept in reference to transnational structures of opportunities for NGOs (Smith, Pagnucco and Chatfield 1997; Smith 1998; della Porta and Kriesi 1999; Passy 1999).[3]

IGOs, particularly the UN, provide access for NGOs because they establish formal mechanisms for cooperating with non-governmental organizations, such as arrangements for consultation, regular meetings, or participation during multilateral negotiations (Joachim 2003). Within the structures of IGOs, NGOs aggregate interests across national boundaries and facilitate intergovernmental policy making by spreading ideas. From closer cooperation, IGOs gain benefits which they often lack, such as knowledge, resources, and international legitimization, since NGOs enhance governmental accountability (Smith 1995: 195; Passy 1999: 155–6). NGOs in return find allies at the UN level such as UN officials, governmental representatives, or individuals and gain symbolic resources because IGOs officially recognize non-governmental organizations (Smith, Pagnucco and Chatfield 1997: 69).

In sum, theoretical approaches to international relations have acknowledged the increasing involvement of NGOs on the global level. Scholars have concentrated on demonstrating the influence of NGOs on world politics and on showing that NGOs that work with IGOs have greater impact. They have identified motives for cooperation between IGOs and NGOs, and have examined the reasons and conditions for, as well as kinds of NGO influence on IGOs. As a result, theoretical approaches to NGOs and their role in international relations have drawn an important but one-sided picture of their relations to IGOs. Specifically, implications *for NGOs* of interacting with IGOs have not been assessed, and that is the aim of this book. In what follows, I will apply societal activism approaches to NGOs, establishing a theoretical framework for the process of NGO institutionalization into the UN.

NGOs in the UN System

Works on societal activism have addressed the implications for societal actors of increasing interaction with official institutions.[4] Such approaches have argued that societal actors respond by adjusting their patterns of activity with the official institution.[5] These adjustments, however, differ in the extent to which organizations institutionalize their relations with the official institution. Institutionalization, in this respect, refers to two notions: (1) an internal factor whereby organizations set up positions and structures that enable them to work together with the official institution; and (2) an external demand, as organizations react to rules and regulations for their recognition which shape their patterns of activity. The degree to which societal actors institutionalize their relations with official bodies also depends on the types of organization and their respective characteristics.[6] Most significantly, NGOs' composition and functions shape the way they institutionalize their relations with official actors.

The following section explores these causal paths. First, I look at NGO activities in the UN system, where I distinguish between policy initiating activities, policy developing processes, and policy implementing practices of NGOs at the UN level. Then, I examine the two facets of institutionalization as the reasons for adjustments in their patterns of activity. Institutionalization as an internal factor refers to NGO representation and representatives to the UN, whereas external demands of institutionalizing the relations between both actors are identified as the NGO's perception of rules and regulations for its accreditation to the UN. In the third section, I explore and categorize the characteristics of NGOs. For the composition of NGOs, I distinguish between a centralist and a federative structure. NGO functions are classified as being either advocacy or service-providing.

From this information, I derive propositions on how the characteristics of NGOs shape their institutionalization of relations to the UN and, accordingly, their likelihood to adjust their patterns of activity with the IGO. These propositions will be presented as competing because they refer to different traditions of research on societal actors. However, since they emphasize facets which are not mutually exclusive, they are in fact complementary. In brief, the line of argument I develop in this chapter is as follows: characteristics of NGOs shape the way they institutionalize their relations with the UN, which in turn influences changes in their pattern of activity with the UN. As each characteristic of an NGO may affect each of the two notions of institutionalization, and each notion of institutionalization may shape changes in the pattern of activity with the UN, the simplistic model presented in the introductory part is now elaborated and shows the range of plausible effects (see Figure 2.1).

NGO activities in the UN system

In social movement theory, different types of activities have been distinguished in order to categorize societal activism and observe changes. Typically, scholars make a distinction between *cooperative* and

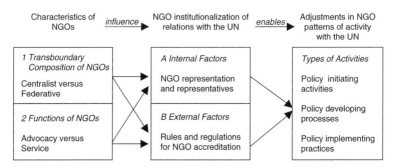

Figure 2.1   NGO institutionalization in the UN system – expanded model

confrontational activities.[7] Similarly, third sector literature identifies different relationships between non-profit organizations and the state. These range from *complementary* to *adversarial*.[8] Such approaches are useful for this study too, but must be adapted to the field of enquiry on NGOs as regards their relationship with the UN. Thus, for the purposes of this study, I distinguish between three types of activities between NGOs and the UN: *policy initiating activities, policy developing processes* and *policy implementing practices* (see Table 2.1).

   (1) *Policy initiating activities* are those activities in which NGOs take the lead in initiating or shaping the political debate. Based on their own goals and objectives, NGOs start a discussion at the UN level or make aware of biases or disrespect of commonly agreed-upon rules. Policy initiating activities include conflictual modes such as agenda or standard setting activities and monitoring, but they can also be moderate and consist of lobby work and diplomatic activities (Gordenker and Weiss 1996: 38–40; Willetts 1996c: 45–6). Thus, the UN and NGOs can have different standpoints and NGOs can be regarded as adversarial because they seek to make changes in public policy (Young 1999: 33).

   (2) *Policy developing processes* include the role of NGOs as advisor and even policy formulator at the UN level. At this stage policies are further developed and put into proposals. NGOs are invited by the UN to contribute during policy developing processes or they are asked to submit their own proposals (Willetts 1996c: 47–8). Thus, they can still bring in their own objectives but they also have to respond to conditions set by the UN. NGOs in this respect often take on supplementary roles, as they fulfil demands which were left unsatisfied by governmental representatives (Young 1999: 33).

(3) *Policy implementing practices* are those activities where both NGOs and the UN work hand in hand towards the realization of a project. This includes NGOs as implementing partners or it involves a contractual relationship in which NGOs fulfil UN tasks (Gordenker and Weiss 1996: 37; Willetts 1996c: 48–9). The precondition for common policy implementing practices is that NGOs and the UN must have similar or even identical goals.

All three aspects of NGO activity can be fulfilled by the same organization, as such tasks are not mutually exclusive. As Young (1999: 33) proposes, '[n]onprofits may simultaneously finance and deliver services where government does not, deliver services that are financed or otherwise assisted by government, advocate for changes in government policies and practices, and be affected by government pressure and oversight'.[9] For the empirical case studies, the distinction between different activities makes it possible to observe and analyse in what kind of activities NGOs are most significantly involved, and more importantly whether their patterns of activity have changed since the mid-1990s.

Table 2.1 Types of NGO activities in cooperation with the UN

Types	Activities
Policy initiating activities	Agenda and standard setting *NGOs try to influence the political agenda and seek to change the debate on a particular issue*
	Information provision *NGOs provide the UN with information which they researched or received*
	Lobbying and diplomatic activities *NGOs lobby officials and seek to convince them about an issue of their concern*
Policy developing processes	Policy advisor *NGOs are asked by the UN or governmental officials for advise on particular issues*
	Policy formulator *NGOs are directly involved during the process of formulating specific policies*
Policy implementing practices	Cooperational relationship *NGOs and the UN cooperate during the implementation phase but work independently*
	Sub-contracting partners *NGOs are subcontracted by the UN for specific tasks and implement them on behalf of the UN institution*

Thus each NGO's activities at the UN level are compared over time and to those of other NGOs in this work.

Institutionalizing NGO–UN relations

Scholars of societal activism identify the changes in the patterns of activity of societal actors as deriving from institutionalization of their relations with the authorities. As mentioned above, the notion of institutionalization can be subdivided into two analytical concepts. On the one hand, changed internal organizational structures account for changes in activities; on the other hand, external recognition triggers such adjustments.[10] From both accounts, I draw analogies to study NGO institutionalization into the UN system. Institutionalization in the first section refers to internal factors, such as societal actors setting up distinct structures and routines within the organization. In the second section, institutionalization is understood as an external demand, in which societal actors and official institutions need to regulate their relationships.

Institutionalization as an internal factor

Implications of increased interaction with the authorities on the part of societal actors have long been a subject of social research. The Weber–Michels model on internal structures of social movements is a classic and often cited approach. Building upon such ideas, others further explored the internal organization of societal actors and its effects on their spectrum of interaction. Since the 1970s, resource mobilization theory, which was developed in reference to American organizations, has been associated with organizational structures of societal actors.

Classic Models.   Classic approaches studying the institutionalization of societal actors are concerned with the dimensions of organizational changes which eventually have implications for their activities. In these approaches, institutionalization is considered a gradual process within social movements, such that they develop through a series of phases. Starting as diffuse and scattered phenomena, they slowly adopt organizational structures and finally end up as large institutions with bureaucratic structures. Michels' (1911/1970) 'iron law of oligarchy' and Dawson and Getty's (1935) 'careers' present ideal-types of this sequence. Various scholars translated such concepts into sociological and political approaches.[11] Moreover, the notion of institutionalization was introduced for the stage in which movements build up internal structures in response to the demands addressed to them (Rucht *et al.* 1997: 39). ·

In his classic study on the sociology of parties in modern democracies, Michels (1911/1970) argues that organizations will always differentiate internally and establish hierarchical structures ('iron law of oligarchy'). According to Michels, this is an organic tendency within each organization, and hence also progressive organizations will establish them, even though hierarchical structures are considered contrary to their ideological principles (Michels 1970: 371). Following this line of argument, the establishment of hierarchical structures within the organization can be seen as a gradual and unavoidable development. Increased size calls for a division of labour, with sophisticated systems of self-administration and professional leadership. At this stage, however, the main objective of the organization becomes its own consolidation: bureaucratic functions prevail over ideological considerations.

In such models, internal factors constitute the reasons for societal actors to adjust their pattern of activity. Due to its intensified interaction with other actors (including governmental institutions), the movement establishes organizational structures to keep up with the demands for coordination. Processes like division of labour, and particularly professionalization and bureaucratization, secure the ongoing success of the movement in society. Eventually, however, these internal rearrangements have consequences for the activities of the movement. Scholars representing this classic approach take a pessimistic view, stressing that the consolidation of the movements prevails over the idealistic or ideological aims and goals on which the movement was founded in the first place.[12]

Resource Mobilization. Resource mobilization theorists presume that political dissatisfaction and social conflict are inherent to every society. Thus, the formation of social movements does not depend on the existence of interests, but on the creation of organizations to mobilize their potential (McCarthy and Zald 1987: 18). In this view, organizations are seen as existing in a changing environment to which they adapt; adaptations, however, depend on the internal structures of the organizations (Zald and Ash 1987: 122). Thus, resource mobilization theory is similar to classic models in that internal aspects represent the significant explanatory factors for the performance of societal actors towards the authorities. Unlike social movement approaches, however, resource mobilization theory is not fatalistic. Rather, it specifies the conditions under which alternative transformation processes take place (McCarthy and Zald 1987: 19–20; Zald and Ash 1987: 122).

Exploring social movements through the lenses of resource mobilization theory, scholars seek to clarify which factors influence the performance of societal actors. They examine availability of critical resources for both mobilization and maturation. To resource mobilization theorists, internal developments do not necessarily make organizations less effective. Zald and Ash (1987) argue in this respect that elaborated internal structures can, in fact, give rise to more radical goals and the use of more aggressive tactics. For example, the establishment of a hierarchy which allows for leadership positions and charismatic leaders may enable individuals to shape the goals and activities of the organization to become radical. Thus, resource mobilization theorists argue that the re-arrangement of internal structures leads to changes in the pattern of activity.

Significant factors in this respect are professionalization and bureaucratization. Through professionalization, issues are dealt with according to subject-specific knowledge in order to maintain quality standards. Moreover, positions which had previously been on a voluntary basis are made into a profession (Rucht *et al.* 1997: 55). Bureaucratization allows NGOs to establish and use particular structures for specific activities, such as a division of labour that aims at performing certain tasks routinely (Zald and Ash 1987: 122; Nullmeier 1989: 4; Rucht *et al.* 1997: 55). Such structures enable NGOs to perform duties routinely and to continue to function with changes in staff (Staggenborg 1997: 425).

From such perspectives *institutionalization* is an internal process of gradual stabilization of institutional structures *within* the organization. It refers to the way organizations increasingly professionalize and bureaucratize their structures. Such internal factors lead to adjustments in patterns of activity toward official institutions. Applying such concepts to this study, I use NGO representation and representatives stationed in UN locations, such as Geneva and New York, as reflecting their degree of institutionalizing relations with the UN internally. Thus, institutionalization is understood as NGO structures regarding relations with the UN. It is the process by which NGOs create organizational provisions for dealing with the UN. NGO representation is the setting up of offices and the division of labour within the NGO to manage relations with the UN. NGO representatives refer to the establishment of positions that deal with the UN. It is here understood as the specialization of a person within the organization to represent the NGO at the UN level.

Institutionalization as an external demand

During the 1970s, dominant perspectives changed to emphasize the impact of external demands on the performance of societal actors. Instead of focusing on hierarchic structures and working processes within the organizations, research on social movement organizations applied the new institutionalist's perspective which highlighted the pressures deriving from external forces, and scholars explored the role played by institutional environments in determining organizations' behaviour (Finnemore 1996: 329; Hall and Taylor 1996: 946). Known as 'isomorphism' (DiMaggio and Powell 1983) and 'institutional channelling' (McCarthy *et al.* 1991), outside pressures lead organizations to change their patterns of activity.

Isomorphism.   Neo-institutionalists put the emphasis on the rules and regulations regarding the relationship between organizations and their environment (DiMaggio and Powell 1991: 12). In contrast to older models of institutionalization, this perspective also contains a sociological perception, emphasizing shared systems of rules that constrain both the inclination and the capacity of actors (Finnemore 1996; Hall and Taylor 1996). Neo-institutionalists often concentrate on examining state-legitimated categories for societal actors, as rules and recognition are structured along the lines of the most legitimate procedures (McCarthy *et al.* 1991: 49; McCarthy 1997: 253). Thus, institutionalization encompasses the formalization of relations between social movement organizations and the state. With the notion of 'isomorphism', scholars captured the significance of external pressures (Meyer and Rowan 1977/1991).

Isomorphism 'is a constraining process that forces one unit in a population to resemble other units that face the same set of environmental conditions ... such an approach suggests that organizational characteristics are modified in the direction of increasing compatibility with environmental characteristics' (DiMaggio and Powell 1983: 149). Applying coercive isomorphism to societal actors changes their activities in relation to governmental institutions. Particularly through official regulations, external pressure is exerted on societal actors seeking to conform to or to meet requirements (DiMaggio and Powell 1983: 150). Isomorphism describes direct imposition of standard operating procedures by powerful organizations in the field as well as more subtle pressure for conformity.

Institutionalists thus argue that increased interaction between societal actors and official institutions lead to 'isomorphism' with the environment because organizations adopt 'legitimated' routines. As a result, institutional isomorphism promotes the success and survival of organizations (Meyer and Rowan 1991). In some approaches, this external environment has been translated as the constraints created by governments. Applying this aspect of institutionalization in the international sphere, intergovernmental institutions, such as the UN can act as 'regulatory systems'

(Scott 1995: xv). IGOs that interact with NGOs exercise pressure on them by creating rules and regulations for their relationship.

Institutional Channelling. Building upon these accounts, others have explored the external conditions in which societal activism takes place. Legal requirements or recognition by official institutions have been described as 'institutional channelling' through an external governmental body (McCarthy and McPhail 1998: 85). That is to say, societal actors receive an acknowledged status awarded by some governmental authority for following state-legitimated practices and obtain special privileges relative to actors without the status (DiMaggio and Powell 1991: 11; McCarthy *et al.* 1991: 49; Meyer and Rowan 1991: 42).

Channelling mechanisms encompass the body of rules and regulations determining the setting in which societal activism is recognized as taking place legally. McCarthy, Britt and Wolfson (1991: 52), for example, refer to the tax-exempt status for organizations, which provides for recognition by an authority and supports recognized organizations with certain rights. Similarly, McCarthy and McPhail (1998: 87) refer to the legal context in which societal activism takes place. In their study of the institutionalization of protest in the United States, they draw attention to the rules governing protest activities by social movement organizations.[13]

Institutionalization is thus the process of creating permanent rules for activities between societal actors and official institutions. It encompasses compliance with a body of law describing such regulation of activities. That body of law can take different forms and includes special benefits. For example, when organizations comply with the rules in Section 501 of the US Internal Revenue Code, they gain the benefits of being tax-exempt, such as special postal rates (McCarthy *et al.* 1991: 56–7). The body of regulations is not static; it continues to evolve and may change over time (McCarthy and McPail 1998: 101). For example, the legal context changes through amendments to the codes, requirement changes, extensive case law and rulings (McCarthy *et al.* 1991: 53).

Organizations do not only benefit directly from the privilege of recognition, status also affords them a good reputation and increased acceptance of their activities (Meyer and Rowan 1991: 49; Kubik 1998: 134). Sometimes recognition by some governmental institution is even a requirement for third parties before they will work with social movement organizations. McCarthy, Britt and Wolfson (1991: 64) argue that '[s]tate-level laws and regulations reinforce these incentives for seeking cover under the *legitimate* form. Also, many elite funding sources, particularly tax-exempt foundations, demand that recipient organizations be *legitimate* in this sense.' In addition, such third parties are more willing to support groups that have a recognized status, because they themselves benefit from supporting legitimate organizations (McCarthy and McPail 1998: 101). However, status also implies additional pressure for groups because it can be revoked (McCarthy *et al.* 1991: 55).

From this view *institutionalization* has been regarded as the process of establishing regulations for relations *between* societal actors and official institutions. Diverse ways of acknowledging and legitimizing societal actors strengthen their recognition. Fulfilling the external demands of recognition, however, implies that societal actors adjust their patterns of activity. To explore this, I consider rules and regulations concerning activities between societal actors and the UN. The UN formally associates NGOs in three ways: consultative status with the Economic and Social Council (ECOSOC), associate status with the Department of Public Information (DPI), and affiliation with the Non-Governmental Liaison Service (NGLS). Of these three, the ECOSOC status has repeatedly been acknowledged as the highest form of 'official recognition', as NGOs have to go through a formalized application process, in which they are tested by UN officials.[14] It is the most elaborate and widely acknowledged scheme for regulating the NGO–UN relationship and constitutes a measurable example of institutional channelling mechanisms. The other two schemes are 'in-house' processes and have only a limited, if any, application procedure.[15]

Categories of internationally operating NGOs

The characteristics of NGOs affect the way in which they institutionalize their relations with the UN. Therefore, I establish categories for internationally operating NGOs. In the first section, I explain the different possible compositions of NGOs in the international arena. The second section focuses on the different functions of NGOs when acting internationally. These categories are not mutually exclusive, but rather helpful for systemizing NGOs by providing tools about specific characteristics influencing institutionalization of relations with the UN.

Transboundary composition of NGOs

The composition of societal actors influences their capacity for institutionalizing relations with official actors (Freeman 1979: 173; Jenkins 1983: 593; McCarthy and Zald 1987: 28–9). International NGOs differ in composition:[16] they can either be international-federative NGOs or transnational-centralist organizations (Young 1991b: 10).[17] In the first case, NGOs follow a bottom-up principle by which autonomous national affiliates with similar aims and goals set up a loose federation in order to better promote common issues on the international level. In the second case, NGOs are guided by a top-down principle; strong international administrative bodies guide the politics of the dependent national sections.[18]

Federative NGOs.   Federative NGOs function as umbrella organizations for single domestic affiliates (White 1933: 30–1). National organizations with similar aims and objectives are loosely connected internationally, so as to better coordinate their concerns or activities. The purpose of these international federations is to provide a platform for mutual exchange between the national affiliates, as it facilitates communication among them (Taylor 1995: 125). Federative NGOs are decentralized and allow for diversity in membership. Decisions are made within the individual affiliate, which usually keeps its autonomy vis-à-vis the umbrella organization. The concerns of the single national organization are very important, and national affiliates can make strong claims to the association as a whole (Young 1991b: 26).

Federative NGOs usually maintain only a small international office which coordinates the communication and cooperation between individual affiliates. As a result, the federative type of NGO is generally considered weak internationally because it is dependent on the consensus of the national members. However, as Gordenker and Weiss (1996: 28) point out, '[f]ederations differ in how much control they can exert over their branches and how much branch activity can be coordinated with worldwide partners as well as how they finance administrative costs for common activities'. Some federative NGOs, for instance, allow the individual name of the same international NGO to vary in different countries; others require adding to the national name the common label of all members.

Often, there are historical reasons for federative NGOs. Many federative NGOs were first active on the national level only and merged together later, because at the time they were founded, international cooperation between them was difficult to establish due to a lack of communication. As a result, such national NGOs joined together only years or decades later when international cooperation became easier. The Fédération Internationale des Droits de l'Homme represents an example of such an international-federative NGO. Independent human rights organizations were founded in different European countries around the turn of the century (Wiseberg and Scoble 1977: 292), but the international federation was not established until 1922. Initially, it was composed of a dozen national human rights organizations whereas today it comprises 141 affiliates.

Many modern organizations also choose a federative structure for governance reasons. As national affiliates have the option to diverge from the overall policy, they can act according to the specific setting in which they operate. Federative NGOs therefore often have broad objectives rather than specializing in a specific purpose so as to encompass the diverse voices of their affiliates.[19] Many prominent NGOs have a federative structure: Oxfam International, International Federation Terre des Hommes or Friends of the Earth International, for example, are typical federative NGOs in that autonomous national NGOs joined together in an international umbrella organization (Smith *et al.* 1994: 135–6; Brand *et al.* 2000: 127; J. Clark 2001: 4).

In the international arena, federations can play an important role. Most importantly, the federation enables its national member NGOs a representation on the international level. Moreover, it provides coordination among the single national affiliates for a common international programme. At the same time, however, federations are limited in the extent to which they are able to support their single national NGOs in their international presence. Since the affiliates retain autonomous decision-making power, the international federation cannot impose on them the content of their international programmes.

Centralist NGOs. Centralist NGOs share common statutes. National sections of a centralist NGO are tied to the transnational body and often share a common mission statement. By and large, all sections have the same name and identify themselves through the transnational body. Centralist NGOs generally have one strong international secretariat from which the national sections are all guided; it sets out the common policy of the NGO as a whole. Moreover, it controls and monitors the quality of the overall work of the NGO (Thränhardt 1992: 226). Centralized NGOs also usually have hierarchical structures and a highly developed division of labour. They therefore often have more specific objectives than federative NGOs and can specialize in particular issues in addition to following broad objectives. Moreover, centralist NGOs maintain a large international administrative body and employ thematic experts or specialists for certain subject matters who work independently.

Centralist NGOs also have a unitary structure. The national sections of a centralist NGO, though working independently in their day-to-day functions, stay in contact with the international office and cannot initiate or carry out a project without its consent. National sections therefore do not operate independently, but need to get permission before launching a campaign or commencing a project. National sections sometimes also receive tasks or information from the international office and carry out a responsibility, such as fundraising (Schmitz 2001: 9).

Unlike the federative NGOs, the national sections of centralist NGOs often did not exist before the transnational body. Instead, many centralist NGOs are established by a person or a group in one country first, and through diffusion the NGO then builds up support in other countries. National and regional sections are subsequently established and modelled on the 'mother-organization' which guides their development.[20] Many post-Second World War or more recently founded NGOs fit into this category. Prominent examples of centralist NGOs, for example, are Amnesty International, Human Rights Watch and Greenpeace International (Smith *et al.* 1994: 135–6). However, centralist NGOs also differ in their degree of centrality. Some have gradually moved towards a modestly centralist structure, in that they share most of the attributes of a centralist NGO. CARE International (Cooperative for Assistance and Relief Everywhere) is a good example for this shift, as it has become more centralist since the 1980s. Similarly, the International Save the Children Alliance has also developed more centralist structures between the members of the alliance over the years (J. Clark 2001: 4; Lindenberg and Bryant 2001: 142).

Centralist NGOs can play a leading role on the international stage. As the international office guides and designs the policy for the entire NGO and all its sections, it also has the authority to direct a common international programme. Centralist NGOs also may present a strong force at the international level and they mobilize a large membership. For this reason, centralist NGOs often develop elaborate strategies and have diverse ways of ensuring their international presence.

> Centralist NGOs are more likely to adjust their patterns of activity than federative NGOs because they have better organizational capacities for their UN representation.

Centralist NGOs have substantial resources at their disposal and a large staff to conduct their affairs (Jenkins 1983: 539). Therefore, they are able to devote a significant amount of resources to their representation at the international level. Moreover, headquarters have the capacity to develop structures within the organization for its UN-related matters. As managerial processes remain in the international office, centralist NGOs reserve the power to decide on the establishment or expansion of their international representation. Thus it is easy for centralist NGOs to ensure their representation at the UN level: they are likely to establish offices in major UN locations related to their field of activity and equip them with full-time professionals.

Federative NGOs, instead, have only limited resources at disposal (McCarthy and Zald 1987: 30). Consequently, they need to budget well with their resources for their UN representation and can dedicate only little means to such purposes. Also, headquarters are too small and weak to develop elaborate structures for UN representation. As the decision-making power lies with independent national member NGOs, federative NGOs are less likely to make strategic choices concerning their international representation quickly. Thus, it is difficult for federative NGOs to establish and maintain professional staff for their UN representation.

In short, centralist NGOs are more likely to institutionalize their relations than federative NGOs, as they have better organizational capacities. According to the theoretical approach, centralist NGOs should thus also be more likely to adjust their patterns of activity vis-à-vis the UN than federative NGOs, as they maintain a higher degree of institutionalized relations. Indicators used to measure the amount of representation are: (1) the number of NGO offices in major UN locations and departments in the international secretariat,[21] (2) number of NGO representatives in UN locations and staff members in the international secretariat working on UN-related issues (or working time dedicated to UN matters), (3) their positions within the organization (voluntary or professional),[22] and (4) other organizational arrangements concerning representation at the UN.

Federative NGOs are more likely to adjust their patterns of activity than centralist NGOs because they seek formal recognition by the UN.

Federative NGOs are particularly interested in gaining and maintaining formal recognition by IGOs, especially the UN. As international federations usually function as umbrella organizations for individual national affiliates, their objective is simply to provide a presence at the international level. Having recognized status as a federation enables member organizations to promote their aims and goals in an otherwise inaccessible international arena. Moreover, a formal status of the federation at the UN level also serves as a sign of prestige because the affiliated members are recognized indirectly.

For centralist NGOs, by contrast, working with IGOs is only one of many ways to reach an international audience. Centralist NGOs direct activities for the whole organization, and national sections concentrate less on work in a single country. Therefore, official recognition by IGOs is not as important as for international federative NGOs because national sections of a centralist NGO have other means for an international representation through headquarters. Centralist NGOs are thus less dependent on formal relations with IGOs: they have other ways of promoting their cause internationally.

In short, federative NGOs are more likely to institutionalize their relations externally because they value formalized recognition. According to the theoretical approach, federative NGOs should thus be more likely to adjust their patterns of activity with the UN than centralist NGOs. Qualitative issues serve as indicators to measure formal recognitions: (1) the significance of having a recognized status at the UN, (2) the importance of maintaining this status and (3) the degree to which status is perceived as a means for a good reputation.[23]

Functions of NGOs

Studies of NGOs usually identify their different 'functions', 'roles', 'or 'objectives' in international politics (Coston 1998: 361). Although the terms for these functions vary, most observers distinguish between NGOs in an 'advocacy' function and NGOs in a 'service' function (Beigbeder 1991: 82; Gordenker and Weiss 1996; Willetts 1996c; Breitmeier and Rittberger 1998; Broadhurst and Ledgerwood 1998; Rittberger *et al.* 1999).[24] Whereas advocacy NGOs seek to influence political processes and introduce their objectives to decision-makers, service NGOs instead aim to provide their target group with support and resources.

Advocacy NGOs. Advocacy NGOs usually have strong causes and seek to change the ideological context of an issue at stake or to bring forward their concerns (Azzam 1993; Brett 1995; Breitmeier and Rittberger 1998; Keck and Sikkink 1998a). For example, they promote themes which governments do not address in order to give them international attention. Advocacy NGOs also try to influence the tone with which specific issues are addressed. For example, they seek to ensure that all aspects related to an issue in question are treated as important, or that specific references are made to issues of their concern.

Advocacy NGOs have various ways of reaching their objectives. They may try to create a public debate about the issue in question, thereby educating the larger public through information campaigns. They may also mobilize and organize citizen protests to show public concern about certain issues (Breitmeier and Rittberger 1998). They try to gain media coverage in order to spread information and awareness about a particular (overlooked) problem. By doing so, NGOs hope to create public pressure to indirectly influence officials. All kinds of 'rights groups' (such as human rights, children's rights, women's rights or minority rights) and also those in the field of disarmament are often categorized as advocacy NGOs (Atwood 1997). Human rights NGOs in particular fulfil advocacy functions (Archer 1983: 323; Brett 1995).

Advocacy NGOs often seek close contact with governmental representatives so that they can place direct pressure on them. Most importantly, NGOs confront governments and IGOs during international negotiation processes and urge states to adopt internationally agreed-upon rules that they can later hold them responsible for implementing (Willetts 1996c: 46). They often address directly the major players who have an important say in the issue in question. Moreover, they try to find allies in order to convince them about the issue at stake.

Service NGOs. Service NGOs provide support to people in need. They are primarily concerned with the well-being of their target group, for which they supply resources such as shelter and food and offer technical assistance and relief work. They seek connections to official institutions because these often have similar objectives, which they can pursue with common strength. Service NGOs may assist other institutions, organizations, or groups involved in their issues of concern, thus helping them fulfil their mandate. Unlike advocacy NGOs, service organizations are less interested in changing ideological contexts than in fulfilling basic needs. '[I]n comparison to advocacy organizations, their focus remains on service delivery, while achieving policy change on the international level remains a secondary task' (Rittberger *et al.* 1999: 117). Since NGOs and states often share aims, they work hand-in-hand. Thus the relationship of NGOs with official institutions is usually one of cooperational partnership.

Service NGOs can most often be found in the social sectors. Prominent examples in the international arena include organizations in humanitarian assistance and development aid (Gordenker and Weiss 1996: 41; Keidel and Koch 1996; Natsios 1996). Service NGOs are often active on the international level, as their target groups are usually outside their home country. Therefore, they are *by definition* internationally operating organizations. Often, they deal with foreign governments and intergovernmental organizations who share objectives, or they work in the same area as these and synchronize their efforts.

Advocacy NGOs are more likely to adjust their patterns of activity than service NGOs because they recruit representatives on the basis of their professional training rather than organizational affiliation.

Advocacy organizations need staff with specialized training in their particular issue areas and subject matter as well as good writing and communication skills for successful representation at the UN (Gordenker and Weiss 1996: 38). The NGOs' ability to bring forward their causes depends on its staff's skills at working the UN system. Representatives need to be highly trained in their field of activity. For example, a background in international studies, most importantly, international law provides the required skills in terms of subject matter; but also language or journalist studies would enable them to have the necessary tools for their position as regards the communication skills. Thus, advocacy NGOs are likely to recruit staff on the basis of professional criteria, like their educational and professional training, rather than due to their organizational affiliation.

NGOs in the service sector are valued for their experience and the resources they can provide to relief efforts. Their representatives must have technical skills and expertise needed to carry out the various phases of the humanitarian project. This includes, for instance, knowledge about providing resources supplies for disaster relief, technology transfer, administration of a treaty secretariat, or the submission of field reports (Rittberger *et al.* 1999: 116). Service NGOs are therefore more likely to recruit inside their organization, as they need representatives to the UN who are familiar with the organizational structure of their own NGO and can assess the options for common projects with the UN. Thus, service NGOs will recruit representatives who have been involved with the organization for many years in diverse situations and who know it well from various angles.

In short, advocacy NGOs are more likely to have highly professional representatives to the UN because they recruit on the basis of professional skills pertaining to their advocacy issues rather than on affiliation or experience with the NGO. In accordance with the theoretical accounts, advocacy NGOs should thus be more likely to adjust their patterns of activity to the UN than service NGOs. To assess this empirically, qualitative differences in the qualifications of representatives serve as indicators: (1) the educational and professional background required for UN-related staff, (2) the necessity of having experience and knowledge of the NGO and the UN system, and (3) recruitment due to long-term work experience for or prior involvement with the NGO.[25]

Service NGOs are more likely to adjust their pattern of activity than advocacy NGOs because they more easily gain access to the UN through formal recognition.

Service NGOs are usually well regarded at the UN. Both NGOs and IGOs seek to work together and combine their strengths, because they often share objectives and exercise similar functions. Thus, service NGOs and IGOs are often equally interested in having mutually binding regulations that formalize their relationship in both directions. Service NGOs have few problems getting and maintaining official recognition by states or intergovernmental organizations as it presents merely the somewhat legalized form of a relationship which would exist anyway.

Advocacy NGOs, by contrast, may not be welcomed at the UN as they often criticize states, so some governments may have an interest in making sure that their access to intergovernmental forums is denied. Because advocacy NGOs seek to change the ideological context, they confront states about delicate and controversial issues. Therefore, it is more difficult for advocacy NGOs to receive the official UN recognition as their application is often opposed by one or more countries. Even after having received status, advocacy NGOs are in greater danger of losing it again because particular states dislike their conduct and seek to revoke their status.

In short, service NGOs are more likely to institutionalize their relations externally than advocacy NGOs because they gain formal recognition more easily. According to theoretical accounts, service NGOs are more likely to adjust their patterns of activity with the UN than advocacy NGOs. Qualitative indicators that test for this are: (1) the type of status the NGO has at the UN, including challenges to receive it, (2) historical development of the status with 'up' and 'down-gradings' and (3) threats of losing status and attempts to withdraw the status.

Case selection

According to the characterization of NGOs, I selected the cases for this study. Since 'functions of NGOs' and 'transboundary composition' are not mutually exclusive characteristics but rather complement each other, Figure 2.2 shows on which basis four case studies can be selected. I chose the following four NGOs for investigation as they fit the characterization well: Amnesty International (centralist composition, advocacy function), Fédération Internationale des Droits de l'Homme (federative composition, advocacy function), CARE International (centralist composition, service function), Oxfam International (federative composition, service function). These NGOs are my primary case studies.[26]

Studies rarely focus on single NGOs in relation to the UN, so I chose another set of four NGOs which also fit into the table.[27] These are meant to support the findings from the main case studies, ensuring that none of

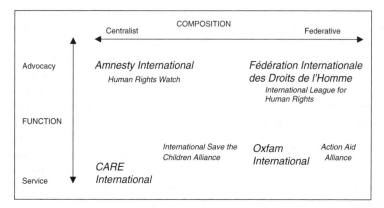

Figure 2.2   NGOs by function and composition

the primary cases were exceptional or extreme. I did not review these back-up NGOs with the same intensity (fewer interviews were conducted), but traced pertinent lines of the argument. This second set of NGOs contains the following organizations: Human Rights Watch, the International League for Human Rights, International Save the Children Alliance and the Action Aid Alliance. The NGOs chosen for deeper study of their relationship with the UN are briefly described in this section. In categorizing NGOs, I focus on organizational structures as well as on objectives of the individual organizations in order to show how the respective NGOs fit into the categories of 'composition' and 'function'. Each section on the individual NGO also contains a brief historical overview.

Amnesty International: centralist composition and advocacy function

Amnesty International is a typical centralist NGO. Its transboundary composition clearly follows the top-down principle as it maintains an omnipotent transnational office which guides the national sections. Moreover, it is an example of an advocacy NGO as it seeks to advance awareness and protection of human rights.

Amnesty International was founded in 1961 on the initiative of Peter Benenson. On 28 May, the British lawyer published an article on 'The Forgotten Prisoners' in the local London newspaper 'The Observer', in which he described Portuguese students who were imprisoned for toasting to 'freedom' in a pub; simultaneously, a French version was printed in Le Monde, and other European newspapers covered the issue in the following days and weeks. With this series of newspaper articles, public awareness to the plight of political and religious prisoners was raised for a campaign called 'Appeal for Amnesty 1961'.[28]

From its early days, AI was meant to be a transnational organization (Smith *et al.* 1994: 129). In the weeks after the series of articles, Amnesty groups were founded in Germany, Belgium, France, Ireland, Switzerland, and the USA. In July of that year, the first international assembly with delegates from various countries met in Luxembourg (Larsen 1978: 17). Today, AI is the largest NGO in the field of protecting and promoting human rights; it has around 1.8 million members and supporters in 150 countries and territories.

Centralist composition. Amnesty International is guided by a strong international administration based in London. It is considered the 'nerve centre' of the organization since all information flows together here and crucial decisions are made. Moreover, the London office is in charge of conducting the NGO's day-to-day affairs. For these tasks it employs a large staff: about 350 people are permanently employed and another 100 volunteers support the permanent staff on a temporary basis. Smith, Pagnucco and Romeril (1994: 134) describe AI's international secretariat as follows:

> Amnesty International is the most centralised. Decision-making is concentrated at the international secretariat level in Amnesty International rather than at the national level. ... The division of labour within Amnesty International is highly complex. Its international secretariat is the central office of Amnesty International which carries out its day-to-day functions.

Amnesty International's membership is comprised of national sections from 56 countries, and some smaller affiliated groups from another 24 countries. The national sections, however, do not work independently of the mother-NGO but act in conformity with the object and mandate of AI. As established in its statutes, 'Sections shall act in accordance with the core values and methods of Amnesty International, as well as any Integrated Strategic Plans, working rules and guidelines that are adopted from time to time by the International Council' (Amnesty International 2001b §11).[29] Moreover, the London office guides its national sections by providing them with directives and methodological instructions for campaigning.

Advocacy function. Amnesty International declares 'a worldwide movement of people who campaign for internationally recognised human rights ... enshrined in the Universal Declaration of Human Rights and other international human rights standards' (Amnesty International 2005). The organization emphasizes awareness of and adherence to human rights standards as espoused in the Universal Declaration of Human Rights and in other legal instruments. It also opposes violations of the rights of individuals, particularly for political reasons (Amnesty International 2001b §5).

Amnesty International applies several strategies to advance the promotion and protection of human rights. Activities range from public demonstrations to letter-writing, from human rights education to fundraising concerts, and from individual appeals on a particular case to global campaigns on a particular issue. The NGO's most important strategy is to raise awareness of human rights violations through large-scale letter-writing campaigns to those responsible for dealing with the respective country's human rights issues: 'The major component of Amnesty International strategy is its letter-writing campaigns that plead with governments for both the release of prisoners as well as for the fair and humane treatment of other prisoners' (Smith *et al.* 1994: 134). For this purpose, AI mobilizes its members, who regularly write letters (and now also use faxes and emails) and send urgent appeals to the 'adopted' prisoners and the authorities.

FIDH: federative composition and advocacy function

As a federative NGO, the FIDH is composed of national affiliates that form a loose federation to facilitate communication, but keep their autonomy. As an advocacy NGO in the field of human rights, the FIDH promotes protection of human rights in accordance with international standards.

The international federation was created in 1922 on the initiative of a few European national organizations, which joined together mainly to coordinate the various national leagues for representation on the international level (Wiseberg and Scoble 1977: 292–3). Disbanded during the Second World War, the FIDH was reconstituted in 1948 with the goal of applying human rights as defined in the Universal Declaration of Human Rights, adopted the same year (Bernheim 1983: 174). In 2002, the Fédération Internationale des Droits de l'Homme represents an international-federative NGO which brings together 141 national human rights NGOs from 90 countries. The affiliates of the FIDH are autonomous organizations and work independently of each other (Interview FIDH-1).

Federative composition. The FIDH is comprised of elected boards that coordinate the federation's approach, and of a small permanent international secretariat which performs the necessary everyday functions. However, these organizational provisions only facilitate the communication between the autonomous, mainly national member organizations. Each affiliate decides on its programmes and projects independently. Every three years, a congress brings together the member NGOs, which elect the International Board and accredit new affiliates. The International Board meets three times a year and defines the political orientation of the organization as well as its strategies. It approves the budget of the organization, and it also appoints the Executive Board based on proposals from the President of the FIDH. The Executive Board manages and runs the organization's daily operations. In monthly meetings, it determines the work for the following weeks and carries out requests of the affiliates.

The international secretariat in Paris is the FIDH's permanent structure. In addition to its own main functions, such as preparing the international triennial report and the report of activities for the UN, it coordinates the activities of the national affiliates. The secretariat also represents the FIDH at the international level and works with intergovernmental organizations to which it transmits information on human rights violations. It also implements the decisions of the International Board and the Executive Boards. As a federative NGO, the FIDH's international office maintains only a small staff: around twelve people are permanently employed in the international secretariat. The major work of the NGO is instead conducted on a voluntary basis within the national affiliates.

Advocacy function. The FIDH states that 'its purpose [is] the promotion of the ideal of human rights, the struggle against their violation, and demand for their total respect' (Fédération Internationale des Droits de l'Homme 1998: 7). It applies a variety of strategies on the international level, such as trial observation, human rights education, promotion of human rights through information campaigns, and mobilization of the community of states for human rights.

For this reason, the FIDH carries out fact-finding and trial observation missions, to which it sends judicial observers. These observers witness political trials and conduct field investigations which provide the public and international organizations with evidence of human rights violations. For the FIDH, such missions are the most effective way of informing and preventing: 'These missions contribute to the realisation of important reforms, to the release of numerous prisoners of conscience, and to informing international public opinion about little known situations' (Fédération Internationale des Droits de l'Homme 2005b).

CARE International: centralist composition and service-providing function

CARE International represents those service-providing organizations which, while gradually expanding over the years, developed moderate centralist structures. Being an organization in the humanitarian field, its main concern is delivering immediate assistance to people in need. CARE was founded in 1945 as an American organization when 22 national US organizations formed a cooperative to deliver packages to Europe. After having fulfilled its primary goal as a post-Second World War relief organization, CARE also began to distribute US surplus food to feed the hungry in the 1950s.[30] A decade later, health care programmes were adopted in addition to the food supply programmes.

Having started as an American organization, the NGO became gradually transnational as new CARE members were founded in the following decades. The first non-American section was established in the late 1970s and gradually others followed, but CARE USA is still the leading organization. CARE International is one of the world's largest secular humanitarian NGO. It operates in 78 countries and provides both emergency aid and long-term development assistance. Over 600 projects are carried out by CARE International and around 45 million people participate each year.

Centralist composition.   Today, CARE International comprises 12 national sections, which share the same name (with the respective national addition) and the common international symbol. Since the 1980s, CARE has moved to a more centralist structure (Lindenberg and Bryant 2001: 142). As more and more national organizations were established, it was clear that the national CARE organizations had to define duties and areas of responsibility. Therefore the NGO decided to maintain a combined structure of coordinated efforts and centralist-administrative procedures. A common governing board was created to unify the organization (Campbell 1990: 197). Today, the modestly centralist body 'exists to promote coordination between the members and to assist them in the pursuance of their aims' (CARE International 2000a). Day-to-day work is conducted at the international secretariat in Brussels which 'is the central hub of the CARE family' (CARE International 2000b). It is headed by the secretary-general who is supported by a deputy secretary-general and administrative staff. The secretary-general is in charge of all operations and represents CARE International at intergovernmental organizations. The international secretariat also coordinates the Brussels-based European Union Coordination Unit and the Geneva-based Multilateral Liaison Coordinator.

The single sections share their tasks and geographic sphere of influence (Campbell 1990: 195). Three of the national organizations are mainly implementing bodies, whereas the other CARE members are more responsible for fundraising (Interview CARE-1). In addition, each CARE specializes in a particular issue or geographic region. When a new project is approved by CARE International, every member organization is free to participate and to contribute to it. All CARE sections operating in the particular country go by the name CARE International, but one member takes primary responsibility for the efficient functioning of the whole project (Interview CARE-2).

Service-providing function.   CARE International distinguishes between its 'vision' and its 'mission'. The vision presents the broader view of the organization as 'seek[ing] a world of hope, tolerance and social justice, where poverty has been overcome and people live in dignity and security' (CARE International 2005). The NGO hereby sees itself as a 'global force' within a 'worldwide movement' dedicated to end poverty (CARE International 2005). The 'mission' is only little more specific. 'CARE International's mission is to serve individuals and families in the poorest communities in the world. Drawing strength from our global diversity, resources and experience, we promote innovative solutions and are advocates for global responsibility' (CARE International 2005).

CARE International follows four paths to reach its goals. These include development and rehabilitation programming that addresses the underlying causes of poverty and social injustice, and delivery of emergency support such as disaster relief to victims. It also seeks to influence policy development and implementation at all levels so that CARE International improves the lives of the poor and addresses discrimination in all its forms. Last but not least, CARE International invests into diverse constituencies that support its vision and mission in all countries in which it is active (CARE International 2005).

Oxfam International: federative composition and service-providing function

Various Oxfams already existed before the international federative body was established to provide a means for better communication amongst them. As a service NGO, Oxfam International sees its purpose as delivering goods to people in need. The first Oxfam was established in 1942 as the

'Oxford Committee for Famine Relief' when a group of Oxford University professors and students discussed reports of starvation among the civilian population in enemy-occupied Europe (Black 1992: 1).

Oxfam's first appeal focused on the problems created by Nazi occupation of Greece. The NGO requested that relief be sent to the country through the blockages and it raised funds for war refugees. In the late 1940s, Oxfam's goals were extended to humanitarian support of all kinds in any part of the world. Since the late 1960s, Oxfam became more businesslike and commercially oriented. It started retail shops which developed to be the main source of income, selling donated items and handcrafts from overseas.

Federative composition. Oxfam International has a federative structure and comprises twelve different affiliates which together work in more than 80 countries. It describes itself as 'a confederation of twelve non-governmental organisations' (Oxfam International 2005), a 'network of individual organisations' (Oxfam International 2000b) or a 'global federation' (Oxfam International 2001). In the early 1990s, it became clear that more coordination was needed among the different Oxfam affiliates, so in 1995 the formal structure for 'Oxfam International' was officially founded. The single affiliates remain autonomous and work independently of each other, but they share a common purpose and have similar goals.

When Oxfam International was established, existing NGOs were integrated into the Oxfam family. Some of them had the name 'Oxfam' already, others had no name affiliation. For example, the Dutch development organization Novib became part of Oxfam International without having had any links to the NGO before. Some Oxfams also keep their own names, such as Intermon or Community Aid Abroad. As noted earlier by Smith, Pagnucco and Romeril (1994: 136), Oxfam International is one of the most de-centralized NGOs: 'Oxfam's organisational structure varies from the other cases in that it is a federation of independent national "sister organisations". These national organisations of Oxfam formally share only the organisation's name, mission and field offices in less developed countries.'

The international secretariat based in Oxford is a small team which organizes the communication and collaboration between the Oxfams. Its goal is 'coordinating, facilitating, and catalyzing Oxfam International's strategies and activities, and improving administrative support' (Oxfam International 2002). Since 1999, the different Oxfams aim at working together closer and Oxfam International planned and developed a campaign with the goal of 'speaking with one voice'. Under this 'harmonization project', teams on the ground are advised to gradually coordinate and integrate their programme activities into a single Oxfam International framework. The aim of such synchronization is to create a common identity and a 'new public face' of Oxfam International (Oxfam International 2000b).

Service-providing function. The individual Oxfam affiliates work in different ways for the same purpose, which they describe as addressing the structural causes of poverty and related injustice (Oxfam International 2005). For this reason, the Oxfams usually cooperate with relevant local organizations to strengthen their own potential.

> In all our actions, our ultimate goal is to enable people to exercise their rights and manage their own lives. For this to happen, opportunities must be created so people can participate in governing all aspects of their lives and they must have their freedom and capacity to organize and take advantage of those opportunities. (Oxfam International 2000c)

Thus, Oxfam International's aims include creating markets for people to meet their needs, strengthening anti-poverty institutions, or preventing and reversing damage to the environment as part of a sustainable livelihood. Each of the Oxfam affiliates shares these aims but has a special approach, focus, or region of the world in which it is particularly strong.

Other NGOs

Human Rights Watch (centralist composition and advocacy function). Human Rights Watch was founded as 'Helsinki Watch' in 1978 to monitor the compliance of the Soviet bloc with the human rights provisions of the Helsinki Accord and to support citizens' groups in those countries. Over the years, the NGO expanded and opened up several offices in other parts of the world; today, it tracks developments in human rights implementation and violations in more than 70 countries. After AI, HRW is the second largest human rights organization. With its headquarters based in New York, HRW is guided by an international secretariat which administers the different 'watches'. It has a large staff of around 150 full-time professionals, most of them lawyers, journalists, academics, and country experts. The organization is divided into different units which specialize in particular regions. The centralist structure was set up in

1988, when the different 'watches' that had grown and developed over the years realized they needed coordination (Korey 1998: 347).

HRW maintains a broad mandate and simply describes itself as being dedicated to promoting the human rights of people. The organization supports victims of and activists against discrimination. It investigates and exposes abuses to hold human rights violators accountable. The NGO works against a broad range of abuses, including summary executions, torture, arbitrary detention, and restrictions of freedom of expression, association, assembly and religion. It is also involved with the protection of civilians during wars, conditions of prisons, refugees, and internally displaced persons. Researchers conduct fact-finding investigations in all regions of the world, from which information and data about abuse are then published in order to raise awareness and to embarrass governments in the eyes of their own citizens and the international community. The organization thereby seeks to hold governments accountable to human rights standards. In addition, HRW presses for the withdrawal of military, economic and diplomatic support from governments that are regularly abusive.

International League for Human Rights (federative composition and advocacy function).   Based in New York, the ILHR encompasses about a dozens of affiliates and partners from around the world. In recent years, it increasingly supported eastern European NGOs, many of them from the former Soviet Union. In many of these countries the ILHR has local partner NGOs (Interview ILHR-1). The ILHR was founded in 1942 as a US NGO,[31] but traces its origins back to a French citizen's league which was created to monitor and criticize the actions of the French government ('Ligue Française pour la Défense des Droits de l'Hommes et du Citoyen').

Today, the organization has a staff of only four full-time employees, a couple of part-time law students, and other volunteers. The full-time staff members each have a main domain of activity (Interview ILHR-2). The ILHR has a broad focus and works to keep human rights at the forefront of international affairs. It sends out missions to explore the human rights situation in a specific country and to support individual human rights advocates.

International Save the Children Alliance (centralist composition and service-providing function).   The ISCA was founded in 1979 and today encompasses 27 organizations from all around the world.[32] They all share the same name but often additionally keep their national equivalent. The ISCA currently works in over 115 countries. The NGO is a moderately centralist organization in that it maintains a medium size international secretariat in London which coordinates the activities of the single nationally based NGOs (Penrose and Seaman 1996: 242). In recent years, cooperation between the member organizations has intensified considerably (International Save the Children Alliance 2002).

The first section was the UK section. It was founded in 1919 in London by Eglantyre Jebb in response to urgent needs of children affected by the First World War. Until today it remains the largest NGO concerned with child health and welfare. Gradually other sections were founded, such as Save the Children USA of New York in 1932, which was created to support the children of Appalachian coal miners hit by the Great Depression. ISCA is a humanitarian organization because its aim is to respond immediately to emergency situations. Unlike many others, however, it caters to children. Its prime aim is to make sure that children's needs are cared for, and therefore it delivers immediate help and lasting aid to children worldwide.

Action Aid Alliance (federative composition and service-providing function). The AAA is a federative organization of seven independent NGOs. Together, they operate in over 40 countries around the world and work with over seven million people in poor communities (Action Aid Alliance, no date). The alliance is a loose federation of national affiliates which share similar objectives and standards, but the different member organizations work independently of each other. The NGO accepts new members sharing its objectives and operational standards. AAA has little common management and only maintains a so-called administrative office in Brussels.[33]

All members of the alliance 'share the same mission of promoting values and commitment in civil society institutions ... with the aim of achieving structural changes in order to eradicate injustice and poverty in the world' (Action Aid Alliance, no date). The alliance's strongest member is Action Aid UK, which also is the biggest and oldest. The Action Aid affiliates share the belief that strengthening the capacities of poor communities and their participation in all levels of decision-making is the best way to address the causes of poverty. Each of the AAA members has a different focus and major geographic area of influence.

Summary

In this chapter, I developed a theoretical and methodological approach for studying NGO responses to intensified interaction with the UN.

Exploring current theoretical approaches to NGOs and their relationship with IGOs in the first section, I showed from what perspective societal actors and their participation in international affairs have been examined so far. The various transnational and transsocietal approaches reveal that exploration of NGO impact on IGOs has been the major focus until now. Therefore in the second section I developed a theoretical framework capable of taking into account the implications for societal actors of increasing interaction with official institutions. Applying concepts of resource mobilization and institutional channelling, I identified the 'NGO institutionalization' into the UN system and resulting adjustments in their pattern of activity as the foci of attention.

In the third section on NGO characteristics, I presented two factors by which NGOs can be distinguished: their transboundary composition and the function they take on. Such characteristics of NGOs indicate the degree to which NGOs have institutionalized their relations with the UN. On this basis, I chose the cases for investigation: Amnesty International, Fédération Internationale des Droits de l'Homme, CARE International and Oxfam International serve as primary case studies and Human Rights Watch, the International League for Human Rights, International Save the Children Alliance, and Action Aid Alliance are chosen as back-up cases.

In short, the guiding theoretical and methodological parameters for the further course of this study have been laid out so that in the following section, empirical data can be filtered and analysed accordingly.

3
Activities in the UN Context – Changing Patterns of Interaction

Since the mid-1990s, NGOs have had more opportunities to work with the UN, and they have adjusted to these by altering their pattern of activity towards the IGO. The dimensions of those NGO adjustments to the UN system are the subject of deeper analysis in this chapter. After having presented a framework for the range of possible activities between NGOs and the UN in the theoretical part, I now employ it on the set of NGOs chosen for this study in order to explore their respective adjustments over the last decade.

In the first section, I will discuss the way relationships between NGOs and the UN system have developed in general, emphasizing changes and additional opportunities for NGO activities during the last decade. In the second section, I explore the specific cases chosen for this study in more detail with reference to adjustments in their particular patterns of activity to the UN.

NGO activities with the UN and new opportunities for interaction

NGOs today have manifold possibilities for interaction with the UN. They assist UN institutions and provide them with information on issues of concern to them, they regularly advise UN commissions and committees, they collaborate with the UN and UN agencies, and implement joint projects. NGOs have been carrying out many of these activities since the founding of the UN, however during the last decade the range and intensity of these activities has broadened. I briefly explore the various old and new avenues of interaction between NGOs and the UN in the following section.[34]

Policy initiating activities

Much NGO activity tries to influence the political debate at the UN level. By providing information, NGOs aim to initiate political processes in their issue-areas, often by feeding information through the official channels. The UN has established mechanisms to take in NGO contributions, such as annual sessions, committees, meetings, or special officers. NGOs are also able to influence UN officials and governmental representatives through informal lobbying. Either way, the information provided by NGOs can be used in official reports by UN staff or by governmental representatives in their statements.

In the human rights area, NGOs contribute to the political debate at the UN level by providing information on the human rights situation and on human rights violations in different countries. Especially before and during the annual six week session of the Commission on Human Rights in Geneva, NGOs are particularly active in supplying information on human rights violations to UN officials and governmental representatives. By doing so, NGOs seek to influence the debate and the policies on a particular country or a specific issue. Sometimes, they even seek to shape the Commission's programme by trying to influence the UN to put a country on the agenda.

In recent years, the number of written statements NGOs have submitted to the Commission on Human Rights and have become official UN documents has significantly increased. Until the early 1990s, NGOs submitted between 50 and 60 written statements to the Commission each session. By 1996, the number of submissions averaged in the 90s, and has grown ever since. In fact, it more than doubled within six years: in 2002 already more than 200 written statements were made by NGOs. One of the reasons for this growth is that the speakers list of participating NGOs has grown significantly since the opening of the UN system for national NGOs. More organizations are accredited to the UN and want to make a statement before the commission. One participant estimated that the number of NGOs involved in each session is usually around 150 (Weschler 1998: 140).

In addition to the annual sessions of the Commission on Human Rights, NGOs work together with UN officials throughout the year. They exchange information with UN country or thematic officers (so-called desk-officers based in Geneva) on a regular basis. These desk-officers are their primary UN reference point on issues concerning NGO work on a specific country (such as China, for example) or thematic issue (like the discrimination of ethnic minorities). Most importantly, NGOs provide these desk-officers with research results on violations so that they can forward them to high-ranking persons in charge or include this information in their reports on the country or thematic issue.

Such NGO reports and summaries of the human rights situation in a particular country often serve UN officials as background material. NGOs have been increasingly acknowledged as the primary sources of information on these subjects, especially since the end of the Cold War. In fact, today

> [c]ommittee members eagerly look for NGO materials before each country review, because it helps make their questioning more precise, factual, and less abstract. Nongovernmental organizations essentially serve as unofficial researchers to committee members, rendering invaluable aid in place of the understaffed, poorly financed secretariat. (Gaer 1996: 56)

In some cases, the UN even relies heavily upon NGO information. In 1995, for instance, 74 per cent of the cases dealt with at the Working Group on Arbitrary Detentions were brought up by international NGOs (Gaer 1996: 55).[35]

In the humanitarian aid field, interaction between NGOs and the UN has also undergone considerable change over the course of the last decade. In the past, both actors worked together almost exclusively on the field level, and there was very little other contact between them. Policy initiating activities occurred only through sessions of the Executive Committee of the High Commissioner's Programme and during congresses at which networks of NGOs participated (Jaeger 1982: 173–4). In recent years, however, the UN has recognized that humanitarian NGOs can contribute to its work in many ways. A UN document on arrangements and practices for the activities with humanitarian organizations states that 'as the comparative strength of NGOs and the potential for their complementarity with the United Nations grew more evident, they have become indispensable partners, not only in development and relief operations, but also in public information and advocacy' (UN Doc. A/53/170 §III 32).

In fact, today information provision and policy development in the humanitarian sector is conducted through institutions especially set up for these purposes. Most importantly, the Inter-Agency Standing Committee (IASC), created in 1992 as the central humanitarian policy making body in the United Nations system, serves as the primary mechanism for coordinating the different actors working in humanitarian assistance. In addition to heads of UN bodies and representatives of the

Red Cross, NGOs are 'also invited on a permanent basis to attend' (Inter-Agency Standing Committee Secretariat 1998). In this body, NGOs do not participate by themselves, but are represented through major NGO networks. The 'NGO consortium thus fully participates in formulating system-wide responses to specific emergencies and in determining priorities and aim to support the work carried out in the field' (UN Doc. A/53/170 §III 36). Together with the UN bodies, NGOs develop and agree on system-wide humanitarian policies, allocate responsibilities among the different actors, and produce common frameworks.

In addition to the formal channels of information provision, NGOs now also have increased options to work with the UN informally or 'semi-formally'. For a few years now, the 'Arria Formula' has provided a new forum for semi-formal information provision by NGOs. Especially for some large internationally operating NGOs, it is an arrangement to work with high-level decision-making officials. The Arria Formula allows the Security Council to be briefed informally about international peace and security issues by non-Council members. In the early phase of its establishment in 1993, the Arria Formula primarily enabled a member of the Security Council to invite other Security Council members to a meeting held outside of the official chambers to be informed on an issue by an expert in a particular area of concern.[36]

In 1996, however, some of the elected Council members sought to broaden the use of the Arria Formula to include NGOs and other non-state representatives. Other delegations insisted on the continued restricted use of the Arria Formula, particularly the permanent members of the Council did not support the idea of broadening the formula. In response, when Chilean Ambassador Somavia organized a meeting between Security Council members and several humanitarian NGOs, it was called 'Somavia Formula'. During this gathering, three humanitarian NGOs met with members of the ECOSOC bureau and the bureaus of the General Assembly's Second and Third Committee and discussed current affairs with members of the Security Council.

After various proposals and much discussion, the Security Council adopted more open and flexible meeting arrangements in 1999, allowing its members to meet with NGO representatives also. In April 2000, it thus held the first regular Arria Formula briefing with NGO leaders. Over the course of the last years, Arria briefings have become an integral part of NGO–UN relations and are now widely accepted by all participants involved. Today, Arria meetings usually take place every month, but sometimes even more often. Next to meetings with private individuals or state representatives, some of these meetings include NGOs as briefing participants. In 2004, at least six meetings occurred in which NGO representatives briefed Security Council members on issues of concern to them. In 2002, five meetings with NGOs on the basis of the Arria formula took place and in 2000, three Arria Formula briefings with NGO representatives took place and another four informal meetings with Security Council members also included NGO representatives (Global Policy Forum 2005a).

Although Arria meetings have become a recognized means of communication between NGOs and the Security Council of the UN, their character remains vague. On the one hand, meetings are typically held at a very high level, as the permanent representative or the deputy of a delegation attends. Usually, all Security Council members send representatives, and only rarely do individual members fail to accept the invitation. Meetings are announced by the Security Council's president at the beginning of each month as part of the regular schedule and no other Security Council meetings are scheduled at the time when Arria Formula meetings take place. Moreover, the Secretariat provides full language translation. On the other hand, however, no codified rules exist as yet concerning the way an Arria Formula briefing should take place (Paul 2003).

In addition to the formal and semi-formal channels of communication, NGOs lobby governmental representatives and UN officials. Through lobbying, NGOs get in touch with UN bodies, UN officials, and government representatives outside the official channels. UN recognition allows NGO representatives to enter UN buildings to meet there with official governmental representatives and intergovernmental personnel. Particularly for advocacy NGOs, lobbying is an important activity at the UN level. Human rights NGOs seek contact with governmental representatives in order to convince them to address an issue of concern to them. When lobbying them, they provide thoroughly researched data on human rights violations in a particular country for use in official forums.

Policy developing processes

NGOs are also involved in UN processes as policy advisors and even policy formulators. UN officials sometimes invite NGO representatives to provide advice on a particular issue or governmental representatives ask them to be part of an official delegation, for example during drafting processes. In the human rights sector, NGO representatives are increasingly involved in the preparation of drafts or sometimes even form part of an official delegation. They are also invited to participate in committees or working groups because they have the necessary legal expertise as well as the technical skills (Schmitz 1997: 53). NGOs, for their part, are interested in being involved in the influential preliminary stages of text development (such as the *travaux préparatoires*) because this is the phase where standards are usually discussed and set for the final documents.

Although NGOs were involved in policy developing processes in one way or the other in the past, they have become particularly valued for their expertise and their provision of technical assistance in the development of human rights standards since the Human Rights Conference in Vienna in 1993. 'Today, human rights NGOs seem on the verge of being offered the prospect of becoming "insiders", working through and with the UN to achieve what has not been possible or desirable for them in the past – the delivery of legal services' (Gaer 1996: 60).

UN officials, instead, often lack the necessary knowledge. As their profession involves rotating between posts, diplomats regularly change their location and tasks, whereas NGO representatives are not changed on a routine basis.[37] Therefore, '[m]any diplomats who deal with human rights soon upon taking up their posts get in touch with representatives of UN-accredited non-governmental organizations as they know that such contacts usually bring in as a result reliable materials and helpful analyses' (Weschler 1998: 153).[38]

As part of a 'new humanitarianism', relief NGOs have also been integrated more closely into policy making forums where they are able to influence the agenda of humanitarian action (Chandler 2001). In the humanitarian sector, however, NGOs usually contribute to policy formulating processes not as single NGOs, but through common networks. One of the most influential NGO networks supporting the UN with advice is the Steering Committee for Humanitarian Response (SCHR), established in 1992 in response to the explosion in numbers of humanitarian NGOs as an alliance of nine of the largest international organizations.

While the network was originally created to improve the synchronization between the single NGOs, it became evident during the 1990s that more coordination with the UN was needed, too. Another aim of this committee therefore became providing a common forum of exchange and management between NGOs and the UN system. By now, the SCHR is a vital participant in the UN's humanitarian inter-agency process and plays a major role on the NGO advisor board to the UN (Interview Oxfam-1). SCHR works closely with the Office of the UN High Commissioner for Refugees (UNHCR), where it advocates for NGO participation during meetings when the UNHCR Executive Committee and governmental members develop policies. It has also been involved in drawing up the Framework Agreement for Operational Partnership, which helps to define what each partner can expect in the field.

The major role of the SCHR in relation to the UN, however, is to introduce the vast amount of field experience of its members into UN humanitarian decision-making processes.

> Such participation is based upon the understanding that humanitarian coordination activity needs to include the participation of all humanitarian actors, both from the intergovernmental organizations and from non-UN agencies which include the NGOs and those from the Red Cross and Red Crescent Movement. ... Likewise, it is important that the extensive field experience of the SCHR agencies who implement a huge proportion of humanitarian assistance both directly and as partners with an IGO, is taken into account when coordination and policy decisions are made. (Steering Committee for Humanitarian Response 2000)

Members of SCHR are particularly valued at the UN for their wealth of experience: because of the diversity of members, the SCHR has gained knowledge through various field situations. 'The strength of SCHR advocacy work is not so much that it speaks with a common voice, but rather that it speaks from common experience' (Steering Committee for Humanitarian Response 2000).

The SCHR and the UN also cooperate in the development of standards for humanitarian assistance. As part of the 'Sphere Project', for example, both jointly issued a common handbook on standards 'in order to develop a common understanding of concepts such as humanitarian imperative, the principle of humanity and their relationship to issues such as protection, security, and access' (Steering Committee for Humanitarian Response 2000). This project also included a common Code of Conduct which defines the legal responsibilities of all parties, such as states, IGOs or NGOs (Sphere Project 2000).

In recent years, additional semi-formal channels for policy development activities at the UN level have been established for NGOs from all fields. The most prominent and influential example is the 'NGO Working Group on the Security Council' (WGSC). Encompassing organizations from different issue-areas, such as human rights, humanitarian relief, disarmament, faith, global governance, and development, the WGSC presents a network of about thirty large NGOs which have a special interest in the matters and issues of the Security Council. It was founded in 1995 when the first private meetings between NGO representatives and Security Council members took place. From 1997 onwards, the working group held such meetings regularly; a year later, the frequency of meetings increased and the number of participating delegations grew. In 1999, for example, more than 33 such meetings took place, and 45 events were held by the WGSC. In 2004, already 50 meetings occurred so that today, the WGSC organizes briefings almost every week, usually in the diplomatic missions, restaurants, or other venues (Global Policy Forum 2005b).

The WGSC has become an influential forum at the UN level, and has astonishingly close access to high-ranking UN officials and government delegates despite having no official status. To maintain such high level of discussion, access to the working group is limited to NGOs that have a direct link to Security Council matters or, as stated in the WGSC's information statement, 'NGOs that wish to join must apply and must prove the seriousness of their purpose and their organization's special program concern with the Security Council' (Global Policy Forum 2000b).

Security Council members value the NGO expertise and experience, as NGOs often have more accurate and up-to-date information about specific situations as well as better and independent sources in the field, particularly during crisis periods. UN delegates also often use the working group's web pages, as these sites may provide the most comprehensive and current source of information. NGOs seek activities with the Security Council because it enables them to better perform their own tasks.

> The Council's decisions directly affect the core programs of many NGOs. NGOs need good information on the Council and its work, so as to better plan and carry out their policy. NGOs also have important information, expertise and experience that they want to offer the Council, to influence its thinking on policy matters. This is particularly true of human rights and humanitarian organizations that are directly in the field during complex emergencies. (Global Policy Forum 2000b)

Policy implementing practices

The UN often works with NGOs during the phase in which projects are carried out, especially in relief work. Since humanitarian NGOs and UN bodies have similar or sometimes even identical goals, they share the workload during field situations. UNHCR, for example, annually signs partnership agreements with over 500 NGOs, and, in 1997 it funded 443

NGOs in 131 countries to implement 931 projects. In recent years, more UN bodies than in the past have recognized the advantage of cooperating with NGOs (UN Doc. A/53/170 §III 36).

The relationship between these operational UN bodies and NGOs in the field are manifold. For example, NGOs and the UN coordinate their activities and divide up the tasks. NGOs, for example, often fulfil supplementary or complementary roles whereby they take over one of the duties, such as the distribution of food or clothes. NGOs can also be subcontracted for specific purposes and implement UN programmes under an agreement with the UN. This puts them in an executive role, carrying out and implementing projects on behalf of the relevant UN body (Gordenker and Weiss 1998: 44).

Both the UN and NGOs have good reason to work with each other in the field. For the UN the advantages of service-providing NGOs 'lie in the proximity to their members or clients, their flexibility and the high degree of people's involvement and participation in their activities, which leads to strong commitments, appropriateness of solutions and high acceptance of decisions implemented' (UN Doc. A/53/170 §III 33). Moreover, NGOs often have more resources at their disposal than the UN. In fact, some of the budgets of single NGOs in the field of humanitarian assistance are higher than the budget of the entire UNHCR – such as CARE International, for example. Cooperation with the NGOs therefore supports the UN to fulfil its mandate.

NGOs, in return, often need the UN for providing the appropriate environment in which they seek to operate. The UN may, for example, be the only body in charge of logistical services and NGOs are dependent on the UN for this, particularly in emergency situations. Most importantly, the UN organizes, controls, and guides all traffic in regions in which the NGO wants to operate. Thus, NGOs must often interact with the UN for security reasons as the UN is the only guarantor of safety.[39]

For more coordination of the activities between NGOs and the UN, the United Nations Department of Humanitarian Affairs (DHA) was set up in 1992. As part of the reform process of the UN, it was established in order to synchronize relief work. When it was renamed the Office for the Coordination of Humanitarian Affairs (OCHA) in 1998, its purposes were extended to include coordination of affairs between the UN and other humanitarian agencies. Today, OCHA is part of the United Nations Secretariat and has the mandate to coordinate UN assistance in humanitarian crises that go beyond the capacity and mandate of any singly humanitarian agency. It makes it possible 'to bring NGOs on board so that they have a voice at the table' (Interview UN-1).

Human rights NGOs, too, have links with operational bodies now. Unlike before, human rights are dealt with not only through the traditional complaint mechanisms in Geneva, but in various operational bodies of the UN system.[40] As Gaer (1996: 58) explains,

> [u]ntil recently UN efforts to report and take action against [human rights] abuses were conducted from afar, through Geneva-based complaint procedures or reporting based largely on NGO information, with occasional short missions by UN special rapporteurs. The situation changed as the United Nations launched human rights operations as part of multifaceted peacekeeping operations in El Salvador and Cambodia, and sent monitoring missions to Haiti. Conceived and run in New York, these human rights missions have opened the door to other on-site UN human rights field operations.

Since the mid-1990s, NGOs have been paying close attention to such operations. Because they have the experience and knowledge to conduct human rights field missions, they are able to provide in-depth analyses and make suitable recommendations; in some instances, UN operations also cooperate with NGOs on the site (Weschler 1998: 145–6).

In sum, NGOs today have various chances to interact with the UN. They can initiate policies, contribute to the development of new policy proposals, and be part of the implementing process. Particularly in recent years, new and additional opportunities have been established to bring NGOs into the UN system. The Arria Formula, the NGO Working Group on the Security Council or the Office for the Coordination of Humanitarian Affairs, for example, enable NGOs to have intense and continuous interaction with high-ranking UN institutions, also on an informal level.

Exploring individual cases of NGOs and their activities with the UN

After having presented some general developments about the NGO-UN relationship in the first section, I now explore individual NGOs and their interaction with the UN in more detail. Special attention is given to changes in their patterns of activity since the mid-1990s. I introduce each case study with a short presentation on the specifics and the significance of that particular NGO's relation to the UN in general. Following from observations made on the four primary organizations studied in detail, I summarize the findings on other NGOs to test whether they resemble the conclusions of the first set.

Amnesty International: shifting priorities in its UN activities

Throughout the 1980s and 1990s, AI consistently describes its activities with the UN, emphasizing that it seeks to make an effective and responsible contribution to the work of the United Nations. The NGO hence considers human rights instruments adopted by the UN central to its work; its major goals are to encourage states to ratify treaties, to promote wider knowledge and understanding of the UN's norms and standards, and to support the UN in implementing them (UN Doc. E/C.2/1982/2/Add.2 §II; UN Doc. E/C.2/1987/2 §4; UN Doc. E/C.2/1991/2/Add.1 §2; UN Doc. E/C.2/1995/2 §3). Amnesty International describes its role as verifying and analysing information obtained on human rights violations and as submitting it to the relevant UN bodies by making statements and being present in meetings (UN Doc. E/C.2/1982/2/Add.2 §II; UN Doc. E/C.2/1987/2 §4; UN Doc. E/C.2/1991/2/Add.1 §2; UN Doc. E/C.2/1995/2 §3). Nonetheless, the NGO continuously develops further its priorities for activities, depending on the opportunities it perceives at the UN level.

Amnesty International considers its relationship with IGOs particularly important: it perceives activities with them as part of its mandate. As laid out in its statute, the NGO seeks to 'support and publicize the activities of and cooperate with international organizations and agencies which work for the implementation of the aforesaid provisions' and 'to make representation to international organizations and to governments whenever it appears that an individual is a prisoner of conscience or has otherwise been subjected to disabilities in violation of the aforesaid provisions' (Amnesty International 1999b). Therefore AI maintains a large IGO programme and conducts intensive activities with a variety of intergovernmental organizations, such as the UN, the European Union (EU), the Council of Europe, the Inter-parliamentary Union and the Organization of American States (OAS). It also works together with specialized agencies of the UN, such as the International Labour Organization (ILO) and the United Nations Educational, Scientific and Cultural Organization (UNESCO).

Amnesty International has a long history of working with IGOs, especially the UN. In the early 1960s, the NGO realized it could use the UN mechanisms to reach its objectives. As a former AI staff member puts it, '[f]rom its earliest days, Amnesty recognised the importance of working directly in and through the UN system, both to expose violations and to advance the frontiers of human rights protection' (Cook 1996: 183).

Over the years, AI established its leading position among the human rights NGOs within the UN context. Even other NGOs recognize AI's outstanding achievements within the UN system. As a Human Rights Watch staff member acknowledges, 'Amnesty International is one of the largest and most active human rights organizations operating within the United Nations' (Weschler 1998: 140).

The relationship with the UN has always played a key role for AI. Various heads of AI's legal office expressed the significance of the UN for the NGO. For example, Rodley (1986: 134) stated in the mid-1980s,

> [l]es Nations Unies occupent une place essentielle dans le travail d'Amnesty International. Les déclarations et les traités adoptées par les Nations Unies comme la Déclaration Universelle des droits de l'homme et le Pacte international relatif aux droits civil et politiques fournissent la base de l'action d'Amnesty International.

A decade later, Cook (1996: 181) confirmed that 'Amnesty's work within the intergovernmental organizations, such as the United Nations, is a core element of its efforts to secure universal observance of the Declaration [of Human Rights] and the organisation devotes considerable time, expertise and resources to these activities'. In fact, of human rights NGOs, AI has by far the most extensive programme with the UN.

> Through its UN work, Amnesty seeks to encourage the development of international standards, derived from the Universal Declaration, regulating the way in which governments treat their citizens; to see that governments respect these international human rights obligations that they themselves adopt; and to ensure that they are held accountable whenever they fail to do so. (Cook 1996: 182)

Amnesty International has always employed a mix of different methods by which to work with the UN. An AI representative at the UN notes, 'obviously the methods used at the UN are different from the methods used when campaigning at street level, and have to be tailored expressly for the UN fora and audience and have to maximize the opportunities that are unique to the UN' (Interview AI-1). These 'methods and strategies were extremely varied, ranging from reading out oral statements at meetings, widely distributing specific documents, to *ad hoc* lobbying of the diplomatic community, either through UN meetings or through formal representation by the AI UN representatives at the respective permanent missions' (Interview AI-1).

The majority of AI's work at the UN regards legal aspects of the human rights mechanism. Amnesty International seeks to encourage states to ratify or accede to international treaties on human rights, like the International Covenant on Economic, Social and Cultural Rights, the International Covenant on Civil and Political Rights, and the Optional Protocol, as well as the Convention against Torture and Other Cruel, Inhuman or Degrading Treatment or Punishment. Such legal work involves trying to incorporate human rights standards into countries' domestic national legislation and practice.

The themes and the range of topics addressed at the UN level are determined by AI's mandate and on the basis of its main concerns; however, similar to the tactics it uses, AI also tailors the themes it pursues to the UN as the addressee. As a representative expressed it, 'as for the themes, these were worked out obviously on the basis of AI priorities in general, but had to take into account the specificities of the UN, as some themes could be pursued there while others had no chance of attracting attention and were not worth pursuing' (Interview AI-1). That is to say, some UN forums provide excellent opportunities to launch new human rights topics, and AI 'exploits' the UN in that way (Interview AI-1). However, the NGO also takes up issues discussed at the UN and develops a standpoint on them; therefore, its choice of topics treated at the UN level often presents a 'compromise between AI priorities and UN priorities' (Interview AI-2).

Policy initiating activities

Amnesty International started providing the UN with data on human rights abuses in the early 1980s. It belonged to the first human rights NGOs to deliver information to the IGO. In fact, 'a kind of unofficial and rather mild breakthrough did take place when Amnesty International and the International League for Human Rights began providing the Human Rights Committee with background Information on individual countries prior to or during the time their human rights reports came up for review' (Korey 1998: 268). In those days, there were no procedures for information provision by non-governmental organizations, nor was there a formalized way of dealing with these sources or for citing them. Thus,

> [t]he intervention of the NGO took the form of personal verbal contact or a mailing sent to individual experts. The circumstance and communications were totally informal and the experts, even when they used the NGO information, meticulously avoided any reference

to an NGO. Should one or another expert challenge a country's presentation, reference might be made to 'reliable attested information'
as the source of the challenge. Insiders frequently understood that
phrase to mean information from an NGO with consultative status.
(Korey 1998: 268)

During the first few years of involvement with the UN, AI did not
have a clear strategy for such activities (Interview AI-3). Rather, it picked
up any opportunity that arose at the UN and sought to either gain information or to supply it itself. On the one hand, the NGO tried to find out
what was taking place at the UN on human rights; on the other hand, it
contributed to a variety of issues and submitted information and position papers to relevant subjects. It participated at the UN even on subjects not within its mandate, such as conscientious objection, the death
penalty, or peace agreements and 'simply tried to get an angle on it'
(Interview AI-3).

Over the years, however, AI developed more precise objectives for its
interaction with the UN. The international secretariat in London set up
an elaborate programme which enabled the NGO to interact more regularly with the UN. As one observer summarized,

Amnesty's early work with the United Nations was directed towards
standard-setting and tended to be carried out at the highest level of
the organisation. By the mid-1970s a more extensive UN programme
was being developed at the International Secretariat, Amnesty representatives were attending UN meetings regularly and cases and information were routinely submitted to the few international procedures
then available. (Cook 1996: 185)

Today, information exchange with the UN is still a major part of AI's
work. Most such information is exchanged on an informal basis. In particular, personal contacts between AI representatives and UN officials
allow the NGO to gain and feed in information which would otherwise
not be accessible or distributed. Despite modern means of communication, such as the Internet and Email, contacts with officials, however,
enable AI to have broader and more intense contact with the UN. An AI
representative in Geneva, for example, spends about three days a week
at the UN trying to find out about current debates and seeking to gain
information, often mainly by 'just chatting around' with the respective
UN officials (Interview AI-4). As the representative puts it, 'I am doing
my tour of duty', seeing and speaking to UN desk officers who are in

charge of the various issues or themes surrounding human rights (Interview AI-4).

A vast volume of information is channelled by AI through the formal mechanisms into the UN system (Cook 1996: 198). In fact, the NGO has been far and away the principal supplier of documentation to all of the formal mechanisms, and no other international NGO approaches AI in the number of submissions (Korey 1998: 260). Until recently, AI there-fore mainly focused on the 'classic' human rights mechanisms within the UN system, which have a clear human rights agenda, such as the Commission on Human Rights, its sub-commission on the promotion and protection of human rights, the Third Committee of the General Assembly and the treaty bodies (Interview AI-5). Until the 1990s, AI adopted a 'neutral' approach in that it worked on the countries already on the Commission's agenda. In its oral statements at the Commission, the NGO did not openly lobby for a particular result or a specific resolution, but rather remained diplomatic without questioning the Commission's agenda.

In the early 1990s, however, Amnesty International changed its strat-egy and began trying to influence the agenda of the Commission. It pushed for specific countries with bad human rights records to be on the agenda instead of following the Commission's recommendations in that regard. AI chose five countries (one per region), to be addressed during the annual sessions of the Commission on Human Rights. Amnesty International selected these countries six months beforehand in order to prepare detailed reports on their human rights situation (Interview AI-5). Researchers in London and in the field worked on these countries, analysed information about human rights violations and transmitted the relevant information to Geneva where it was presented. At the same time, AI mobilized the membership and openly campaigned for the Commission on Human Rights to take action on these countries.

In the mid-1990s AI reconsidered its priorities for work through the formal mechanisms. As part of a revised UN approach, the NGO signifi-cantly reduced its submissions to the Commission on Human Rights. Due to the enormous rise in written statements at the Commission since the opening of the UN to national NGOs, AI regarded single statements as less significant. In response to such developments, the NGO brings forward less information through this formal mechanism. Whereas throughout the 1980s and early 1990s, AI always made a number of written statements at the Commission on Human Rights, it has in recent years dramatically reduced the number of statements submitted during the sessions (Interview AI-5). Until the mid-1990s, the NGO prepared and delivered three to five single-authored statements before the commission each year in which it addressed the countries chosen. Since 1997, AI has not contributed any individual statements and only delivered joint statements with other NGOs, if at all.

Amnesty International chose instead to increase its information provision to the treaty bodies it considers better in using its information. The treaty bodies of the human rights system have long been neglected by UN officials as well as by NGOs. Although they are the major bodies for monitoring the human rights treaties, they were becoming peripheral to the UN system as they were not provided with sufficient information (Clapham 2000: 175). In the past few years, however, these bodies have become more aggressive in monitoring the human rights obligations agreed to by states. Therefore, AI today supplies them with its research and is cited in UN reports. Of the six committees which monitor the treaty bodies, the Committee Against Torture (CAT) and the Human Rights Committee (CCPR) are the main addressees of AI information. The information is also sometimes used in the Committee on the Elimination of Racial Discrimination (CERD).

AI researchers often feed questions and information to CAT members which find their way into the Committee's reports and conclusions. A good example in this respect is Amnesty International's work on Russia in late 1996. Prior to CAT's examination of Russia, AI released reports on torture and the human rights abuses there. The international secretariat wrote to Russian NGOs asking for additional information to be forwarded to CAT. Four Russian NGOs reacted and submitted their reports to the CAT; one of them even sent its own representative to the meeting (Clapham 2000: 181). Before the meeting, AI's Russia researcher also met with CAT's rapporteurs on Russia as well as with other Committee members.

In their subsequent questioning of Russia, Amnesty International was directly referred to many times and other inquiries were based on the NGO's report (UN Doc. CAT/C/SR.264 §15, 33–4, 37, 41), also recognizing the information that AI had encouraged Russian NGOs to submit. Moreover, the hearing was transmitted by a Russian radio station and throughout its prison system (Clapham 2000: 182). When AI researchers met with members of the Russian delegation in the context of this session to discuss the NGO's concerns about the human rights situation in Russia, 'it was apparent that they [the delegates] felt caught off-balance by the extensive use of the non-governmental material and there was some anger at the use of these reports' (Clapham 2000: 182).

In addition to the formal UN mechanisms for submitting information, AI is also very active through semi-informal channels, such as the meetings with the Security Council through the Arria Formula. In fact, AI was the first NGO to brief the Security Council on a Arria/Somavia Formula briefing in 1997 (Global Policy Forum 2001b). In October 2001, another Arria Formula meeting took place convened by the Permanent Mission of Jamaica in which the humanitarian situation in Liberia was addressed. This time, together with Médecins sans Frontières (MSF), Global Witness, and Oxfam, AI was one of the participants to address the Security Council on the matter (UN Doc. S/2001/1298 §30). In 2004, two of the six Arria meetings included presentations by Amnesty International (Global Policy Forum 2005a; Amnesty International 2004a; Amnesty International 2004b). Such work with the Security Council is considered highly valuable for the NGO and has become more important in recent years. AI's work at the Security Council has taken up a prime position in its annual reports over the last years (Amnesty International 2002; Amnesty International 2001a).

Amnesty International has also recently reconsidered its priorities for the development of new human rights standards. Until the mid-1990s, it had been one of the major actors pushing the development of new standards on human rights. In particular, AI put a lot of effort into the promotion of declarations and conventions on human rights at the UN level and pressuring states to ratify them. As Cook (1996: 189) explained, 'Amnesty's criticisms of a particular government's practice and its recommendations for improvements carry far greater weight when they are based on norms set up by the UN. Amnesty has, therefore, actively encouraged and participated in the development of new treaties and standards.' In recent years, however, AI exerts less effort on standard setting activities. In fact – as a representative called it – the NGO purposely shifted away from such 'conference room activity' (Interview AI-6). For example, AI did not take part in the campaign against landmines in which more than 1000 NGOs were active (Winston 2001: 34).

In the past, instead, Amnesty International had been a dynamic and active NGO in standard setting within the UN context. In fact, its campaign and activism on banning torture has been repeatedly interpreted as 'one of the most successful initiatives ever undertaken by an NGO' (Korey 1998: 171; see also Rodley 1986: 130–3, similarly Cook 1996: 189; and A. Clark 2001). In December 1972, AI started its first worldwide campaign to proclaim a total ban on torture. An element of this campaign was to pressure governments to enforce Article 5 of the Universal Declaration of Human Rights which forbids torture. Its sections around the world appealed to the UN to draw up a convention prohibiting torture. The campaign also included publicizing the extensive practice of torture in all regions of the world, for which Amnesty International produced a detailed report on countries which torture people. In 1973, for example, AI organized a conference on the ban of torture with 300 participants from governments, UN officials and NGOs. The conference was to be held at UNESCO headquarters in Paris, but was cancelled on the very last minute:

> [T]he very nature of Amnesty's global report on torture created a problem for officials of UNESCO. In the initial arrangement for the conference, Amnesty officers had given assurance that no member states of the UN would be publicly attacked at the conference. From the perspective of UNESCO's Director-General René Maheu, the publication of the torture report was itself a breach of the agreement. But UNESCO's refusal of its facilities for the conference served only to embarrass itself. Front-page stories in Le Monde and Le Figaro stirred public sympathy for Amnesty even as they challenged the integrity of UNESCO. (Korey 1998: 172)

In November of the same year, when the UN General Assembly adopted a first resolution against torture, AI, in response, started its 'Urgent Action' against torture so that cases could be made public and the NGO could pressure governments. 'To meet the new and continuing political opportunities, Amnesty arranged for its so-called urgent action network, heretofore limited in character, to be the centrepiece of its strategy. The campaign against torture, largely focused upon the UN, now was integrated into the organizational structure of Amnesty itself' (Korey 1998: 173). Partial success was reached when in 1975 the General Assembly adopted the 'Declaration on the Protection of All Persons from being Subject to Torture' in response to the brutality of the regime in Chile. However, the declaration was not binding, and AI continued to call for a more rigid treaty which was eventually declared in 1984.

A more recent example of AI's activities in standard setting is its efforts to establish a High Commissioner for Human Rights (HCHR). During the preparations to the Vienna Conference on Human Rights and at the conference itself, AI campaigned extensively for the establishment of this post (Cook 1996: 194; Ziegler 1998: 90). The idea to set up a post of High Commissioner was first introduced in October 1992 at an African regional meeting, when AI called for the creation of such a position at the preparatory meeting in Tunis (Azzam 1993: 92; Clapham 1994: 558–9; Cook 1996: 194), and at every regional preparatory meeting, it was endorsed by the NGO community (Gaer 1996: 60). Not only did the

NGO forum in Vienna strongly encourage the establishment of the post, but 60 official speakers at the plenary session referred to this concept. About two-thirds of the governments favoured the idea, whereas most of the Asian participants preferred to reconsider the establishment and to call for further study (Gaer 1996: 60). During the conference, AI continued its intensive lobbying for the NGO community to observe the working group on the issue (Cook 1996: 192).

Although AI considered the establishment of the post a landmark decision (Amnesty International 1995: 32), the actual results proved disappointing to the human rights community. The *problématique* which arises when an NGO like AI is intensely involved in such a creation process is that criticism about the actual work of the post is difficult to express. Since AI participated in creating the position of High Commissioner, it refrained from publicly criticizing the post for three years. Its 1995 annual report covering the first eight months of the work of the High Commissioner devotes five paragraphs to the 'new opportunities' opened up by its appointment, being mainly descriptive about the tasks and goals of the position (Amnesty International 1996: 37–8). The 1996 report only makes indirect references to the work of the HCHR (Amnesty International 1997). Not until 1997 did Amnesty review the High Commissioner's activities more critically and make known the deficits in the work of the UN body (Amnesty International 1998: 46–7).

Instead of focusing on developing new international standards, the NGO has shifted its efforts to the creation of mechanisms that monitor the *implementation* of human rights. Most importantly, AI was particularly active in the creation of the International Criminal Court (ICC). The NGO began working on the ICC in 1994 when it started publishing position papers and documents advocating the establishment of the ICC. Between 1998 and 2001, the NGO also involved its networks and associations of lawyers who, according to AI, played a key role in campaigning for the international criminal court and had a significant impact on the adoption of the Rome Statute. In fact, AI was one of the main NGOs pushing for the establishment of the ICC, as it lobbied the UN and member states and collected over a million signatures to a petition (Winston 2001: 27). During the plenary meeting in June and July 1998, AI was also one of those NGOs which contributed to the debate about the establishment of the court (UN Doc. A/CONF.183/SR.9 §118–19).

In addition to standard setting and information provision, AI's policy initiating efforts at the UN have always included lobby work. AI approaches UN officials and governmental representatives to the UN and supplies them with material. As a former representative expressed it, informal talks with official representatives can provide 'a way to get AI's concerns through' (Interview AI-2). For this kind of work, however, it is necessary to have a clear understanding of how the whole diplomatic system works and 'who is talking to whom' (Interview AI-2). Lobbying is well prepared when a researcher has profoundly studied the situation and the NGO representative at the UN has a friendly relationship with a government. That is to say, AI makes use of the researcher's expertise in order to prepare a report and recommendations for the UN, and provides a 'friendly government' with the information. Former partners of this kind include the Netherlands, Jamaica, Portugal, or Sweden, depending on the issues in question (Interview AI-2).

Many activities thus take place on an informal basis, so personal relations between AI staff and governmental representatives are important factors. Often it is not the entire government or all diplomats of a delegation interacting with Amnesty International, but only an individual delegation member who has good relations with a single AI representative. As one representative mentioned, communications to the EU went mostly through Austria for a period of time because AI staff in New York had particularly good connections to that nation's representative (Interview AI-2). As a result of these tight bonds between the UN and AI, information provision is mutual; in fact, AI is often given information UN officials are unable to use. They supply it with the details and let the NGO take the initiative. The reasons for this practice can be due to a lack of resources at the UN to deal with additional matters, but it is more often that AI is provided with this information for political reasons. For example, when a topic is too sensitive to be discussed in a forum of governmental delegates, UN officials encourage AI to write an open letter to the High Commissioner who then has to respond to the issue.

In addition to informal lobby work, AI's efforts at the UN also involve diplomatic activities and networking, particularly in recent years. Just like diplomats from governmental missions to the UN, AI is often represented at various meetings and receptions held by the missions surrounding the UN system. Unlike other NGOs, AI is more consistently invited to these receptions, during which the NGO meets and talks with other official representatives 'on ten minute schemes, just like governmental representatives' (Interview AI-4). Attendance at these receptions is intended to allow NGO and UN representatives to get to know each other, to establish networks and to 'simply make oneself known' (Interview AI-4). For AI, networking and mutual identification is particularly important as it facilitates lobby work and informal exchange of information (Interview AI-4).[41]

Policy developing processes

Unlike other NGOs, AI had for a long time an official policy of not being directly involved in drafting processes of international documents produced in the UN context so as not to compromise its independence. During the Cold War period in particular, AI abstained from drafting processes because it did not want to be caught between the superpowers (Interview AI-7). As a former head of AI's legal office explains

> [u]nlike several other NGOs ... Amnesty refrains, as a matter of policy, both from supporting specific draft texts and from putting forward its own drafts. Instead, it concentrates on promoting and lobbying for the essential principles and issues that it considers ought to be included in the text. This enables it to maintain a certain distance from the process of government negotiation that is involved in reaching final agreements on a text, a process which often results in weakening compromises. (Cook 1996: 191)[42]

Nowadays, however, it is acceptable for AI to participate openly in drafting processes (Interview AI-7). In fact, it has become an integral part of Amnesty International's activities at the UN to contribute its expertise and knowledge as advisor. Today, AI is involved in more drafting processes than other NGOs and usually participates throughout the entire process, whereas other NGOs neither have the resources nor the means to do so. Although usually between five and 15 NGOs participate in drafting processes, Amnesty is present more consistently and constantly (Interview AI-5). As Cook explains about the Declaration on the Protection of All Persons From Enforced Disappearances, '[a]mong NGOs, the International Commission of Jurists took the lead on advancing this text through the system, but Amnesty remained closely involved in the drafting and in lobbying until the adoption by the General Assembly' (Cook 1996: 193).

Since AI's information is often used as a first source, the UN also approaches the NGO and requests more detailed advice on specific topics. Especially since the mid-1990s, when the post of the High Commissioner for Human Rights was established, Amnesty International has often been asked for its advice. An AI representative describes that

> a lot of activities were also geared at the OHCHR [Office of the High Commissioner for Human Rights] and making demarches with the High Commissioner herself or her staff, either in response to specific requests from her Office (for example before a country visit) or on

AI's own initiative. Such meetings were either on a bilateral basis or along with other NGOs for group pressure. (Interview AI-1)

NGOs like AI are eager to be asked to brief the High Commissioner because it is an excellent opportunity to supply information. Often, such a briefing takes place on very short notice. For example, before a mission of the High Commissioner to a particular country, she may give the NGOs 48 hour notice to brief her on certain subjects. In general, only a limited number of NGOs – four to six organizations – are invited to these informal consultations, and AI is usually one of them (Interview AI-4). In addition, Amnesty International is regularly involved in semi-formal consultation processes with the Security Council. As a founding member of the Working Group on the Security Council, it participates actively and regularly at its meetings in New York (Global Policy Forum 2003; Global Policy Forum 2001a).

Policy implementing practices

In recent years, Amnesty International has put more effort into expanding its contacts with the operational bodies of the UN. As human rights have become an integral part of many UN bodies and organs as well as UN projects and programmes, NGOs now have more opportunities for thematic linkages to the operational side of the UN system.

The establishment in 1991 of the UN Observer Mission in El Salvador (ONUSAL) to verify a human rights agreement between the government and the armed opposition was a new departure that attracted the attention of Amnesty and other human rights NGOs. Suddenly, human rights appeared to be at the heart of a new area of UN operations. (Cook 1996: 207)

In response to such developments, AI broadened its spectrum of interaction with the UN and started working with a variety of other UN institutions it had had no contact with before. Since today human rights are considered an integral part of implementation processes in many issue-areas, the NGO searches for relations to operational UN bodies. In the past, many of them refused to work with human rights NGOs like AI because such UN bodies are not 'human rights' organizations but rather concerned with other issues, such as development (Interview AI-2). Now, however, human rights are not seen as a distinct subject, but as an essential component of other policies. Development, for example, is only possible with a minimum of human rights standards.

As other parts of the UN system embraced human rights language, AI built up relations with them and discussions with these institutions became much more substantial (Interview AI-5). Today, AI cooperates with a wide range of UN institutions including United Nations Development Programme (UNDP), United Nations Children's Fund (UNICEF), OCHA and the UNHCR (Interview AI-5; Amnesty International 1999a: 54). The NGO also established and continues to develop systematic strategies for interaction with world financial institutions, particularly the World Bank, as well as with business, concerning issues of trade and human rights (Interview AI-2; Interview AI-6). Moreover, it has built up a programme on human rights education with UNESCO and collaborated on human rights education programmes with WHO regarding the role of medical personnel in the treatment and protection of prisoners (Cook 1996: 188). The NGO expects to intensify its activity with these bodies over the next years (Interview AI-5).

Unlike the political bodies, the implementing bodies of the UN system have operational functions and larger resources at their disposal than the traditional human rights mechanisms with which AI usually interacts. This offers new opportunities for linkages to the UN. NGOs like AI can now build up different types of relations with the UN, for example being subcontracted for projects. In his case study on AI, Clapham (2000: 193) explains:

> Large projects aimed at 'democratisation' or 'good governance' organised through specialised agencies such as the World Bank may provide huge opportunities for improving human rights in the relevant country. ... Part of the attraction is obviously the fact that many of the projects for training, education and development are subcontracted out to NGOs by the donors and agencies.[43]

As a result of its new range of activities with the UN, AI addresses additional topics which the NGO does not usually deal with outside the UN context. For example, women's rights or the role of the Security Council are topics AI needs to work on due to its broadened approach to the UN (Interview AI-8; Amnesty International 1999a: 64–5). The most significant consequence of the NGO's activities with the UN and UN agencies is its involvement in peacekeeping. In fact, AI has made peacekeeping an integral component of its recommendations on human rights at the UN level. 'Amnesty International has set forth human rights principles to be followed in designing all peacekeeping operations, calling for UN peacekeepers to be more than silent or indifferent witnesses, demanding

that troops be impartial, properly trained and ready to uphold international law and to adhere to it in their own conduct as well' (Gaer
1996: 58).[44]

Addressing these new issues and topics has in turn caused AI to
change its way of dealing with the UN. Today, it writes reports for a variety of addressees, for instance, recommendations on the human rights
situation in a particular country are sent to the Security Council, but
also include suggestions for the operational bodies on the ground. As a
former AI representative describes this kind of activity at the UN level,
'the approach is different as one is not dealing with violators for the
most part. Rather one is seeking to integrate human rights thinking and
standards in areas where it has traditionally been excluded' (Interview
AI-8). A former head of AI's legal office summarizes the complexities
human rights NGOs deal with at the UN level:

> It has not been easy for Amnesty and other human rights NGOs to
> make an impact in the area of UN peace-keeping. Traditional meth-
> ods of action are not necessarily effective. The political negotiations
> proceed in the strictest secrecy. Proposals for UN actions are formu-
> lated at the highest political levels and are debated and ultimately
> approved by the Security Council. Peace-keeping operations involve
> interlinked components – military and civilian – operating in a
> highly volatile political context. Human rights are too often subordi-
> nated to political or military imperatives. The UN's own human
> rights bodies have been largely excluded from the design, planning
> and implementation of peace-keeping operations, including those
> with a full human rights component. So there has been no opportu-
> nity for NGOs to influence the process through their normal chan-
> nels of operations within the human rights sphere. While it may be
> preferable for NGOs to keep some distance from the political deals, it
> means that positive influence at an early stage is much more difficult
> to achieve. Yet, if human rights are not dealt with early on, it is infi-
> nitely more difficult to address these issues after the settlement and
> implementation plans are in place. (Cook 1996: 208)

In sum, AI responded to the changing UN context of the 1990s by
adjusting its pattern of activity towards the IGO. While the NGO had
been active at the UN for many decades, it had approached the UN
mainly in policy initiating activities. That is to say, it focused on activities
such as agenda setting and information provision in order to advance the
debate on human rights and influence decision-making bodies of the

UN. In recent years, however, AI has become involved in policy implementing practices and today keeps up links to a variety of UN bodies,
including those on the ground. Thus, AI now maintains a broader range
of interaction with the UN and has also shifted its priorities since the
mid-1990s. In brief, the NGO extended its pattern of UN activities to
include policy implementing practices, while simultaneously reducing
its policy initiating activities.

FIDH: deepening established areas of activity

The main objective of the FIDH at the UN level is to facilitate dialogue
between the intergovernmental body and its member NGOs engaging in
the human rights field. As described in one of its quadrennial reports,
the FIDH's purposes is 'to promote dialogue and cooperation between
human rights defenders and representatives of States and to develop the
best possible cooperation between non-governmental organizations in
the field and the bodies and procedures of the United Nations' (UN Doc.
E/C.2/1999/2/Add.14 §6). Although the FIDH has sought to strengthen
its contacts with the UN since the 1980s, it has intensified them to a
considerable extent only over the course of the last decade.

The relationship to IGOs plays a major role for the FIDH, as they are a
main addressee of its efforts to influence the promotion and protection
of human rights. For this reason, the FIDH maintains activities with
a variety of IGOs, such as the European Union, the United Nations,
the ILO, the European Council, the OSCE or the OAS. As a Paris-based
organization, it also maintains close links with UNESCO. Of these IGOs,
the FIDH maintains its most extensive contact with the EU and the UN.

At the UN level, the FIDH acts as a coordinating organization for its
member NGOs. It provides the link between headquarters in Paris, local
NGOs, and the UN (Interview FIDH-2). Whereas the single affiliated
members of the FIDH work independently of each other on the country
level, all activities at the UN level are channelled through the common
federation (Interview FIDH-3). The NGO provides services to its member
organizations which enable them to interact directly with the UN. For
example, it familiarizes them with the mechanisms of the UN, it provides the means for information exchange, and it observes the UN in the
name of its member leagues.

The FIDH is primarily concerned with bringing forward information
to the UN that has been submitted to the international body by its affiliates. Therefore, the FIDH follows the sessions of the Human Rights
Commission and the sub-commissions, and submits written and oral
presentations, whereby it forwards the information provided by the

member NGOs. Similarly, it acts as a monitoring body for its national affiliates and transfers back the information it receives from the UN. Thus, the FIDH keeps its members informed about what is going on at the UN on issues of concern to them and lets them know about upcoming events and projects (Interviews FIDH-4, FIDH-2).

Moreover, the FIDH enables direct contact between its affiliates and the UN. For example, when a national member NGO representative comes to Geneva, the FIDH arranges to meet with UN officials, governmental representatives and the media. Especially, during the six-week session of the Commission in Geneva, the FIDH creates opportunities for the affiliated members to lobby diplomats and to meet journalists. Moreover, the FIDH invites member representatives and UN officials for a lunch reception so that contacts can be established and informal discussions can take place. During presentations before the commission, the FIDH hands over its mandate to the individual member organization whose country or thematic issue is on the agenda. As a representative mentioned, 'every time we take the floor we give the floor to our member organisations' (Interview FIDH-4). In practice, this often takes the form of a joint request for presentation, and someone from a member league delivers a statement ('FIDH and its member league X' or 'the FIDH represented by its member organization Y').

Due to its broad mandate, the FIDH does not focus *per se* on any specific set of rights, but addresses a range of human rights issues. Its priorities are vast and the themes it addresses at the UN level are varied (Interview FIDH-2). As shown in a recent quadrennial reports, the FIDH covers many aspects:

> [t]he Federation has regularly transmitted reports and complaints through special rapporteurs on summary or arbitrary executions, torture, religious intolerance, the promotion and protection of the rights to freedom of opinion and expression, contemporary forms of racism, racial discrimination, xenophobia and the intolerance associated with it. It also has a working group dealing with forced disappearances and arbitrary detention. (UN Doc. E/C.2/1995/2/Add.1 §4)

Policy initiating activities

The FIDH's efforts at the UN as information provider have increased over the years. In the 1980s, relations between both were limited to occasional contacts with the formal mechanisms. Most of the FIDH's work at the UN concentrated on the annual six week period of the

Commission on Human Rights and its sub-commissions (UN Doc. E/C.2/1982/2/Add.1 §VII). The FIDH and its affiliated member organizations conducted missions of inquiry and legal observation to countries in which human rights violations were reportedly occurring. The FIDH then transferred this information to the UN and made statements before the Commission mainly during the annual assembly of the Commission on Human Rights. Apart from following the sessions of the Commission, the FIDH participated only *ad hoc* at special events, such as international conferences (UN Doc. E/C.2/1982/2/Add.1 §VII; UN Doc. E/C.2/1987/2 §9).

Since the mid-1990s, however, the FIDH has significantly intensified interaction with the UN. Most importantly, the NGO increased its presence at the UN bodies by having many representatives from national member leagues participate directly at the UN level. 'At those sessions the IFHR [*English abbreviation for* FIDH] delegation was composed mainly of representatives of its member organizations. IFHR seeks to facilitate access by national organizations for the defence of human rights to the deliberations of those bodies' (UN Doc. E/C.2/1999/2/Add.14 §6). As a result, the NGO notably increased its contributions to the formal mechanisms of the UN. For example, the FIDH has delivered significantly more contributions to the Commission on Human Rights since 1996. In fact, it tripled the number of written statements at the Commission compared to the 1980s. Until the mid-1990s, the FIDH delivered four statements on average at the Commission on Human Rights; since 1996 it increased its contribution to around 12 statements per session. It is therefore one of the most active NGOs represented during the sessions of the Commission on Human Rights.

In recent years, the FIDH has also contributed to the treaty bodies of the UN human rights machinery. For example, it provides information to the CAT, the CERD, the Committee on Economic, Social and Cultural Rights and the Human Rights Committee. On several occasions, it also coordinated its affiliated organizations attending these sessions so that they could meet directly with expert members of those bodies (UN Doc. E/C.2/1999/2/Add.14 §6). As with its statements at the Commission, the information provided by the FIDH to the treaty bodies today finds consideration in the reports of the expert bodies. A report of CAT on Tunisia, for instance, referenced an FIDH report concerning human rights violations in the country.[45] In comparison to AI, however, the FIDH plays a comparatively minor role as information provider to the treaty bodies. AI's information is considered roughly five times more often than reports provided by the FIDH.

Policy developing processes

Like its information provision, the FIDH has also expanded its activities in policy developing processes in recent years. Starting in the 1990s, it has occasionally participated in working groups with comments and proposals (UN Doc. E/C.2/2001/2/Add.13 §8). It contacts its local member NGOs and asks for their contributions to transfer to the UN (Interview FIDH-2). For example, the FIDH participated in working groups of the Sub-commission of the Commission on Human Rights as an advisor and passed on suggestions provided from its member leagues. For the Working Group of the Sub-commission on Prevention of Discrimination and Protection of Minorities, for example, it responded to an appeal launched by the group and contacted all its member leagues around the world to send in contributions on the themes of minority rights in education (UN Doc. E/C.2/1999/2/Add.14 §6).

Since the establishment of the position of the High Commissioner for Human Rights, the FIDH now occasionally functions as policy advisor during informal meetings. From time to time, the High Commissioner asks the FIDH for advice and the NGO provides the post with the relevant information. However, the FIDH regards it as a privilege to be invited. Unlike AI, the FIDH is not automatically asked for advice by the High Commissioner. As the representative mentioned, 'you never know whether you make it to the list [of invited NGOs]' (Interview FIDH-4). As there is no formal procedure for being invited, much depends on informal relations with the 'desk-officer' in charge of the specific country or thematic issue in question and his or her recommendation to the High Commissioner regarding invitees (Interview FIDH-3).

In the 1980s, instead, the FIDH had contributed only sporadically as policy advisor to the UN. It provided advisory opinions when the UN requested NGOs to reply to issues raised in the General Assembly. In 1984, for instance, the FIDH emphasized the importance of assistance in any form by states and international and non-governmental organizations to victims of racism, racial discrimination, and apartheid (UN Doc. A/39/505 §VI). It also contributed to the draft of the Code of Medical Ethics, suggesting the inclusion of specific concepts, like requiring all doctors placed in situations of torture to make it known publicly that torture has taken place (UN Doc. A/35/372 §IV; UN Doc. A/39/480 §V).

Besides human rights-related bodies of the UN system based in Geneva, the FIDH deals only rarely with the UN. Therefore, it did not expand its range of activities with the UN during the 1990s beyond the established types of policy initiation. Unlike AI, the FIDH is not part of the Working Group on the Security Council in New York, nor does it participate at any Arria/Somavia Formula gathering; it maintains only weak contact with the operational bodies of the UN system and has only limited links to the ILO.

Over the last decade, the FIDH responded little to a changing UN context and continued to maintain the same type of activity with the IGO. Its UN approach has always been to concentrate on policy initiating activities; that is to say, the NGO addresses the human rights bodies of the UN and supplies information about human rights violations. Since the mid-1990s, the FIDH increased such policy initiating activities, but still rarely works with the UN in other circumstances. In short, the FIDH did not change its spectrum of interaction with the UN, but rather deepened its established pattern.

CARE International: broadening the spectrum of interaction

CARE International and the UN maintain a variety of linkages and often share similar objectives. The NGO works with the UN and various UN agencies whenever their activities overlap and also receives funds from them. Its traditional approach has been to interact with the operational UN bodies on the field level; in recent years, however, the NGO has broadened its spectrum of interaction beyond such project work. In addition to the UN, CARE International also cooperates with a few other IGOs, such as the European Union.

Most activities with the UN take place on the operational level and contain a financial component. As a humanitarian agency, CARE International constantly seeks funding for its projects. The UN, however, has never played such an important role as a donor to make the NGO dependent on its contributions. In comparison to other private and public donors, the UN's financial contribution is rather small. Only between 4 and 7 per cent of funding in 2000 came from the UN and this figure has not changed significantly over time.

More importantly, the UN functions as the provider of adequate working conditions. This is the main factor of interest for the NGO, as the UN often supports or even substitutes local authority. Particularly during emergency and crisis situations, the UN provides logistical services and administrative capacities. It manages traffic, gives out permits for passage, and generally ensures that humanitarian agencies can operate in a safe environment. Thus, CARE International maintains most contact with the UN because it is the provider of security.

On the field level, activities between CARE International and the UN fall under the responsibility of the national sections of the NGO (Interview CARE-3). Since CARE's country officers are responsible for managing all relations with multilateral institutions, they are thus also responsible for UN relations. The single officers decide when, where, and to what extent the NGO will work together with the UN. Moreover, they are responsible for deciding on the modes and content of activities with UN bodies and they also work out the details of a contract when the UN subcontracts the NGO. CARE International has no formal guidelines governing the relationship with multinational institutions like the UN, however there are rules for managing relations on the country level which serve as guidance (Interview CARE-3).

When a contract is discussed, the country manager makes a proposal which is then submitted to the UN, and after a period of negotiation over the controversial issues, the proposal is revised, and it is signed when all differences are resolved. This procedure of discussing details concerning the relationship and delegating tasks between both organizations can take between two days in emergencies and six months in a development project. The NGO rarely changes its strategic plan to fit UN proposals, but rather tries to influence the UN to include issues that it believes are important to better conduct a project and to fit CARE International's needs. As a result, the NGO and the UN bodies often make compromises (Interview CARE-4).

CARE International sees its activities with the UN as a partnership and is supportive of the UN. The NGO's experience with the UN is generally very positive, especially with smaller and implementing bodies. In particular, CARE International maintains a good relationship with 'technical agencies of the UN as they tend to be easy to work with' and have a 'tightly focused area of expertise' (Interview CARE-4). For example, relations to the United Nations Fund for Population Activities (UNFPA) are particularly good, as it appreciates the resources NGOs bring into the country, and 'tends to view NGOs more as professional peers' (Interview CARE-4).

Policy implementing practices

CARE International and the UN interact with each other predominantly in the field. Single sections of the NGO cooperate with the IGO on the ground or implement projects on behalf of or jointly with the UN. In particular during the 1980s, CARE International's relationship with the UN was characterized by such a clear service function. As emphasized in one of its early quadrennial reports on its activities with the UN, '[m]uch of the organization's consultative and collaborative efforts vis-à-vis the United Nations take place in the "field" where CARE operates development and emergency assistance programmes in 38 developing countries'

(UN Doc. E/C.2/1987/2/Add.1 §6). Many such projects with the UN were conducted on a contractual basis and the NGO cooperated with the operational bodies of the UN system (for examples see UN Doc. E/C.2/1982/2/Add.2 §V).

Due to the nature of its work, CARE International's activities with the UN have always been dominated by cooperation with UNHCR. Both organizations have been working together for a long time. Unlike other UN bodies, UNHCR is an implementing partner and subcontracts NGOs like CARE International (Interview CARE-4). When implementing a project for the UNHCR, CARE International conducts the project 'in its own name, but on the UN's behalf' (Interview CARE-4); that is to say, UNHCR is not in the field itself, but contact with the UN is necessary, often on a daily basis for logistical reasons (Interview CARE-4).

Already in the 1980s, field activities between the NGO and UNHCR were manifold. Both organizations interacted in the field in various parts of the world. Activities took many forms and types of cooperation from contract work for the UN to complementary provision of services to mutual administrative support (UN Doc. E/C.2/1982/2/Add.2 §V). For example, CARE provided services to the Chad in 1982 under a contract with the UNHCR. The project assisted Chadian refugees returning from Cameron and activities included the transport, operation, and distribution of relief supplies like blankets, household utensils, soap, tools, and equipment for housing repairs (UN Doc. E/C.2/1987/2/Add.1 §6). In the 1990s, CARE International continued to implement projects on behalf of UNHCR in different parts of the world and on a range of activities reaching from pure implementation work to coordination links for logistical support (UN Doc. E/C.2/1997/2/Add.2 §6; UN Doc. E/C.2/2001/2/Add.3 §2).

Although the NGO has always maintained closest links to UNHCR, it also collaborates with various other UN bodies. In the early 1980s, for example, CARE worked together with the World Food Programme (WFP), UNICEF, UNDP and the International Bank for Reconstruction and Development (IBRD). In the late 1980s, it also started interacting with the Food and Agriculture Organization (FAO) in forestry projects in various parts of the world. At the field level, there was likewise intense communication when FAO projects and CARE's activities had similar purposes and locations as 'such exchange is mutually advantageous' (UN Doc. E/C.2/1987/2/Add.1 §6; UN Doc. E/C.2/1991/2 §7). CARE also worked quite often with UNICEF in field projects. Again, in the 1990s, CARE International continued to cooperate with several of these bodies of the UN system. Today, as a staff member put it, the NGO maintains tightest links with UNHCR and WFP, but also UNICEF, UNFPA and FAO are important partners for CARE International; the NGO rarely work with UNDP these days, as its interest in humanitarian NGOs is limited (Interview CARE-3).

Policy initiating and developing processes

As CARE International and various UN bodies and agencies share similar goals and objectives, they often fulfil complementary tasks in the field work. Since the 1990s, collaboration between CARE International and the UN has not been limited to field work only: the NGO is today continuously and regularly involved in policy discussions at the UN level in addition to its operational links. Unlike before, a 'close working relationship [between CARE International and the UN] takes place both at the field and at the headquarters level' (UN Doc. E/C.2/1993/2 §11).

Before the 1990s, CARE rarely worked together with the UN in any context other than on the field level. The NGO hardly ever used the UN as a forum to transmit political statements as policy advisor or information provider. In the early 1980s, its involvement at the policy initiating level was limited to sporadic attendance of UN conferences and other meetings, usually simply following these sessions, but rarely did the NGO make statements or comments. On average, CARE made one or two statements a year within the UN context (UN Doc. E/C.2/1987/2/Add.1). On any regular basis, however, there was not much activity between the NGO and the UN as information provider. CARE maintained only some limited contact with the DHA, the predecessor of OCHA. Being the first coordinating body for humanitarian affairs in the UN system, 'it was somewhat natural' for the NGO to liaise to this body, but at that stage, the organization was not deeply involved with the UN system as there was no interest in it from the national member sections (Interview CARE-2).

In recent years, however, the UN has gained significance for CARE International as a policy discussion forum. Since the mid-1990s, it has increased the amount of effort it devotes to policy initiating and development. As mentioned in a quadrennial report,

> CARE International and its members value its expanding partnership with the various bodies of the Council very highly. The close working relationship promoted by regular consultation with all its members is very much appreciated. Through such cooperation, CARE International can work to achieve the goal of helping those in need throughout the developing world, which is the common purpose of the Council and CARE International. (UN Doc. E/C.2/1997/Add.2 §6)

In fact, CARE International made policy initiating activities a goal when it broadened its programme strategies to target intergovernmental institutions (CARE International 2001; Interview CARE-2). As a consequence, the CARE sections started sharing the additional workload: some attended various UN conferences in the first half of the 1990s, others gradually established regular links with the UN system (UN Doc. E/C.2/1997/Add.2 §6). As part of its strategic plan, it also decided to maintain regular contact with UN bodies in Geneva and New York. The NGO now gradually develops strategies for choosing the topics it wishes to address within the UN context. As a representative of CARE International expressed it, so far, the NGO seeks to be 'faithful to what we do in the field' and thus, in order to stress when it is taking a stand on something, does not contribute simply to every issue (Interview CARE-3).

Similarly, before the mid-1990s, CARE only occasionally cooperated with the UN in advisory functions. Today, the NGO is regularly involved with the UN as policy advisor on various committees and boards. For a long time it had been perceived as the 'sleeping giant in the NGO community' whose potential for involvement lagged behind its formal institutional capacities (Interview CARE-3). In recent years, however, CARE International has recognized its role within the NGO community and participates in policy developing processes.

Unlike NGOs in other issue-areas, the organization does usually not act as CARE International only, but rather represents the community of private humanitarian agencies. It holds positions in different humanitarian NGOs representing networks before the UN. As one CARE representative expressed it: 'I don't believe I overtly tried to "influence" UN agencies as strictly a "CARE Person". However, being in Geneva allowed CARE to play an important role *together* with other international humanitarian NGOs' (Interview CARE-5). For example, CARE International has led the NGO community in the SCHR for some years. Most importantly, a CARE representative served on the Sphere Management Committee (Interview CARE-5). Through this position in SCHR, the NGO was influential in the development of the Sphere Humanitarian Charter and Minimum Standards for Humanitarian Response.

In addition, CARE International and the UN share common standards. For example, the UN uses the NGO's manuals where appropriate:

CARE International and the United Nations Mine Action Service joined together in 1998 to develop a landmine safety manual and training programme for United Nations and NGO personnel working in countries with mines around the world. The manual and programme are based on ones CARE International developed for its own staff. The programme has received support from the United Nations Foundation support. (UN Doc. E/C.2/2001/2/Add.3 §2)

CARE International's activities with the UN today involve information sharing on a day-to-day basis. The NGO is regularly represented at UNHCR Executive Committee meetings in New York, for instance. It brings its data from the field into UN bodies and returns information from the UN to field offices (Interview CARE-6). It also holds regular consultation meetings with the various UN bodies and agencies and their representations in Geneva and New York, such as UNHCR, UNDP, WFP, UNICEF or the joint United Nations programme on HIV/AIDS (UNAIDS) (UN Doc. E/C.2/2001/Add.3 §2). As a result, CARE International addresses a greater variety of issues in the UN context. Since the NGO was mainly involved with the UN through service delivery before the mid-1990, topics and modes were defined in terms of service contracts. This has changed over the last five to seven years. Nowadays, the NGO also needs to address issues such as poverty and social injustice due to its representational functions (Interview CARE-3).

Since 1995, CARE International is also increasingly involved in informal briefings as policy advisor, because the NGO has given the Security Council highest priority in its activity (Interview CARE-6). In 1997, CARE was one of the first humanitarian NGOs to brief the Security Council on the Great Lakes Crisis. Together with MSF and Oxfam International, CARE International was invited to a briefing 'because of its deep involvement in humanitarian assistance to the war-torn region' (Global Policy Forum 2001c). The high attendance of the meeting showed its significance: in addition to those three NGOs, about a dozen individuals participated from the NGO side, including several which came specifically for this meeting from field operations. Moreover, 27 delegations of member states attended the meeting, including all 15 Security Council members and another 12 delegations as well as Secretariat staff. After the briefing, the three humanitarian agencies held a joint press conference in which they 'welcomed the historic opportunity' (Global Policy Forum 2001c).

In 2000, CARE International gave the first regular Arria presentation together with other humanitarian NGOs. Its secretary-general at that time, Guy Tousignant and others urged the Security Council members 'to separate humanitarian concerns from political considerations when mandates for United Nations missions are drafted, and stressed that greater priority should be given to the plight of internally displaced persons' (UN Doc. A/54/942-S/2000/707 §3; see also Global Policy Forum 2000a). CARE International was recently again involved in Arria briefings (see CARE International 2004).

In brief, CARE International responded to a changing UN context by adjusting its pattern of activity toward the IGO over the last years. Until recently, the NGO's main activities with the UN took place in policy implementing practices as it maintained a long history of links with the operating UN bodies in its given field of activity. Since the mid-1990s, however, CARE International shifted from a mere operational relationship with the UN to include policy initiating and policy developing processes in its pattern of activity. Today, CARE International also serves as an advisor and information provider to UN bodies in Geneva and New York, often representing the humanitarian agencies as a whole. In recent years, CARE International was thus able to adapt to greater opportunities at the UN level and broadened its spectrum of interaction with the UN. That is to say, the NGO took up additional areas of activity while keeping its core.

Oxfam International: acting individualistically with the UN

Oxfam International's activities with the UN are more diffuse than those of the other NGOs examined in this study. The individual Oxfams work with the UN through the international body, but also have other separate links with the IGO. Whereas the operational members maintain a long history of activities with the UN in the field, other activities with the UN take place on an *ad hoc* basis. Like CARE International, Oxfam International primarily interact with governments, with whom they work out the details of cooperation during projects and contractual relations. Of the activities with IGOs, Oxfam International works extensively with the World Bank and other financial institutions, as the NGO focuses mainly on trade issues when working with IGOs (Interview Oxfam-2).

The international body of the Oxfams enables the members to maintain a link to the UN. Through this common umbrella organization, the affiliates are informed about what is taking place at the UN and what the UN is planning to accomplish in specific emergency situations. In return, the Oxfam affiliates are able to deliver information which they receive from their field staff to the UN level. Such exchange of information enables the NGO to support its field people and staff members in headquarters better (Interview Oxfam-3). Thus, on the whole, most of the common activities between the international body and the single

Oxfam affiliates regarding the UN focus on sharing information (Interview Oxfam-1).

However, besides the common exchange of information, the single members of Oxfam International also interact with the UN individually. Unlike other NGOs in this study, affiliates of Oxfam International, establish their own linkages to the UN and cooperate individually and separately with UN-related bodies or through other networks. Thus, Oxfam Great Britain (Oxfam GB) and Novib/Oxfam Netherlands, for example, have common links with the UN, but also their own separate ones. Thus, the international body is only one channel among many through which single affiliates can be active at the UN.

Similar to CARE International, Oxfam International's contacts with the UN in field operations maintain a financial element. However, in comparison to other donors, the UN is a small contractor for Oxfam International. It is only one among a variety of multinational institutions which provide the NGO with funds, making up a small percentage of Oxfam International's budget as a whole (Interview Oxfam-4). Even for Oxfam GB, which is by far the biggest of the operational Oxfams, only a small amount of funding hails from multilateral institutions which include the UN (Interview Oxfam-1).

The NGO's activities with the UN are dominated by Oxfam GB, the largest branch of the Oxfams. Within the international body, the British member maintains the most contact with the UN; its humanitarian department and its policy department have most relations with the UN on a daily basis, as staff working in these departments spend 'a fair bit of time' on UNHCR matters (Interview Oxfam-5). When analysing the relationship between Oxfam International and the UN, it is thus often difficult to differentiate between the international body and the national British member NGO, because 'sometimes it is Oxfam International and sometimes it is Oxfam GB' which conduct the activities for the NGO with the UN (Interviews Oxfam-1, Oxfam-5). In particular, much of Oxfam's involvement with NGO networks consulted by the UN is initiated or driven by Oxfam Great Britain and feeds back predominantly or sometimes even exclusively into the British affiliate of Oxfam International. In other situations, affiliated members may profit from Oxfam Great Britain's activities with the UN, for example they receive information about UN activities through Oxfam Great Britain when it concerns all the Oxfam members.

As Oxfam GB is the largest of the Oxfam affiliates, it also drives its own relations with the UN, particularly when there is disagreement within Oxfam International which line the NGO as a whole should take.

If Oxfam GB has an approach different from that of Oxfam International, it may thus take its own steps at the UN level; however, there is a tendency within Oxfam International to find common agreement (Interview Oxfam-5). On the whole, the relationship with the UN usually is very cooperational. Sometimes Oxfam GB and the UN are allies when they share similar aims, and in fact the NGO can be closer to the IGO than to many governments. Moreover, Oxfam International would not lead any campaign against the UN (Interview Oxfam-1).

Policy implementing practices

Like CARE, Oxfam International's activities with the UN have been mainly on the field level over the last decades. It has cooperated with a variety of operational UN bodies during the implementation phase of various field projects. Oxfam's 'first and most regular contact with UN agencies' was in the disaster field, helping refugees through the UN Relief and Work Agency for Palestine Refugees (UNRWA) and with the Office of the High Commissioner for Refugees (Stamp 1982: 99; see also UN Doc. E/C.2/1982/2/Add.1 §14; UN Doc. E/C.2/1987/2 §47). As Stamp (1982: 100) reports in the 1980s for the British branch of Oxfam,

> Oxfam's most extensive contact with the UN has been at the grassroots level. Projects have been funded with UNRWA, UNHCR, FAO, WHO and with UNICEF. The Field Director often establishes a close working relationship with the UN Development Programme Resident Representative and at times have gone on tour to inspect projects together. In emergency relief operations, where the UN now designates a 'lead agency' to provide field coordination for its many programmes and specialized agencies, co-operation may be particularly close and frequent. ... UNICEF along with the International Committee of the Red Cross, coordinated most non-communist, governmental assistance, while Oxfam administrated the international NGO consortium. UNICEF, ICRC and Oxfam made sure their work was complementary.

Even today, mainly the operational members of Oxfam International maintain activities with the UN in the field. Unlike CARE International, the NGO usually does not operate as 'Oxfam International' in the field, where single Oxfam affiliates lead activities individually. Therefore, field level activities between the NGO and the UN take place between the operational Oxfams in a respective country and the operating UN bodies. Non-operational Oxfams have little or no activities with the UN on the field level. For example, Novib/Oxfam Netherlands maintains activities in the field only through local partners as it has no own field offices (Interview Oxfam-6). Thus, the respective programme officer in the headquarters in The Hague only keeps limited contact with the UN.

In the field, activities between the Oxfams and UN bodies or agencies can take different forms. Member NGOs may take up complementary roles, or the UN will subcontract an Oxfam affiliate for particular services. For example, the operating Oxfams may take over parts of the UNHCR operation, such as water and sanitation facilities for which the UN gives local contracts depending on the situation (Interview Oxfam-1). The Oxfams maintain links with the UN system in a variety of ways. The most important are UNHCR, OCHA, UNICEF (in emergency response programmes) and WFP, for which the NGO delivers food as a contractor. Most activities have taken place with UNHCR, for which Oxfam International often is an implementing partner. The two bodies often share technical knowledge about a specific issue matter and work together in the planning and implementation of projects (Interview Oxfam-5).

Policy initiating and developing processes

Until the 1990s, policy initiating and developing activities between the Oxfams and the UN took place rarely and on an *ad hoc* basis. Only at conferences and through networks of NGOs did Oxfam go beyond a mere contractual and field relationship with the UN. As Stamp (1982: 100) reported,

> only once has Oxfam used the formal channels to lobby at the UN in New York and that was to call for more aid for the Bengal refugees in India in 1971. Even Oxfam's lobbying tends to occur at the grass-roots. In 1980 when the UNDP representative in Uganda suspended the UN's convoys of relief lorries into Karamoja, it was pressure in Kampala from Save the Children and Oxfam, which helped to get supplies resumed. Normal contact between Oxfam and the UNDP would not involve public appeals of this type. Discussion, co-operation and exchange of information may result in influence of a less immediate or obvious kind.

In the late 1970s and throughout the 1980s, Oxfam only sporadically attended conferences and meetings of the UN related to its area of activity (UN Doc. E/C.2/1982/2/Add.1 §XIV; UN Doc. E/C.2/1987/2 §47; UN Doc. E/C.2/1991/2 §68). It sent representatives to attend NGO forums organized alongside these conferences. Oxfam GB, for example, attended some conferences as an observer (UN Doc. E/C.2/1982/2/Add.1 §14).

In the early 1990s, Oxfam GB continued to participate occasionally at a variety of international conferences (UN Doc. E/C.2/1995/2 §58), but did not maintain regular contact with UN bodies. The NGO only produced a few statements for the UN upon request when being asked its opinion on a particular issue. Occasionally, it also functioned as a consultant. Oxfam's Development Policy Adviser, for example, advised the World Bank-NGO Committee (UN Doc. E/C.2/1991/2 §68).

Before the mid-1990s, Oxfam's activities with the UN outside the field level were directed through NGO networks. Most importantly, the International Council of Voluntary Associations (ICVA) provided a key network for the NGO. In the 1980s,

> contact with the UN is more readily made through the International Council of Voluntary Agencies, which now is among the small number of NGOs with Category I consultative status. Joint statements with other NGOs are regularly made when developing issues are debated in New York or Geneva and Oxfam's views will usually be in accord with the ICVA position, even if Oxfam has not been directly involved. (Stamp 1982: 100)

In fact, Novib/Oxfam Netherlands maintained all of its activities with the UN on a policy level through ICVA until the mid-1990s. Novib's contributions and statements were submitted to this network, which then presented them at the UN (Interview Oxfam-6). However, since ICVA only had limited time slots for contributions, it had to choose among the contributions of many member NGOs what to deliver at the UN level. Therefore, not only did Novib depend on its network, its own contributions were not all considered (Interview Oxfam-6).

Novib's participation during international conferences was also directed through an NGO network. In the early 1990s, for example, the NGO followed a variety of conferences. Most importantly, it attended the Summit on Social Development in Copenhagen in 1995 (Interview Oxfam-6). As the NGO knew the agenda of the conference early on in the preparatory process, it tried to get its Southern partners involved and together with them the NGO developed a common position paper for the Summit. With the help of the Non-Governmental Liaison Service, Novib formed a development caucus which continued to exist as the Social Watch initiative and monitors the implementation outcome of the summit (Interview Oxfam-7).

Though it is a member of Oxfam International, Novib does not necessarily seek close contact to the other Oxfams when attending conferences, as it can be very helpful to be represented separately: every individual Oxfam member is then able to lobby its own government. Similarly, government representatives sometimes prefer to come to the individual national Oxfam affiliate and ask for advice. Thus, during conferences 'there can be eleven Oxfams' being active individually and separately (Interview Oxfam-7). For example, at the Conference on the Least Developed Countries in 2001 two of the Oxfams (Novib and Oxfam Solidarité) were present individually and also simultaneously accredited through Oxfam International (UN Doc. A/CONF.191/13; UN Doc. E/C.2/2000/2/Add.1 §10).

Since the mid-1990s, Novib regularly follows the sessions of the Commission on Human Rights and those of the Commission for Social Development. Novib and other NGOs established common networks so that they could coordinate their efforts and bring forward a more influential stance to promote the topics in question (Interview Oxfam-6). Again, these networks also often include smaller and Southern NGOs which would otherwise have no opportunity to be represented in international events. Novib also accredits representatives from other Southern NGOs so that they can speak at the UN level (Interview Oxfam-6). Other than the sessions of the commissions, Novib maintains only irregular activities with the UN. For example, it has limited contacts with UNDP and UNICEF as policy advisor, for which from time to time a Novib representative is invited to provide suggestions (Interview Oxfam-7).

Oxfam GB, instead, maintains most relations with the UN in New York through the IASC and as a founding member of the Working Group on the Security Council. As Oxfam GB has the greatest experience of the Oxfams in humanitarian response, it is the 'natural representative' within Oxfam International in these UN forums (Interview Oxfam-5). Consequently, Oxfam GB also represents Oxfam International at the SCHR. Moreover, it associates with the UN through OCHA. However, it uses its contact mainly as a mechanism to feed in and receive information on current affairs (Interview Oxfam-3). Unlike CARE International, Oxfam GB puts no particular effort into its work with the humanitarian institutions in Geneva (Interview Oxfam-1), providing information only rarely (UN Doc. E/CN.4/1998/24 §III).

Although Oxfam GB alone is a major player in the humanitarian aid sector, it seeks to work together with other NGOs to have greater impact. As a staff member mentioned, 'we seek to avoid being Oxfam by itself' (Interview Oxfam-1). As such, Oxfam has – together with other humanitarian NGOs – participated in Arria/Somavia Formulas and briefed the Security Council on current issues (Global Policy Forum 2001c; UN Doc.

A/54/942-S/2000/707 §3). With CARE International, for example, Oxfam International participated at the first Formula in September 1997, briefing Security Council members on the Great Lakes situation. For this historic meeting, the NGO had sent the director of Oxfam GB to lead the organization's delegation (Global Policy Forum 2001c; Global Policy Forum 2002; see also Oxfam International 2003).

In the future, Oxfam International seeks to have a more coherent face at the UN level. Activities with the UN are intended to be more regular rather than *ad hoc*. For example, Oxfam International seeks to establish more systematic contact with the UN in advisory boards (Interview Oxfam-4; Oxfam International 2000a: 29). In this context, the NGO plans to shift some of its current focus on monetary institutions, such as IMF and World Bank, to the UN instead (Interviews Oxfam-4, Oxfam-2).

Oxfam International responded to a changing UN context to a limited extent and adjusted its pattern of activity only slightly. The Oxfams' main activities with the UN have been in policy implementation processes on a field level, where the NGO has been cooperating with a variety of UN bodies and agencies. In the 1990s, the Oxfam affiliates continued to keep their operational links with the UN, and added some policy initiating and policy developing processes to their activities, as some Oxfams occasionally function as advisors or information providers to the IGO. However, its relationship with the UN remained diffuse and took place mainly on an *ad hoc* basis, as single Oxfam affiliates work with the UN separately or through various other networks that have no direct link to the international body of Oxfam. In short, over the course of the 1990s, Oxfam International changed its spectrum of interaction at the UN level only modestly.

Other NGOs

After having examined the four main cases in detail, I will briefly present an additional set of NGOs and their adjustments to the UN context, showing some broad features of each in order to control the findings of the first set. This indicates that other NGOs adjusted differently to the UN context in recent years also. While some shifted their spectrum of interaction or broadened it, others rather concentrated on their existing activities and adapted only to a limited extent.

Human Rights Watch

Human Rights Watch started interacting with the UN in the early 1990s when it changed its perception of the UN after it had played a valuable role in ending the raging civil war in El Salvador and in the mediation process on human rights (Korey 1998: 352). Before the 1990, HRW did not have 'such a clear agenda for its UN work as AI' (Interview HRW-1). Over the last decade, however, HRW has established an impressive record of policy initiating activities. Whereas in the late 1980s and early 1990s, 'HRW was inexistent on the Geneva scene' (Interview AI-9), many of HRW's efforts at the UN today, actually focus on providing information during the sessions of the Commission on Human Rights and the treaty bodies (Interview HRW-2).

Since 1995, the NGO makes comparatively many written statements and oral presentations at the Commission at its annual session. All year round, it provides the country and thematic specialists of the UN with information it has researched during its field missions. Moreover, through activities driven by the legal office in London and the New York office, it does legal work at the UN level (Interview HRW-2). Also, HRW attends the sessions of the Third Committee of the General Assembly, different commissions (for example, the Subcommission on Prevention of Discrimination and Protection of Minorities or the Commission on the Status of Women) and various conferences (UN Doc. E/C.2/1999/ 2/Add.7 §4).

Human Rights Watch also functions as a policy advisor to the UN. The NGO maintains regular contacts with the High Commissioner for Human Rights and provides information and expertise on a range of issues (UN Doc. E/C.2/1999/2/Add.7 §4). HRW provides 'technical assistance', for example, when asked to brief the commissioner before missions (Interview HRW-2). HRW has been asked for consultation by various UN bodies. For example, in 1996 the UN invited the NGO to a consultation on HIV/AIDS and human rights to which HRW proposed its own formulations (UN Doc. E/C.2/1999/2/Add.7 §4).

HRW was also invited by UNHCR to be part of an editorial group drafting the NGO Guide to International Standards on Refugees and Human Rights (UN Doc. E/C.2/1999/2/Add.7 §4). Moreover, HRW frequently consulted with UNICEF on a number of issues concerning children and their rights. In addition, HRW regularly provided human rights material to UN bodies and departments, particularly to UNHCR, UNDP, OCHA and to the Secretariat in response to specific requests (UN Doc. E/C.2/1999/2/Add.7 §4). HRW also is a member of the Working Group on the Security Council and has briefed the Security Council on Arria Formulas (Human Rights Watch 2004a; Human Rights Watch 2004b).

Similarly to Amnesty International, HRW recently expanded its spectrum of interaction with the UN and established links to UN implementing bodies. As a result, Human Rights Watch became more involved in peacekeeping; in fact, it has made this issue a component of its recommendations and, for example, urged among other things Kofi Annan to integrate human rights into all procedures and programmes of the UN soon after he became UN secretary-general. HRW has also published extensively on this issue (Weschler 1998: 145).

International League for Human Rights

The International League for Human Rights was one of the first NGOs to conduct activities with the UN. In fact, the UN has always played a significant role for the ILHR in its purpose to promote and safeguard human rights. Since the foundation of the United Nations, the ILHR has maintained relations with it. First contacts between the NGO and the UN can be traced back to 1946 when ILHR representatives transmitted written statements to the IGO and gave oral presentations (ILHR 1949). The ILHR also maintains relations with the OSCE and the Council of Europe.

The ILHR seeks 'to promote the development at the United Nations of international human rights standards and measures of implementation ... to promote ratification and compliance' (UN Doc. E/C.2/1982/2/Add.4 §7). The ILHR's predominant activity within the UN system is the provision of information. It regularly submits statements in compliance with the international treaties and covenants. As a representative described it, the ILHR seeks 'to strengthen the Human Rights mechanisms, present alternative reports, give speeches before the Commission, sending inquiries and alert rapporteurs, help rapporteurs on their missions' (Interview ILHR-2).

As with the FIDH, the ILHR regularly advocates on behalf of its affiliated members and partners around the world. It also functions as a transmitter of information for its members. Already in 1949 a document states that '[t]he League has extended its contacts with affiliated national groups throughout the world in order to serve as a means of communication between them and the United Nations' (ILHR 1949: 137). Consequently, the ILHR follows the sessions of the Commission on Human Rights, and makes contributions such as written and oral statements (UN Doc. E/C.2/1987/2 §33; UN Doc. E/C.2/1991/2/Add.1 §18).

Today, the ILHR presents statements at the Commission on Human Rights more regularly than in the 1980s, though it did not deepen such activities as much as the FIDH. Rather than the single national affiliates, it is the principal international body of the NGO that delivers information to the UN. The members provide the ILHR with information on human rights violations and the international secretariat prepares and submits information and statements to the UN.

Similar to the FIDH, the League too creates possibilities for its affiliated members to meet with UN officials. For example, it convenes every year a series of workshops each for 30 to 45 delegates from its affiliates on human rights issues prior to the sessions of the Third Committee of the General Assembly. As a New York based NGO, it concentrates on activities at the UN headquarters. Therefore, the ILHR is also a member of the WGSC. In Geneva, the international body only convenes a short special briefing for delegates to the Commission (UN Doc. E/C.2/1995/2 §44; UN Doc. E/C.2/1999/2/Add.10 §8). Other than such policy initiating activities, the ILHR has very limited contact with UN bodies.

International Save the Children Alliance

The International Save the Children Alliance has always had strong relations with IGOs. In fact, the NGO even interacted with the predecessor of the UN because its first national section approached the League of Nations in 1922 (Freeman 1965: 42). The Alliance has a long history of links with the UN and UN agencies, having done a lot of implementing work with different operational UN bodies. Already in the 1980s, it implemented a variety of projects on a contractual basis with UNHCR in various regions of the world (UN Doc. E/C.2/1982/2/Add.3 §22; UN Doc. E/C.2/1987/2/Add.1 §41). UNHCR also funded a Save the Children-administered refugee education programme and the NGO implemented one of UNHCR's programmes (UN Doc. E/C.2/1987/2/Add.1 §41).

However, as with CARE International, the relationship between the ISCA and the UN did not go beyond the field level until the mid-1990s. Describing the British section's relationship with the UN for the 1970s and 1980s, Penrose and Seaman (1996: 153) note that '[i]ts relationships with UNHCR and other UN agencies were at field level, sometimes at national level and less frequently at regional level. Rarely did SCF-UK engage with UN agencies at an international level.'

Due to its focus on children, the NGO also implemented contracts for the UN Children's Fund in different parts of the world and on a variety of issues. Moreover, a great amount of collaboration in training and implementation also took place together with UNICEF (UN Doc. E/C.2/1982/2/Add.3 §22; UN Doc. E/C.2/1987/2/Add.1 §41). In fact, the Executive Director of UNICEF sent letters to all country representatives encouraging them to find ways of working with the ISCA (UN Doc. E/C.2/1987/2/Add.1 §41). In addition, activities with UNDP became more intense in the late 1980s, when this UN body provided funding for a ISCA programme, and NGO staff participated in UNDP meetings (UN Doc. E/C.2/1991/2 §74). Other activities followed with WFP, UNRWA, the World Bank and the WHO (UN Doc. E/C.2/1991/2/Add.2 §19). In the 1990s, the NGO continues activities at field level with various UN bodies and agencies and now cooperates on a regular basis with UNHCR, UNICEF or UNDP, for example (Interview ISCA-1).

Other than the field level, the NGO and the UN's activities were limited in the 1980s; it participated only at some conferences to which it sent individual representatives (UN Doc. E/C.2/1987/2/Add.1 §41). However, in the early 1990s, the ISCA started working with the UN on other levels. For example, it coordinated the subgroup on outreach and advocacy for the NGO-UNICEF Coordinating Committee on Activities for Children in Eastern Europe. It also served on the NGO Committee on UNICEF, whereby the US section held the position of the chair. By now, UNICEF and the NGO even regularly review their progress in extensive collaboration on all levels (UN Doc. E/C.2/1997/2/Add.1 §9).

In fact, over the course of the last decade, the ISCA became increasingly involved with the UN in policy developing processes. Since the mid-1990s, the NGO has been a member of SCHR and fulfilled the role of the chair, representing the SCHR on the IASC. The NGO is also a member of the WGSC. Moreover, part of the ISCA is on the International Campaign to Ban Landmines (ICBL) Steering Committee (UN Doc. E/C.2/1997/2/Add.1 §9). Relations with UNHCR also strengthened over the course of the 1990s. After a joint effort resulted in UNHCR Guidelines on Refugee Children in 1991, the two organizations continued to develop relations, particularly on promoting the use of these guidelines (UN Doc. E/C.2/1997/2/Add.1 §9; UN Doc. E/C.2/2001/2/Add.19 §7). As part of this effort, in 1996 the joint refugee assistance programme and a protection and capacity-building programme became established.

Since 2000, the ISCA also seeks to become more involved in policy initiating activities in major UN locations. In New York, for example, the NGO will work in monitoring and information gathering and pro-actively bring forward children's issues while responding on country and thematic issues which reflect its programmes on the ground (Interview ISCA-1).

Action Aid Alliance

As with Oxfam International, the activities of the AAA with the UN are dominated by the largest of the Action Aids, which is the UK affiliate (AA UK). However, even AA UK has limited contacts with the UN. In its activities with IGOs, it rather focuses on the European intergovernmental organizations, and maintains closer contacts with the EU institutions

(Interview AAA-1). Like Oxfam, the NGO's main activities with the UN take place on the field level; AA UK country programme directors cooperate directly with UN programmes and bodies or specialized agencies in various ways. For example, in 1994 and 1995, the Action Aid Logistics Support Unit, operating under and partially supported by the UNCHR, delivered relief supplies to Rwandan refugees in Zaire (UN Doc. E/C.2/1997/2/Add.2 §1). AA UK also maintains activities with UNICEF and UNDP, but does no contractual work with the UN (Interview AAA-2; UN Doc. E/C.2/1997/2/Add.2 §1).

Other activities with the UN are irregular, and interaction mostly takes place during conferences or through programmes which are the results of conferences (Interview AAA-2). AA UK, for example, participated at various conferences throughout the 1990s and sent representatives (UN Doc. E/C.2/1997/2/Add.2 §1). During conferences, AA UK usually lobbies on its own or through other strategic alliances. For example, at the Social Summit in Copenhagen in 1995, AA UK participated through Eurostep, the Development Caucus and the South Asian Caucus. Similarly, the alliance participated in the Conference on Women in Beijing in 1995 through the Asian Caucus and the African Caucus (UN Doc. E/C.2/1997/2/Add.2 §1).

The Action Aid Alliance functioned occasionally also as a policy advisor to the UN. For example, during the Earth Summit 1992 in Rio, AA UK was represented on the official UK delegation. Moreover, one of its staff members was seconded for two years to work as NGO Affairs Officer at the European office of UNDP in Geneva (UN Doc. E/C.2/1997/2/Add.2 §1). AA UK however, is not a member of the SCHR, and takes no part in the Working Group on the Security Council. AAA does not have permanent contacts with the UN in Geneva (Interview AAA-2).

Summary

NGOs today have many ways to interact with the UN. They are able to work with the UN in many circumstances and on a large variety of issues. Particularly in recent years, the opportunities for NGOs to work with the UN have notably increased. NGOs have taken advantage of such possibilities in all fields of policy initiating activities, policy developing processes, and policy implementing practices. The NGOs examined in this study have all been active within the UN context over a long time, but they have adjusted their activities vis-à-vis the UN differently in recent years (see Table 3.1).

Table 3.1 Patterns of interaction between NGOs and the UN

		Amnesty International	Human Rights Watch	FIDH	ILHR
Policy Initiating Activities	Agenda Setting/Standard Setting	Most efforts in the past (e.g. Convention against Torture, establishment of HCHR), now less 'conference room activities'			
	Information Provision	Reports serve as source, but AI puts less efforts to channelling information through the formal mechanism, e.g. CHR *Briefed Security Council on the basis of Arria Formula*	Reports serve as a source of information, HRW channels a lot of information through the formal mechanism *Briefed Security Council on the basis of Arria Formula*	Reports occasionally serve as source for UN work, significantly more input through formal mechanisms	Reports occasionally serve as source for UN work
	Lobbying	Lobbying of governmental representatives and UN officials, diplomatic interaction	Lobbying of governmental representatives and UN officials	Significantly more lobbying of delegates	Lobbying of governmental representatives and UN officials
Policy Developing Processes	Policy Advisor	Sought for advisory functions from the UN and single governments	Sought for advisory functions from the UN and single governments	*Occasionally requested for advice*	
		Member of the WGSC	*Member of the WGSC*		*Member of the WGSC*
	Policy Formulator	*Shift in policy, now participant in policy formulation processes*	Involved in drafting processes and in consulting functions		
Policy Implementing Practices	Cooperative Relationship	*Shift towards more interaction with field organisations*	*Interaction with field organizations*		
	Subcontracting Partners	*Subcontracting considered beneficial*			

Continued

Table 3.1 Continued

	CARE International	ISCA	Oxfam International	Action Aid Alliance
Policy Initiating Activities — *Agenda Seeting/ Standard Setting*	*Representational functions in IASC*			
Information Provision	*Briefing of the Security Council on the basis of the Arria Formula*	*Information provision on Children's issues*	*Briefing of the Security Council on the basis of the Arria Formula*	
Lobbying	*Lobbying of UN officials and governmental representatives in New York*	*Lobbying of UN officials and governmental representatives*		
Policy Developing Processes — *Policy Advisor*	Advisory and representational functions for NGO networks, such as SCHR	*Advisory functions, SCHR*	*Limited representational functions*	*Limited advisory functions*
	Member of the WGSC	Member of the WGSC	*Member of the WGSC*	
Policy Formulator	*Shared development of common manuals for activities*	*Shared development of common guidelines for activities*		
Policy Implementing Practices — *Cooperative Relationship*	Cooperation with a variety of UN field agencies	Cooperation with a variety of UN field agencies, particularly UNICEF	Cooperation with a variety of UN field agencies	Cooperation with the UN in the field
Subcontracting Partners	Contract work for UNHCR	Contract work for UNHCR	Contract work for UNHCR	

 ——— Lines denote the intensity of activities
 → Arrows denote tendencies in activities since the 1990s
 Italics denotes new types of activities since the mid-1990s

Until the early 1990s, the patterns of activity between NGOs and the UN were restricted to a specific type of interaction. Amnesty International and the FIDH, for instance, concentrated on policy initiating and – to a lesser extent – on policy developing activities when working with the UN. That is to say, these NGOs usually focused on a few decision-making bodies of the UN in the field of their concern and intended to influence their decisions. Most importantly, they provided information, lobbied governmental representatives and participated as advisors in official procedures. Amnesty International regularly provided the Commission on Human Rights and other UN bodies with information on human rights violation and lobbied governmental representatives; similarly, the FIDH channelled information received from its affiliated member NGOs about human rights violations to the UN. CARE International and Oxfam International, instead, mainly worked with the UN at the stage of policy implementation. These NGOs maintained contact with field organizations of the UN which were concerned with the same issues, and their common goal was to provide services to their target groups. Therefore, they had links with a variety of UN bodies and agencies in the field and implemented projects in cooperation with them.

During the course of the 1990s, however, the options for NGOs to work with the UN were extended. Amnesty International and CARE International exemplify how these NGOs have reacted to the changing opportunities. Those NGOs demonstrated that they were capable of adapting to new opportunities at the UN level and expanded their spectrum of interaction with the UN. Today, Amnesty International is not only involved in policy initiating and developing process, but it also considers taking on policy implementing practices. It added complementary areas of activities at the UN level which broadened its spectrum of interaction with the IGO. CARE International, too, expanded its activities with the UN and today, the NGO increasingly works with the UN in policy initiating and developing activities. While doing so, it represents various NGO networks at the UN level which are involved in standard-setting processes and advises UN bodies. At the same time, the NGO maintained its activities with the UN on a field level.

Other NGOs, instead, were less able to respond to new or changing opportunities when interacting with the IGO and did not adjust their patterns of activity with the UN significantly. Interaction between the FIDH and the UN has not changed much since the mid-1990s; the NGO still works with the UN mainly in policy initiating processes. However, the NGO has significantly increased its information delivery and thus deepened existing activities. Oxfam International did not develop a clear pattern of activity with the UN. Some Oxfam affiliates maintain links through the international body but also independently of it; some Oxfams work with the UN through various networks not coordinated by the international branch. Thus, Oxfam International's interaction with the UN is diffuse. It added only few new types of activities with the UN predominantly maintaining its existing practices of project implementation.

In brief, the NGOs in this work differ in how they have adjusted their patterns of activity with the UN during the 1990s. The opening up of the UN to more interaction with NGOs provided the necessary condition for a shift in their activities with the intergovernmental body, but additional factors must be considered to explain the difference among individual NGOs and their responses to these opportunities. As determined in the theoretical part, these factors are the subject of further research in the following two chapters.

4
Representation and Representatives to the UN – Institutionalization as an Internal Factor

As explored in the theoretical section, adjustments in the patterns of activity between societal actors and official institutions are dependent on internal factors. In such a view, institutionalization refers to the structural provisions within the organizations with regard to the official institution. For the purposes of this study, these internal factors have been identified as the organizational arrangements within NGOs for their relations with the UN. Therefore, I examine NGO representation and representatives to the UN as forms of internal institutionalization of relations with the UN.

This chapter is split into two sections. In the shorter first section, I discuss general features of NGO representation to the UN to place the selected cases in a general context. In the second section, I present eight examples of NGOs in detail. Consistent with the theoretical framework I laid out earlier, increasing investment in internal arrangements of NGOs for representation to the UN is the indicator of adjusted patterns of activity with the UN.

General observations about NGO representation to the UN

The picture of NGO representation in relation to the UN has changed considerably over the last two decades: whereas in the 1980s, NGOs and their representatives were often regarded as unprofessional, they are now valued for their expertise and knowledge about their area of interest and participate regularly during UN sessions. In this section, I outline such general observations about the increasing professionalization of NGO representation at the UN.

The image of NGOs at the UN in the past

For a long time, NGO representation at the UN was predominantly conducted by volunteers who had little professional affiliation with their organization. Archer (1983: 303) notes that '[m]any of these people are volunteers, retired, or representing their organizations in their spare time'. NGO representatives were associated with the image of 'little old ladies in tennis shoes' (Archer 1983: 303) or 'politicians on the downward slope' (in Chiang 1981: 235). The representation of NGOs at the UN therefore had little value because it 'seemed confined to collecting documents and attending meetings', while many 'come just for the ride, with expenses paid'. Only few UN officials or governmental delegates attended meetings or sessions when NGO representatives gave oral presentations, while others read newspapers (Chiang 1981: 235).

Due to their low degree of professionalization, NGO representatives did not have a good reputation at the UN. In his 1981 study of NGOs in the UN system, Chiang (1981: 235) reports that 'Secretariat officials, for example, characterized most NGO representatives at the UN as "idle old ladies" who know little, are not to be taken seriously, and who, by talking about irrelevant things, waste their time as well as UN resources'. NGO representatives were a source of embarrassment, irritation and resentment because of their astonishing naïveté and ignorance of international affairs. Although early research showed that NGO employees are often highly skilled people who have full-time professional appointments within their organizations (Skjelsbaeks 1975), representation at the UN, apparently, was not considered important enough by many NGOs as to send specifically trained personnel.

Therefore being a representative to the UN was more a source of status, prestige, and ego satisfaction to single individuals than it provided an opportunity for NGO work at the international level. Many representatives simply enjoyed having access to international diplomats, UN officials and governmental representatives because they were able to meet them in the lounges, chat with them and have coffee or lunch in the UN cafeteria. Accordingly, they interacted at levels 'rarely rising above the purely social kaffee klatsch level' (Chiang 1981: 236). Because of this low calibre, relations with NGOs were often regarded as ineffective and many secretariat and governmental delegates did not take NGO representation at the UN seriously (Chiang 1981: 328).[46]

NGO representation at the UN today

Over the years, NGOs increasingly recognized the potential of activities with the UN and gradually invested in their international representation.

Many NGOs shifted from voluntary representation at the UN to professional personnel for this purpose. Some NGOs, for example, nominated a regular staff member to conduct all the UN-related affairs of the organization. Others divided up their representation such that staff members took over the representation of the organization when their issue-area or subject of expertise was on the agenda of the UN. Some NGOs even decided to establish independent offices in major UN locations and devoted professional full-time personnel to their representation.

Such shifts led to a greater recognition of the capacities of NGOs, and they grew to be perceived as serious actors in international relations. Particularly in the 1990s, NGOs became tremendously valued for their contributions, and their advice and expert opinions have increasingly been taken into account at the UN level. They contributed significantly during the series of world conferences, whereby they delivered not only valuable information on the matters discussed, but also assisted in drafting the resolutions and documents. NGOs were highly regarded for their subject knowledge and expertise on details, which often exceeded the preparation of governmental representatives.

The growing professionalization of NGO representatives working at the UN level also meant that career paths in the two types of organizations grew to be similar. NGO staff shifted to UN jobs and vice-versa. As Weschler (1998: 154) reports for the human rights sector,

> owing to their long existence, non-governmental organizations have by now created a sizable group of human rights professionals. When at the beginning of the 1990s, the United Nations for the first time needed within a fairly short period of time a relatively large number of properly prepared staff to fill many human rights posts in peacekeeping operations, and then in human rights field operations, NGOs became the main source of experts, both at the rank-and-file and the managerial levels.

At the same time, it became increasingly acceptable for NGOs to recruit former government or UN employees for positions similar to those they were to take in NGOs, for instance as researchers on a particular specialized topic or in the field. Whereas in the 1980s, it would have been unthinkable for NGOs to recruit such former officials, as the organizations feared to question their integrity and independence, in the 1990s, it became commonly accepted to recruit governmental or UN staff for positions in NGOs (Interview AI-7). Many professionals had taken office in the early 1990s when the UN increased its field presence and they left it by the mid-1990s to start working for NGOs.

Part of the change in perception was also due to the fact that NGOs needed specialists for complex issue matters with very specific skills. Sometimes, the NGOs could not provide such knowledgeable persons themselves and these specialists could only be found in other organizations, such as intergovernmental organizations or governmental institutions. For this reason, NGOs increasingly employed persons who offered these skills even if they acquired them through working for governmental actors and had no prior record of NGO engagement.

NGO representatives at the UN in total

The UN requires accredited NGOs to nominate at least one liaison person of their organization to be in charge of all administrative purposes. If an NGO has a permanent representative based in a major UN location, it is usually this person, who is named on the UN's list. In case an NGO does not have a representative in any UN city, someone from headquarters – often a person who is in charge of the external affairs – is nominated for the position. Hence, in theory, there should be at least as many NGO 'liaison persons' as there are accredited NGOs. Since there are currently around 2600 NGOs accredited to ECOSOC, the same number of official NGO representatives should be found on the database, hosted by the UN Liaison office in Geneva.

However, the total number of NGO representatives and their status within the organizations they are representing is difficult to estimate. Although the UN demands NGOs to nominate their 'representatives' each year, it keeps limited track of these records (Interview UN-3). For example, in the UN's data base of NGOs, there are only about 900 persons mentioned as NGO 'liaison persons'. In addition, that database concentrates on contacts in Switzerland and allows for only one representative per NGO. If an NGO has more than one representative to the UN, and one of them represents the organization in Switzerland, only that person is listed on the database. Moreover, the records make no distinction between professional and volunteer representatives.

NGOs may nominate up to 15 different representatives, five in each of the three UN locations where the IGO maintains NGO liaison offices (New York City, Geneva and Vienna). For special events like international conferences, they are allowed to nominate additional representatives, sometimes even without any upper limit (Interview UN-3). NGOs often use up their allotment of representatives so that different people can enter the UN without the bureaucratic hurdles, even if they do not represent the NGO on a regular basis. One or two positions are often reserved for top NGO positions (president, secretary-general or vice-president) though they rarely actually make use of it (often for special occasions like conferences only).

In brief, NGO representation at the UN has shifted over the years from being voluntary to professional. Today, NGOs increasingly allot resources to their international presence. However, NGO representation at the UN is under researched, particularly as far as it explains NGO–UN interaction. Current statistics on NGOs are usually used for other, administrative purposes and leave open the qualities and quantities of organizational resources for their representation at the UN.

Exploring individual cases of NGO representation to the UN

In this section, I explore in detail the individual organizational provisions of the four main NGOs chosen with regard to the UN. Each section contains data about the number of offices and representatives in major UN locations and at headquarters level, provisions for their division of labour, and information about other internal organizational arrangements for representation at the UN. Moreover, I discuss the individual representatives' respective educational background, prior involvement with the respective NGO or nongovernmental work in general as well as required experience with the UN. In a fifth section, I explore briefly the four additional NGOs in order to ascertain whether the phenomena observed for the prime set of case studies seem generally applicable.

Amnesty International: mobilizing resources for its UN representation

Amnesty International has representatives in major UN locations to present and promote the NGO's aims and goals before the human rights-related UN bodies on a continuous basis. Most importantly, having these representatives allows AI to maintain constant contact with UN delegates, agencies and other institutions.

People in UN locations

The number of staff AI dedicates for relations with the UN and its increase over the years reflects the NGO's broadened UN approach. It has gradually invested in its personnel, and today maintains permanent representatives in Geneva and New York. Such representation allows the NGO to keep constant interaction with the UN in the two major human rights locations.

In Geneva, AI has two representatives working exclusively on UN matters. AI's official 'UN representative in Geneva' and the 'deputy representative' conduct the NGO's daily representation there. Moreover, nowadays the office is usually supported by a few volunteers (Interview AI-4). Thus, all in all, there are at least three people permanently based in Geneva who work on the NGO's relationship with the UN. Their work is occasionally supported by one or two country specialists from the international secretariat. These AI staff members are specifically flown in to Geneva each year during the six-week session of the Commission on Human Rights in March and April (Interview AI-4).

AI's UN representation in New York has been increased by another person in recent years (Interview AI-6). Until 2000, the NGO had two permanent representatives in New York, but in spring 2001 it added a third. These representatives have different grades and divide their tasks and duties (Interview AI-6). As with the AI office in Geneva, the NGO also always employs at least one intern who works for its office in New York on a six-month basis.

Offices in UN locations

The increasing professionalization of its staff dealing with UN matters made it possible for AI to play a greater role in UN matters. The offices in New York and Geneva both started on a voluntary and informal basis. In both cities the representation was first led by local Amnesty members who represented the NGO at the UN in their spare time. As more prospects for activities with the UN became evident, the NGO expanded and invested into its UN representation. As a result, the offices became an integral part of Amnesty International and are today led by professional staff members.

Representation in New York, for example, started in the early 1960s and was led by volunteers and individual AI sections. In those years, the Danish section of AI first took over to represent the NGO at the UN – a member of that section was listed as its representative. A few years later, when the US section of AI established a national office in New York, it maintained the NGO's representation at the UN as 'ordinary monitoring and liaison work from the mid-1960s devolved for a time to a one-person office staff of the U.S. section and volunteer appointees, with occasional visits from London staffers' (A. Clark 2001: 7).

Examples of representatives at that time include a retired Amnesty member who represented the NGO in his spare time. Because he had previously worked for the FAO, he was thus familiar with the UN system and its procedures and had various personal contacts with UN officials

(Interview AI-3). A professor for Russian history also volunteered as AI's representative in the mid-1970s, starting the first AI 'office' in his personal home in New York, together with a graduate in international relations (A. Clark 2001: 8). Amnesty International's representation in Geneva also started on an informal basis in the early 1980s. Founded by a volunteer local member (Cook 1996: 185; Interview AI-1), it was supported by the Swiss section of AI based in Bern. Later, an Irish diplomat and lawyer acted as a volunteer liaison for Amnesty International while in his professional life, he was secretary-general of another NGO (A. Clark 2001: 7).

In the late 1970s the international climate for human rights issues began to change, the discourse on human rights advanced significantly, and more options for promoting human rights at the UN opened up. Amnesty International correspondingly changed its strategy by increasing its UN work (Schmitz 2001: 10). Most importantly, the NGO recognized it could do more work at the Commission of Human Rights. In addition, more and more mechanisms came into force, and the CAT was created. It became clear that representing AI at the UN required more efforts than volunteer members or staff flying in from London for special occasions could handle (Interviews AI-3, AI-9).

As a result, the offices in New York and Geneva changed and became fully equipped with professional staff members. In New York, the first permanent professional representation was established in 1977 (A. Clark 2001: 8); the Geneva office became a substantial part of the NGO in 1988 when the first professional representatives were hired (Cook 1996: 185). This change had an immediate effect on AI's UN approach. As a representative in Geneva during those first years notes, 'our very presence enabled us to spot avenues where AI could have an impact' (Interview AI-9). Permanent representation in Geneva, for example, enabled a continuous flow of information so that AI immediately knew 'what was going on at the UN level' (Interview AI-9).

In fact, the NGO's stabilized presence at the UN also influenced intra-organizational work procedures, as other parts of the organization became more involved in UN matters. Researchers in London started to prepare background information, specifically designed for the NGO's UN work, such as reports intended for presentation to the treaty bodies of the UN. Thus, the establishment of representatives in UN locations generated more work within the organization, but also helped staff in London to focus on where the NGO could have an impact (Interview AI-9).

Today, Amnesty International's UN work forms an integral part of the researchers' duties. When working on country reports, for example, they now take into account the UN presence there and address their recommendation to the Security Council as well as the implementing bodies and agencies on the ground (Interviews AI-6, AI-2, AI-3). Also when conducting research in the field, they visit UN operations in their missions (Interview AI-6). Researchers are crucially involved in the presentation of the country-specific data on human rights violations. For example, they present their own data in New York or Geneva when their country is on the agenda of the Commission on Human Rights. Since the level of debate often requires very specific country knowledge, AI researchers speak with governmental representatives because they have been in the country most recently and have specific information (Interview AI-4).

The physical location of AI's offices also attests the significance of UN relations for the NGO. Its current offices in New York and Geneva are both located very close to the UN. In fact, of all the NGOs examined in this study, AI is the 'closest' to the UN in geographical terms. AI's office in Geneva has always been located in the northern part of the city, where all UN institutions and other intergovernmental organizations are based. It is only walking distance from the UN main building, close to the side-entrance of the *Palais des Nations* housing the UN bodies concerned with human rights. In fact, AI even shares a building with some UN institutions and other intergovernmental organizations. Such close proximity allows for intense and continuous interaction with the UN.

Similarly, AI's office in New York is located across the road from UN headquarters in a building housing many other organizations' international secretariat or New York office. Unlike other NGOs, AI's representation at the UN is kept particularly separate from other AI affiliations in the city. AI's UN representation does not share any facilities with its US section based in New York. While many other NGOs which maintain permanent representatives in a major UN location and, at the same time, also have a section or affiliate in the city, share services or split costs, AI's representation at the UN does not have more communication with its US office in New York than with any other AI office.

People and organizational provisions at the international secretariat

Unlike in other NGOs, some of AI's staff in its international secretariat in London also work almost entirely on UN relations. Three people at headquarters level are permanently involved with the UN as part of AI's programme on 'Legal and International Organizations'. One is in charge of the special mechanisms of the UN and two work on the treaty bodies (Interview AI-4). On the whole, the department maintains a permanent staff of around 20 people and some trainees (Interview AI-4, AI-5). Depending on their individual tasks, all of them may occasionally spend up to 30 per cent of their time on IGO-related matters (Interview AI-5).

The international office provides legal advice, and drafts and supervises legal documents. As part of this work, it also leads and guides AI's work with international organizations like the UN and the EU. For example, it provides legal advice on special procedures as well as political recommendations on how to shape strategies for interaction with the UN (Interview AI-5). As part of its work, it also seeks to develop new standards and to contribute to country and thematic discussions on human rights in order 'to make the UN human rights machinery more effective and efficient' (Interview AI-5).

Amnesty International set up clearly defined positions for its representation at the UN in the late 1970s when it had grown to such a significant size that more intra-organizational structuring was needed. It established organizational units, such as the board composition and the legal department, as well as research departments, including the thematic and country specialists. As part of this reorganization of work and divisions, the representation in UN locations was more formally structured and incorporated within the overall structure of the NGO (Interview AI-3). The positions became an integral part of the legal and intergovernmental department of Amnesty International's headquarters in London, and today represent – what representatives call – its 'outposts' or 'satellites' in New York and Geneva (Interviews AI-4, AI-5).[47]

Amnesty International's legal advisors approve all documents, statements and press releases 'to make sure that everything is ok' (Interview AI-5). In practise, this means that statements by AI on a particular issue concerning human rights may take up to several weeks. For example, when the representative in Geneva prepares a statement, it is first sent to London to be checked through by the legal department and then sent back to her to be delivered. Similarly, when the initiative for a statement to the UN comes from a researcher, it goes through the same process. Also, when national sections make a suggestion as to what they want to be addressed at the UN level, it goes through London first, as decisions regarding the international representation rest with the international secretariat (Interview AI-5).

Educational background

The skills and capacities of AI's representatives to the UN explain the NGO's broad and intense involvement with the IGO. Amnesty

International hires extremely well-trained people as UN representatives, many of them with legal expertise, because '[f]ull-time professional staff, including legal experts, enable Amnesty to field well-briefed, experienced representation at the United Nations. They have the necessary political, technical or country specialization and can build and maintain contacts with governmental delegates, UN staff, NGOs and the media' (Cook 1996: 186). Current AI representatives at the UN have gone through higher educational programmes and hold post-graduate degrees. They have usually studied law or subjects with an international focus, such as international relations or development studies. The majority hold an LLM degree in international law, and an increasing number is even specialized in human rights studies.

For example, one AI representative in Geneva studied law as an undergraduate and worked as a lawyer for her home government for several years before doing a Masters in international human rights law. This educational background was highly valued when she applied for the position, making up for her lack of foreign language knowledge (Interview AI-4). An AI representative in New York during the 1990s also emphasized the importance of his law training, as his work on UN peacekeeping and the International Criminal Court was 'very legal' (Interview AI-8). Moreover, his training in languages and as an actor enabled him to have the necessary communication skills for the work at the UN and for public speaking engagements, including interviews with domestic media (Interview AI-8).

Amnesty International has long been valued for its professional approach to its UN relations. In the 1970s, when AI participated during the sessions where standards against torture were developed, the NGO was particularly strong due to its professional approach. 'These preparations drew on the considerable strengths of Amnesty International: a well-organized and professional international secretariat, a Legal Adviser of outstanding competence trained in international law and an extensive network of national sections' (Leary 1979: 202). AI stood out from other organizations because of its exceptionally professional staff. As Leary (1979: 206) reports, '[f]ew NGO's have the tremendous advantage which Amnesty International has of a full-time competent and committed international lawyer on their staff'.

Although a background in law is not formally required, it is vital to a UN representative to have a good knowledge about legal affairs. As AI's representative in New York asserts, the NGO's staff members for UN-related matters do not necessarily have to be lawyers, but for AI's kind of work at the UN and the experience and knowledge needed for this job, 'it happens to be in most cases people trained in law' who represent AI before the UN (Interview AI-6). Staff members of the Legal and International Organizations Programme based in London also generally come from an academic background and are trained in legal or international studies. In fact, similar to the representatives in UN locations, a majority of them holds a post-graduate degree, often in human rights law (Interview AI-7). Some of them also have a few years of experience in working with legal matters (Interview AI-5).

Experience and knowledge of the UN System

Amnesty International's representatives must have a variety of skills for the post as UN representative besides educational background. Most importantly, they are required to know the system and mechanism of the UN well to make use of the machinery for AI's goals and to develop appropriate strategies for campaigning and action. 'In order to make an impact, it is important for an NGO to send delegates with a real grasp of the issue and with expertise in drafting and, as far as possible, to maintain continuity in its delegates, building on their familiarity of the issue, the process and the other players involved' (Cook 1996: 192).

Experience with the UN is another desirable qualification for the position of AI's representative at the UN. For example, an AI representative in Geneva gained experience with the UN before taking up her post by first interning with the UN High Commissioner for Refugees. Another AI representative in New York who had previously cooperated with the UN in the field in the implementation of children's rights emphasized the importance of having experience with the UN before starting the position (Interview AI-2). London-based researchers, too, need to acquire significant knowledge about the UN system, as they have to prepare recommendations for the Security Council and for the implementing bodies on the ground.

Experience with NGOs

Whereas experience and knowledge of the UN system are extremely important when dealing with IGOs, prior involvement with Amnesty International or having had a leading position in the NGO is not a precondition for the post as AI's representative at the UN. In fact, most professional representatives were not actively involved with AI before taking up the position as a UN representative. Rather, they often only sympathized with the NGO or supported the organizations as a paying member (Interview AI-2).

Only rarely have AI's representatives gained some sort of experience on the local level,[48] and if so, this was not the decisive factor for their recruitment. Moreover, UN representatives usually do not have experience with AI on the international level, like in the secretariat, nor have they done research for AI as thematic or country specialists in either the secretariat or in the field.[49]

Instead, since its positions as representatives to the UN have become an integral part of the NGO, AI is hiring people on the basis of professional criteria, even if they come from 'outside the NGO' (Interview AI-3). As a representative mentioned, when the first AI representatives in Geneva were hired in 1988, it was remarkable that they were chosen even though neither of them had a background with AI (Interview AI-9). Although the salary for the position was low ('less than an assistant in a department store') around 700 people applied for the two positions, as they were seen as prestigious. The list of applicants also included many former or retired diplomats who apparently mistook the advertised position as an honouree post or good-will ambassador rather then a full-time job (Interview AI-9). The selection criteria were actually very objective and the applicants had to go through an action-oriented test of their abilities for analysis and administration: given UN documents announcing a series of meetings, the candidates had to filter out the relevant events as well as write memos to London and recommend strategies (Interview AI-9).

General experience of working in a membership organization in the international sphere is valued over prior involvement with AI *per se* (Interview AI-6). As an AI representative stressed, what got him into the job out of 600 applicants was his knowledge of the UN system and his experience in working in and with non-governmental organizations (Interview AI-2). Similarly, in the legal department, prior work for AI is no precondition for being hired, but 'some volunteer experience' with NGOs, in particular with human rights NGOs or with a rights-based approach, is required (Interview AI-5).

As a result, new recruits must be introduced to the NGO's work and receive training on AI's guiding principles. They attend coaching on the NGO's techniques and policies in certain issue-areas. For example, if peacekeeping is a topic dealt with at the UN for a certain period, representatives are sent to headquarters to attend an internal seminar on peacekeeping. New recruits usually spend a short period of time in London to get to know the staff members with whom they will be working closely (Interview AI-6).

In sum AI's representation at major UN locations reflects its broad spectrum of interaction with the IGO. AI's investments in its representation enabled it to maintain continuous and consistent contact with the UN and to respond to new opportunities for interaction.

As a centralist NGO, AI is able to dedicate considerable resources to its UN representation and has gradually developed organizational structures for it. As it has steadily invested in its representation over the last 10 to 15 years, it now maintains permanent representatives in major UN locations and has staff members at headquarters for UN-related matters. Over the years, the NGO has developed a clear division of labour between the international secretariat and its UN offices.[50]

As an advocacy NGO, AI increasingly recruits people for relations with the UN on the basis of professional criteria. Many of them are trained in international human rights law, as the work requires knowledge of legal affairs. Moreover, AI's representatives must have either academic or working experience with the UN. Prior involvement with the NGO itself, instead, is not a factor which plays a role for the appointment as AI's representative at the UN.

FIDH: using limited resources to its advantage

The Fédération Internationale des Droits de l'Homme maintains offices and permanent staff in major UN locations to coordinate its representation at the international level. The federation provides the common channel through which individual national affiliated members participate on the international scene (Interview FIDH-4).

People in UN locations and bureaucratic structures

The FIDH has adjusted very little to the new opportunities for UN interaction. This can be explained by the amount of resources it devotes to its representation there: FIDH has invested little in its representation at the international level, employing just one professional representative for relations with the UN. This 'permanent delegate to the United Nations' is based in Geneva and represents the NGO and all its affiliates full-time. Since most human rights-related UN bodies are based in Geneva, the Swiss city is regarded as particularly important and the NGO decided to place its representative there. (Interview FIDH-3).

At the UN's headquarters in New York, however, the FIDH is represented irregularly. Someone from the FIDH's headquarters in Paris may fly to New York when a major event is taking place there, and once a year a representative flies over for the session on women's rights in the

UN headquarters. Another representative went to New York three times in one year for issues related to the establishment of the International Criminal Court (Interview FIDH-3).

Until 1999, an FIDH volunteer who lived in New York represented the NGO whenever needed (Interview FIDH-5). Because his budget covered only phone and fax expenses, it was not possible to establish a stable UN representation, and the post was less successful than the international secretariat hoped. Moreover, the post was disconnected from Paris head-quarters and thus satisfactory New York representation was impossible (Interview FIDH-3).

Offices in UN locations

The FIDH does not have a full office in Geneva, but rather shares one with other NGOs in order to reduce costs. Representation in Geneva started in the early 1990s, led by a conscientious objector doing his com-munity service (in lieu of military service) as a representative of the FIDH in Geneva. He was succeeded by another civil service provider before the NGO established a full-time paid post in Geneva in 1994 (Interview FIDH-3).

In contrast to AI's representation in Geneva, the office of the FIDH is in the south-east of the city, a good distance from the UN building com-plex. Thus, intense activities with the UN can be difficult as the discon-nect makes transaction costs high. As a representative emphasized herself, a permanent representation at the UN and daily office duties may limit the FIDH's opportunities for intense work at the UN (Interview FIDH-4).

People and departments at the international secretariat

As the FIDH's means dedicated to UN relations are limited, there is for-mally no particular section, department, or person at the international secretariat working exclusively on relations with the UN or international institutions. The representative in Geneva therefore works together with different staff members in Paris. Depending on the issue at stake, the representative contacts the relevant person in headquarters dealing with the country matter or the thematic issue (Interview FIDH-2). However, the FIDH's director also deals with UN-related issues when they are relevant to the whole organization and concern its future activities with the UN. Most importantly, he takes over the NGO's representation at key moments, for example, by going to Geneva for three or four days during the session of the Commission on Human Rights (Interview FIDH-3).

Representation through multipliers

The FIDH's intensified approach in its established areas of interaction can be explained by how it uses its resources to work with intergovern-mental organizations. Despite its limited funds, the NGO is able to ensure an intense representation at the UN level: the FIDH functions as a facilitator for direct activities between its affiliated members and the UN, and ensures that its national members are familiarized with the UN mechanisms on human rights. Since 1995, the FIDH has trained its affil-iates in UN processes and procedures. 'These seminars are aimed at pro-moting dialogue and cooperation between human rights defenders and representatives of States, and developing optimum cooperation between non-governmental organizations in the field and the organs and proce-dures of the United Nations' (UN Doc. E/C.2/1999/2/Add.14 §6).

Through this training the FIDH mulitplies its activities at the UN level. As mentioned by an interviewee who implemented the first training programme, 'national NGOs wanted to come to the UN to have a resolu-tion on their country, but they did not know how to do it. The idea of this programme was to train these human rights defenders' (Interview FIDH-3). The main purpose of this programme is to aid national repre-sentatives of affiliated members so that their impact and lobbying at the UN level is more effective. These training programmes provide them with the necessary tools to work with the UN independently.

With these seminars, the FIDH seeks to reach a broad participation by a large number of affiliated members. When the programme started, national NGO representatives from ten different countries were trained in UN mechanisms over a two-week period so that they were able to fol-low the six-week session of the Commission on Human Rights (Interview FIDH-3). During the training sessions representatives of the member leagues were taught UN procedures for protecting human rights and familiarized with the rules for bringing forward human rights violations. As part of the programme, the FIDH even invited UN officials who explained the UN mechanisms. All in all, between January 1995 and December 1997 almost 300 individual representatives of national mem-ber organizations benefited from the services of the FIDH at the UN level in one way or the other (Fédération Internationale des Droits de l'Homme 2005c). The NGO stopped this programme in 2001 because a large num-ber of its national member organizations had already learned how to use the different mechanisms of the UN system for their own purposes (Interview FIDH-2).

Instead the FIDH installed a new training programme in the late 1990s that familiarizes member NGOs with the treaty bodies of the UN

(UN Doc. E/C.2/2001/2/Add.13 §8). As part of the training, an FIDH representative teaches the national affiliates how to prepare and write reports, and how to adapt their language to UN standards and procedures (Interview FIDH-2). Through this training, the respective members of the FIDH are thus able to prepare their 'alternative' reports parallel to government reports in which details on human rights violations are presented in UN required manner (Interview FIDH-4).

The FIDH also pays for affiliates to go to Geneva so that they themselves present their report to the UN and the governments. The FIDH's representative coordinates such visits of national affiliates to Geneva. In this context, their knowledge about the UN human rights mechanisms is evaluated through a questionnaire beforehand so that they can receive additional training during their stay if necessary. Moreover, the FIDH ensures that its national members meet with local governmental missions, UN officials, as well as other NGOs, and are trained in lobbying tactics (Interview FIDH-2).

Educational background and experience with the UN

Knowledge about legal affairs concerning human rights has become increasingly necessary for the post as representative of the FIDH at the UN. As a representative emphasized, 'a serious legal background' was the main requirement for the recruitment (Interview FIDH-2). The person had studied law and specialized in human rights law in post-graduate studies. Similarly, another representative had studied law and holds a Master's degree in international human rights law (Interview FIDH-4). One former representative had even written her Master's thesis on the UN mechanisms for human rights NGOs (Guillet 1995).

Experience with the UN system and the human rights mechanisms is also an essential criterion for the position of the FIDH's UN representative (Interview FIDH-2). Background knowledge and the practical experience of how the UN system works are considered a necessary tool for the position (Interview FIDH-4). One former representative of the FIDH in Geneva noted that she needed to be familiar with the human rights mechanism of the UN before taking up the position as permanent representative. She had studied the UN on an academic level and acquired practical experience through an internship.

The profile of the post as FIDH's representative today requires a number of other personal and analytic skills. For example, knowledge of various official UN languages has become increasingly important. In addition to English and French as the working languages, familiarity with Spanish is necessary as many of the FIDH's affiliates who wish to use the federation's channel to the UN come from Latin America and often only speak Spanish (Interview FIDH-2). In addition, a representative emphasized that his prior work for the French government showed him how to work with authorities and the way in which administrative language is used. Such skills have proven to be important for writing and interpreting reports and UN documents (Interview FIDH-2).

Experience within the NGO

For the position as the FIDH's representative at the UN, prior involvement with the NGO is not considered as important as the educational background. One representative, for example, mentioned that he was not involved with the NGO before taking up his position in Geneva (Interview FIDH-2). Similarly, a former permanent representative had not worked for the NGO on a professional basis before, either in the international secretariat or on a voluntary basis.

Instead, the representatives were briefly introduced and trained in the organizational principles of the FIDH before taking up the post. That is to say, future representatives spent three weeks in the international secretariat before taking up their positions in Geneva. One representative mentioned that during this time in Paris he was introduced to the various posts and positions there, and also worked together with staff members on a report for presentation at the UN concerning the human rights situation in Algeria, so that he became familiarized with the processes and procedures of the organization's headquarters (Interview FIDH-2).

The FIDH's paucity of resources for its international representation reflects its spectrum of interaction with the UN. As a federative NGO, the FIDH has limited funds to spend on its UN representation. It maintains only one professional representative in a major UN location and counts on voluntary representation whenever possible. However, the NGO uses its limited resources as a multiplying factor in that it trains its member NGOs so as to deepen its activities with the UN in selected areas. As an advocacy NGO, subject knowledge has become highly important for the post as the NGO's representative, and academic achievements as well as specialization on the issue matter are more valued than experience and groundwork for the NGO.

CARE International: increasing investment in its UN representation

The primary function of CARE International's UN representatives is to keep close contact with UN bodies and agencies related to humanitarian issues. 'The Multilateral Liaison Coordinator is tasked with the responsibility to maintain regular contacts with the Geneva- and Rome-based multilateral agencies and representational bodies – including UNHCR, WFP, Red Cross – and to represent CARE in the general humanitarian debate' (CARE International 2000a). The functions of the office include making the UN bodies and agencies more familiar with the NGO, and gathering information about their ongoing and planned activities. It also settles disputes between individual CARE members and the UN system. The offices enable CARE to be a more important player in international humanitarian policy by being in daily contact with UN humanitarian agencies, ensuring the NGO's representation in important bodies and meetings in Europe (Interview CARE-5).

People in UN locations and organizational
structures of representation

CARE International's extended spectrum of interaction with the UN is evident considering its greater amount of resources dedicated to that purpose. Since the late 1990s, the NGO invested significantly in its representation to the UN in Geneva and New York, so that today it maintains permanent professional representation in both major locations where it deals with humanitarian issues. Before CARE International was represented at the UN as one internationally operating NGO, CARE USA had already installed some individual voluntary representation. In 1991, the American branch recognized that more synchronization was needed for the NGO's UN representation, as at one point 12 people worked on UN-related issues, without any coordination. This became a problem when the quadrennial reports were due because it was difficult to take together the various ways in which the NGO related to the UN. In response, a volunteer was designated to coordinate CARE's UN work (Interview CARE-2).

As one international NGO, the organization maintains representation at the UN since the early 1990s, when the voluntary representative who had been representing CARE USA before, became accountable to CARE International. Although representation had thus officially been transferred to the international body, responsibilities were not clear for the first years and only gradually shifted over to the Brussels office. The voluntary representative remained officially a member of staff of CARE USA, and reported to CARE USA and CARE International simultaneously. For the first few years, the US member organization also primarily paid her basic salary, but CARE International was billed for the 'advisory work' at the UN (Interview CARE-2). In mid-2000, CARE International then hired a professional to represent it at the UN in New York. As part of a new strategic plan, formal representation at the UN became a matter of greater importance, so financial resources were allocated to this new post by the international headquarters (Interview CARE-2). As an independent section within CARE's New York office, CARE International established its UN representation only three blocks away from the UN.

In Geneva, CARE International has been represented by a full-time professional since 1997. This position was allocated to CARE International when established, as the international body financed it through contributions from various national CARE sections. Thus, the representative in Geneva is formally employed by the international secretariat in Brussels and also reports back to the secretary-general of CARE International. Prior to 1997, the NGO was only represented in Geneva on an *ad hoc* manner. Various senior staff members travelled to Switzerland on UN matters that were of concern to their specific CARE only. Thus, the importance of the Geneva office is that it represents all CARE sections as one common CARE International and 'does not just advance the vested interests of one specific CARE member' (Interview CARE-5). Establishing an office in Geneva had been under discussion for some time.

> Off and on over many years CARE discussed setting up a liaison office in Geneva, but nothing ever came of it. There was always some disagreement among various national CAREs regarding the value of such an office and cost was an important factor ... it is quite expensive to support an office in Switzerland, even a small one. (Interview CARE-5)

Eventually, the establishment of the office significantly influenced the activities of CARE International at the UN level. 'The most influential part of this [permanent representation] was because having a CARE person on the ground in Geneva meant that CARE for the first time played a large and important role in the Steering Committee for Humanitarian Response' (Interview CARE-5).

People and departments at the international secretariat

In addition to the permanent representatives, the secretariat of CARE International now plays a much greater role in representing the NGO at the UN than before. Most importantly, the secretary-general of the NGO is heavily involved in the representation of the organization. He goes to Geneva regularly, representing CARE International in important matters and at high meetings before the UN. In his function as Head of the Steering Committee for Humanitarian Response, CARE's secretary-general represents the network on the Inter-Agency Standing Committee (Interview CARE-4).

Prior to his position as secretary-general of CARE International, he was Head of the UN peacekeeping operation in Rwanda. Being an ex-UN official, he therefore knows the UN system very well and maintains personal contacts with UN officials. (Interview CARE-1). Thus, unlike other NGO secretary-generals, he has additional channels to the UN due to his previous career and personal connections. Otherwise, however, there are no staff members specifically dedicated to UN-related matters. Rather, various people work on UN-related issues according to the subject matter. For example, an assistant secretary mentioned that he usually spends 10 to 15 per cent of his time on UN-related issues (Interview CARE-4).

The New York and Geneva UN representatives are 'nominally' part of the CARE International office (Interview CARE-3) and 'technically' the offices and their staff members are supervised by the NGO's headquarters in Brussels (Interview CARE-4). However, the international secretariat does not have an official policy or strategy for the nature of CARE's representation at the UN, or as one staff member expressed it, there is 'no book of rules' on this issue (Interview CARE-3).

Educational background and experience with the NGO and the UN

For the post as the representative of CARE International before the UN, the educational background does not play a role. In contrast to advocacy NGOs, most of CARE's representatives are not chosen for their academic studies, but their affiliation with and knowledge about the NGO have been the deciding factors for their recruitment for the position as the NGO's UN representative.

In general, CARE's representatives have a long history of involvement with the NGO in many different positions and in various areas. For example, one representative in Geneva obtained training as a geologist, but he had been working for CARE in a field position for about 15 years before becoming the NGO's Geneva representative (Interview CARE-1). Another representative had been working in the humanitarian field for 15 years, serving among other positions as a country director in three countries and coordinated all of CARE's humanitarian work in Zaire in 1994–95 (Interview CARE-5). Similarly, a representative in New York had also been involved with the NGO for about 20 years working for CARE USA in different positions and in various regions of the world (Interview CARE-2).

Rather than academic training on the subject matter, CARE International's representatives at the UN must have experience with the organization and knowledge about how the UN system works. As a representative (Interview CARE-5) mentioned,

> CARE puts high priority in having a very experienced 'mature' person in the position. It has to be someone with extensive humanitarian field experience, senior humanitarian management experience and the type of person who the UN agencies could view as an 'equal', a person who could comfortably work with and communicate with very senior UN officials. It also has to be a person who is highly respected by all national CARE members.

Thus, for the post as CARE International's representatives at the UN, the NGO recruits senior people from inside the organization on an informal basis; usually they are 'asked' to take up the position. For example, the Geneva representative speaks for the NGO in Geneva because of his knowledge of CARE International and because he knows the UN structures well (Interview CARE-1). Similarly, the volunteer representative had also been asked to continue to represent CARE International in New York City because a person was needed who knows the organization and its programmes very well.[51]

In brief, CARE International's increasing representation at the UN accounts for the expansion in its activities at the UN level. Representing a case of a modestly centralist service NGO, it has gone through increased internal institutionalization of its relations to the UN. In recent years, the NGO invested to a comparatively high degree in its representation before the UN and established full-time posts in different UN locations. Moreover, its representation became increasingly formalized and tasks and duties are divided between the national sections and headquarters. Due to its function as a service NGO, CARE International mainly recruits its representatives from inside the NGO as they have the necessary knowledge about the NGO and expertise about the field which is necessary for interaction with the UN.

Oxfam International: only few resources mobilized

Until recently, Oxfam International was represented at the UN by a single Oxfam affiliate only. Oxfam Great Britain, intending to maintain a post in New York, set up the position because it sought to interact on a more permanent basis with people from the missions to the UN in order to discuss issues related to humanitarian aid (Interview Oxfam-3).

Offices and people in UN locations

Oxfam International's limited and diffuse activities at the UN level are explained by examining the NGO's resources and organizational structures for its work with the IGO. Oxfam International dedicated few resources to its representation at the UN until 2002, as it had no official office in any major UN location.[52] Its UN representation was limited to one representative in New York for the British affiliate to the NGO. Besides representing Oxfam at the UN, he simultaneously represented another humanitarian NGO.

This representative of Oxfam conducted this job on a voluntary basis after retirement from leadership positions in other humanitarian organizations. Similar to CARE's representative, he came to the post on an informal way: he was asked by Oxfam staff members to represent the NGO in New York City (Interview Oxfam-3). Leading members from the British Oxfam affiliate approached him with the idea of representing the NGO in New York City because of his experience with humanitarian agencies (Interview Oxfam-3).

Organizational structures of representation

Oxfam International's representation at the UN is less formally structured than other NGOs which work with the UN. When the voluntary representative took up the position in 1993, Oxfam International did not yet exist as a federation of all Oxfam affiliates. Thus, he was only representing Oxfam Great Britain and later also Oxfam USA, the two Oxfams which at that time both were working independently with the UN. Since Oxfam Great Britain initiated his post, it also covered his small budget.

As a result, it remained ambiguous which of the Oxfam affiliates the post was representing. Novib, which joined the Oxfam family in 1995, for example, did not consider itself represented through Oxfam's volunteer representative in New York as very little information is channelled through him. As one Novib/Oxfam Netherlands representative remarked, 'he [Oxfam's volunteer representative in New York] is more of an observer and works mainly for Oxfam GB and is not perceived as a representative of Novib at the UN level' (Interview Oxfam-6). Instead, Novib named its own contact person at headquarters, however this is only a formality as this person simply distributes incoming information from the UN due to her position in headquarters in The Hague (Interview Oxfam-7).

Conversely, in addition to the British affiliate of Oxfam, the representative in New York also developed informal contacts with some of the other Oxfam affiliates due to his personal relations with staff members. As such, he sometimes took on the role of representing the different Oxfams at the UN when they approached him with a particular matter.

However, not all information concerning the NGO's relations with the UN necessarily went through him; single Oxfams might deal with the UN independently (Interview Oxfam-3). Moreover, not even all representation of Oxfam GB at the UN went through the volunteer representative in New York. Oxfam GB sometimes interacts directly with the UN in New York, and Oxfam International may also send a representative from its office in Washington (Interview Oxfam-1).

As for Geneva, a host of different people represent the NGO there; depending on the issue at stake, the appropriate person from headquarters of Oxfam GB goes to Geneva to represent the NGO (Interview Oxfam-5).

People and departments at the international secretariat

There is no particular section in the international secretariat of Oxfam International or in Oxfam GB's office dedicated to UN-related matters. Oxfam GB's representation at the UN differs in this respect from its representation to the EU and the UK government, for which it employs specifically designated persons. The UN, instead, is addressed by different people working on UN-related issues depending on the subject matters (Interview Oxfam-1).

About ten people in Oxfam GB's headquarters deal with UN-related matters in one way or the other. Also, the director of Oxfam can be much involved with UN-related matters and goes to New York for important meetings. Novib/Oxfam Netherlands, too, has two people in its headquarters who are to some extent involved with UN-related matters selected on the basis of their duties within the organization. Particularly during the three years prior to the Social Summit in Copenhagen in 1995, Novib's contact person had a strong connection with the UN because she coordinated the participation of the NGO's Southern partners (Interview Oxfam-7).

*Educational background and experience within
the NGO and the UN*

Experience in the sector of humanitarian emergency relief is the decisive factor for recruitment of Oxfam's representatives to the UN. The voluntary representative in New York has been involved with international humanitarian organizations for a long time. He was president of another network of US-based humanitarian NGOs for almost ten years before taking up the position at Oxfam (Interview Oxfam-3). During his career he gained experience in NGO–UN relations by initiating activities between many NGOs and the UN in the humanitarian sector (Interview Oxfam-3). As a result, he was able to acquire the knowledge as well as the experience for interaction with diplomats necessary for his position as Oxfam's representative.

Such skills are highly important as UN representative in the humanitarian field because the job demands the maturity and self-confidence to take initiative, as well as the capacity to understand issues surrounding complex emergencies very clearly, both from a diplomatic and a field perspective (Interview Oxfam-3). Since many diplomats are often not experts in the issue matter, humanitarian NGOs gain more from their relations with the UN when they have a competent representative who knows the organization and its capacities well (Oxfam International 2000a: 29).

In sum, Oxfam's diffuse activities at the UN level are explained by its representation at the intergovernmental organization, which was barely internally institutionalized. As a federative NGO, Oxfam International spent few resources on its representation at the UN and only one affiliated member NGO maintained volunteer representation in one major UN location. Within the international federation, representation is less coordinated than in centralized NGOs, as responsibilities are unclear and not all representation goes through the single representative. Similar to other service NGOs, that representative was qualified for the post because of his knowledge about the service sector and his capacities due to his long involvement with humanitarian organizations.

Other NGOs

In addition to the four examples chosen for intense study, I briefly explore the second set of NGOs and their representation and representatives to the UN. I show that other NGOs largely conform to the observations made about NGO representation and representatives in the primary set of NGOs. The backup NGOs also demonstrate a general tendency towards professionalization of NGO representation to varying degrees depending on the functions and composition of the NGO.

Human Rights Watch

Human Rights Watch, too, dedicates resources to its representation at the UN. Two people have been working exclusively on UN matters in New York headquarters since 1994 (Interview HRW-3). In Geneva, Human Rights Watch is also represented by a staff member since 2000. The position was first led by a volunteer who worked on a part-time basis and supported HRW during the sessions of the Commission on Human Rights (Interview HRW-2). In 2001, HRW made this position in Geneva a full-time professional representative post as the NGO wanted to intensify its UN relations (Interview HRW-1).

Before being represented in Geneva with local staff, the New York representative commuted between both UN locations (Interview HRW-2). She went to Geneva about five times a year to represent HRW at the UN and also spent a considerable period of time there during the sessions of the Commission (Interview HRW-3). However, HRW still considers New York the 'key to the UN': this is where the IGO's headquarters is based, so the main office for HRW's representation at the UN will always be in New York (Interview HRW-3). It forms a separate unit within the international secretariat of HRW. Like Amnesty International, HRW too maintains a Legal and Policy Department in which UN-related matters and legal affairs are dealt with.

Educational and professional training is valued by the NGO for the position of HRW's representative to the UN. One of the New York representatives, for example, has a background in language and area studies as well as journalism. Unlike AI, however, this HRW representative acquired her knowledge about human rights and legal affairs through practical experience as she was involved with the NGO in various positions for about two decades (Interview HRW-3). Similarly, the Geneva representative has a strong background in journalism which is highly valued for the position as she often deals with the media. Her negotiation skills acquired as part of her post-graduate degree in public administration are also helpful in working with diplomats. Although she does not hold a degree in human rights law, she took several courses and specialized in it as it became 'vital' to have such technical skills for her job as HRW representative to the UN (Interview HRW-2).

The International League for Human Rights

As with the FIDH, the ILHR can dedicate only few resources to its representation at the UN level. The NGO has only the required 'nominal' representative to the UN, and maintains no professional staff working on UN matters exclusively (Interview ILHR-2). Instead, since the ILHR has its headquarters in New York City, all staff members spend time on UN-related activities.[53] In addition, for some period of time, the ILHR was allied with other NGOs for legal advice. As Wiseberg and Scoble (1977: 308) reported in the late 1970s,

> [s]ince the League does not have the research and verification manpower and competence that Amnesty International has established with respect to political prisoners, nor does it have the legal-professional and jurisprudential prestige of the limited-membership International Commission of Jurists, the League has sought to develop its own style

of response. ... Reference here is to the Lawyers' Committee on International Human Rights, a joint effort begun in 1976 by the International League and the Council of New York Associates.[54]

In 1998, the ILHR established some volunteer representation in Geneva. Like the FIDH's last representative in New York City, the volunteer in Geneva operates on a 'grant basis' and represents the League whenever necessary (Interview ILHR-1). Thus, the NGO has no official office in Geneva, and the representative works out of his personal home. Like other human rights NGOs, the representative of the ILHR in Geneva did not work for the League before, but had been involved with other human rights NGOs.

International Save the Children Alliance

Similar to CARE International, the ISCA has in recent years invested considerably in its representation to the UN, and set up permanent representation in New York and Geneva. The post of 'Head of UN office New York', for example, was established in September 2000, and his work is supported by two more permanent full-time professional staff members (Interview ISCA-1).

Before this position became established, national sections of the ISCA conducted UN representation in New York individually. The US section of the NGO, for example, used to have its national headquarters in New York and sent representatives to the UN; also the UK section was represented by a part-time voluntary representative who was a former ambassador. However, they only represented the objectives of the single national sections, rather than the alliance of them all (Interview ISCA-1). Driven by the UK section, the creation of a representative post for the whole Alliance was initiated. Individual sections may still seek to advance their objectives in New York individually, however. Since the 1990s, the NGO has had a volunteer representative in Geneva. Like with CARE International, one section of ISCA took over the payment and administration of the post. The representative was working for the Swedish section (Rädda Barnen), but – without formal mandate – she 'was wearing the Alliance's hat'. In early 2001, the post became professionalized and now represents the whole alliance (Interview ISCA-2).

Also similar to CARE International's strategy for recruiting its representative for relations with the UN, the ISCA appointed its representatives because of their involvement with the NGO, knowledge about the UN, and experience rather than for their educational background. For example, the New York representative has been working for the ISCA for four years in the field and had also been active for other NGOs. He also worked as an advisor in the diplomatic service in Geneva and gained experience in the diplomatic world which was valued highly (Interview ISCA-1).

Action Aid Alliance

The Action Aid Alliance maintains no volunteer or professional representative at the UN level (Interview AAA-1). Single member NGOs, predominantly Action Aid UK, represent the NGO in Geneva or New York on an *ad hoc* basis instead. Depending on the particular issue, a staff member of AA UK, for example someone from its food team, attends a meeting with the UN. In other circumstances, different team members may also represent the NGO in other UN bodies. Thus, AA UK maintains only the nominal 'contact point' in its headquarters in London, and all incoming UN-related information is channelled through her (Interview AAA-2). This person was appointed the contact point because of her position within the NGO as the 'Food Policy Adviser' and the 'Head of UK advocacy team'. Because it was already an internationally active post, it made sense to channel UN-related information through it (Interview AAA-2). The educational background thus did not play a great role for her appointment. Rather, her experience with the UN after having followed the Earth Summit and various other meetings caused the organization to nominate her. Thus, 'it is more a practical reason rather than because of the knowledge that she has the position' (Interview AAA-2).

Summary

Representation of NGOs at the UN goes through three steps. First, NGOs are initially represented by a volunteer or only one national NGO maintains an individual representation. In a second step, this voluntary representation is professionalized or the individual representation of one NGO becomes a substantial part of the whole organization. The third step contains an expansion of the NGO representation to the UN. Additional representatives in other UN locations are accredited or the existing offices enlarge their body of staff. Again, these additional posts may first be filled with volunteers and become professionalized gradually (step one and two; see Figure 4.1).

NGOs differ in the time at which they choose to invest more heavily in UN representation. While advocacy NGOs have set up their representation at the UN for some time and now are able to expand, service NGOs

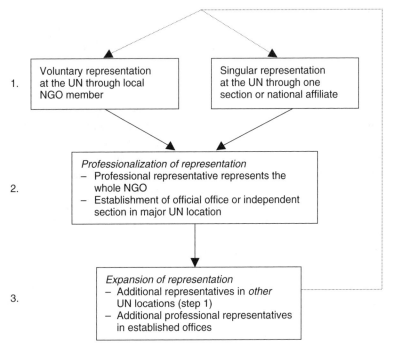

Figure 4.1 Steps of representation at the UN

instead invested in their representation and professionalized such posts only recently. Most advocacy NGOs have been represented at the UN since the early 1990s (and in some case even earlier) on a voluntary basis, and they gradually professionalized their representation over the years. Earlier than service NGOs they recognized that for continuous interaction with the UN it is necessary to have permanent representatives. Service NGOs, instead, did not regard representation at the UN as particularly useful until recently and thus humanitarian NGOs did not provide for such posts in New York City or Geneva. Since their activities with the UN took place almost exclusively in the field, it did not seem necessary to have representatives in UN locations. As more avenues for activities with the UN opened up in recent years, however, humanitarian NGOs 'caught up' and invested comparatively much in their representation to the UN. In this context, they often skipped voluntary or singular representation (step 1): NGOs that had no representation before the mid-1990s have recently established official offices in major UN locations and equipped them with full-time professionals.

Moreover, the NGOs examined in detail differ as to the stage at which they institutionalized their representation at the UN level internally. The empirical analysis shows that centralist NGOs are more likely to professionalize the positions of NGO representatives to the UN than federative NGOs because they can devote more resources to relations with IGOs. In recent years, centralist NGOs, such as AI or CARE International are increasingly augmenting or investing in their UN-related staff. In doing so, they take better advantage of the possible spectrum of interaction with the UN. International federations like the FIDH or Oxfam International instead have the disadvantage that because of their international composition they have only a small number of staff altogether and are not able to maintain many representatives. As they have only a small budget, they calculate their possibilities and split representation or rely on voluntary representation.

Advocacy NGOs are likely to recruit people on the basis of professional criteria such as their specific knowledge about the subject matter; service NGOs, instead, are likely to recruit representatives for their involvement and practical experience with the NGO. That is to say, advocacy NGOs like AI or the FIDH are increasingly recruiting specialists because of the educational and professional background, and less for their involvement or former commitment with the NGO. Service NGOs, like CARE International or Oxfam International recruit their representatives from within the organization for interaction with the UN. Representatives of humanitarian NGOs need to have considerable knowledge about the

Table 4.1 Recruitment factors today

	Involvement with NGO	Experience with the UN	Academic Training in relation to post as representative
AI	Very Low	High	Very High
HRW	Medium	Medium	High
FIDH	Very Low	Medium	Very High
ILHR	Medium	Medium	Medium
CARE	Very High	Very High	Very Low
ISCA	Very High	Very High	Low
Oxfam	High	High	Very Low
AAA	Very High	Medium	Very Low

NGO, its programmes and projects in the fields. As they have been working in the humanitarian field or for the NGO for many years or decades, they know how the organization operates on the ground (see Table 4.1).

In short, over the course of the last decade, NGOs have invested significantly in their UN representation. However, depending on the type of NGO, there is variance in how and to what extent they have installed provisions for such representation.

5
Accreditation to the UN through Rules and Regulations – Institutionalization as an External Demand

Changes in the patterns of activity between societal actors and official institutions can result from external demands. As discussed in the theoretical section, the notion of institutionalization also refers to formalized principles by which interaction between societal actors and official institutions is officially recognized. In this study, external demands are understood as the rules and regulations for the relationship between NGOs and the UN.

In this chapter, I first present some general observations about formal NGO recognition by the UN. This part provides the context for the responses of individual NGOs to such external demands. In the second part of the chapter, I examine the eight NGOs in greater detail. The UN's main regulated form of NGO accreditation is consultative status with the ECOSOC, so I focus on the significance of that status for the different organizations and explore its impact on their patterns of activity with the UN.

General observations on consultative status of NGOs at the UN

Both NGOs and the UN have good reasons for entering into an official relationship. NGOs gain access to the UN which enables them to meet with delegates, obtain and spread information, and participate in meetings. The UN receives additional information, valuable advice, and support from NGOs. Moreover, both parties may gain legitimacy. While NGOs are recognized as actors on the international level by an official institution, the activities of the UN gain a democratic component since civil society organizations take part in their official processes. In this section, I discuss facets of consultative status with particular reference to its latest revision in 1996.

Previous resolutions on NGO–UN relations and current legal foundations

The relationship between the UN and NGOs dates back to the founding period of the UN. NGOs have been formally involved in the UN system since 1945 when in Article 71 UN Charter it was provided that

> [t]he Economic and Social Council may make suitable arrangements for consultation with non-governmental organizations which are concerned within its competence. Such arrangements may be made with international organizations and, where appropriate, with national organizations after consultations with the Members of the United Nations concerned.

The article, however, only generally allows for UN relations with NGOs, and several resolutions were needed to lay down their relationship in more detail. In fact, relations between the UN and NGOs were a topic of discussion at the very first session of the UN General Assembly. Early East–West tensions led to a struggle over the right of admission to consultative status (Ziegler 1998: 30; Stephenson 2000: 273–4). A temporary committee was established to work out a resolution on how the NGO–UN relationship should be regulated (UN Doc. E/43/Rev.1 §37; UN Doc. E/C.2/23). Based on the committee's recommendations, ECOSOC introduced a 'three class system' of NGO consultation by which NGO categories A, B, and C had different demands, rights, and duties respectively.

In 1950, Resolution 288 (x) replaced these *ad hoc* regulations for NGO consultation (UN Resolution 288 (x)). Two labour organizations, the American Federation of Labour and the World Trade Union Congress (WTUC) argued about the right to submit questions to the agenda of ECOSOC, which led to difficulties in the NGO community. As a result, the NGO Committee functioned as a selection instance, which either submitted the request of an organization directly to ECOSOC or it rejected it (Hüfner 1991: 627). In addition, some governmental representatives felt that NGOs misused their status and thus called for it to be more restricted (Ziegler 1998: 31).

In 1968, Resolution 288 (x) was replaced by Resolution 1296 (XLIV) which went on to regulate the consultative status for almost 30 years. This revision of NGO access to the UN had become necessary when it was made public that single NGOs were secretly financed by the CIA and others were suspected of being financed by governmental sources (Hüfner 1991: 627; Willetts 1996c: 41). The new resolution replaced the ABC system with a roster and categories I and II. Moreover, NGOs had to make statements concerning their financial resources and submit a report about their activities every four years.

Since 1996, Resolution 1996/31 has governed the relations between NGOs and the UN. The enormous NGO participation at the series of UN conferences in the first half of the 1990s made a reform of the almost three decade old resolution necessary. National NGOs are now also eligible to apply for accreditation to the UN. Other than a broadening of access, however, there was no fundamental change in terms of the legal foundations for NGO consultation. Although categories I and II were renamed 'general consultative status' and 'special consultative status' (the roster stayed the same) the rights and duties of NGOs vis-à-vis the UN, particularly the criteria for eligibility for status, remained almost the same as before the resolution.

The UN's requirements for NGOs to attain status are: an established headquarters, an executive organ and officer, a democratically adopted constitution (providing for the determination of policy by a representative body), an authority to speak for the members, and financial independence from governmental bodies. Furthermore, the UN requires the NGOs to fulfil some criteria which remain only vaguely specified, such as 'international standing', 'independent governance', and 'geographical affiliation'. For example, NGOs need to have a recognized standing within the particular field of their competence or to be of a representative character, and they should represent large sections of the population. In terms of composition, NGOs may include members designated by governments, but only if this does not interfere with the free expression of the organization's view (UN Resolution 1996/31 §9–13).

The criteria for determining which status an NGO should receive, however, are vague. The resolution states that general consultative status is reserved for organizations concerned with most of the activities of the Council and from which sustained contribution to the achievement of the objectives of the United Nations can be expected. NGOs with general consultative status must also represent major segments of society in a large number of countries of different regions of the world (UN Resolution 1996/31 §22). In return, the rights and privileges pertaining to this status are the most far-reaching of the three categories. NGOs with this status have the right to attend meetings of the ECOSOC and its subsidiary bodies and speak and circulate statements of 2000 words.

Table 5.1   Status-specific privileges

General	Special	Roster
Able to consult with officers from the Secretariat on matters of interest to the NGO	Able to consult with officers from the Secretariat on matters of interest to the NGO	Able to consult with officers from the Secretariat on matters of interest to the NGO
Allowed to make oral statements based on recommendations by the Committee	Allowed to make oral statements based on recommendations by the Committee	
Allowed to submit brief written statements (2000 words)	Allowed to submit brief written statements (1500 words)	
May designate representatives to sit at meetings of ECOSOC and its subsidiaries	May designate representatives to sit at meetings of ECOSOC and its subsidiaries	May designate representatives to sit at meetings of ECOSOC and its subsidiaries
Have the right to place items on the agenda of ECOSOC and its subsidiaries		

They are also allowed to make proposals to the provisional agenda of ECOSOC or its exercising bodies (UN Resolution 1996/31 §28–31; see Table 5.1).

For organizations with a smaller scope of activity, special consultative status applies. It is similar to general consultative status, except that NGOs can neither submit proposals to the agenda nor speak at meetings of ECOSOC. Written statements NGOs of this status may circulate are limited to 1500 words (UN Resolution 1996/31 §23, 29–31). Other organizations which do not fulfil the criteria for either general or special status are put on a 'roster'. Roster NGOs are limited to attend meetings only within their field of competence. Moreover, they need an invitation by the Secretary-General to make a written contribution, which may not exceed 500 words (UN Resolution 1996/31 §24, 31).

NGOs and the consultative status today

The number of NGOs maintaining official relations with the UN has risen tremendously since the establishment of the accreditation scheme.

When consultative status was introduced in the 1940s, 40 NGOs were accredited. In the late 1960s, this number grew to 377 and by the early 1990s the figure of accredited NGOs had gradually increased to 744. It was in the mid-1990, however, that the number of accredited NGOs exploded. Whereas in 1996, 1226 NGOs were enrolled on the consultative status, only five years later the number had almost doubled and by mid-2005, 2614 NGOs had official relations with the UN (Department of Economic and Social Affairs 2005). The most dramatic growth in numbers occurred in 1999 when more than 400 new NGOs became enrolled at once (see Table 5.2).

There are two main reasons for this exponential growth. First, in the aftermath of the UN conferences in the first half of the 1990s, many NGOs which before only had informal relations with the UN, applied for consultative status in order to formalize their relations. Other NGOs became aware of the benefits of working with the UN and therefore also applied for the status, particularly many national NGOs (Interview UN-3). Second, the various UN bodies and agencies, which sometimes have their own mechanisms for NGO accreditation, were asked to provide

Table 5.2 Number of NGOs with consultative status

Year	General	Specific	Roster	Total
1948	7	32	1	40
1949	9	77	4	90
1968	12	143	222	377
1969	16	116	245	377
1983	31	239	422	692
1992	38	297	409	744
1994	40	334	410	784
1995	69	436	563	1068
1996	81	499	646	1226
1997	88	602	666	1356
1998	100	742	663	1505
1999	111	918	909	1938
2000	122	1048	880	2050
2001	124	1132	895	2151
2002	131	1197	906	2234
2003	131	1316	903	2350
2004	134	1474	923	2531
Mid-2005	134	1545	935	2614

Sources: UN Doc. E/1998/43 (1998); Department of Economic and Social Affairs (2005); Interview UN-3.

lists of associated NGOs which then automatically became enrolled on the consultative status scheme (Interview UN-3).

NGOs that want UN affiliation submit their application for consultative status to the Department of Economic and Social Affairs (DESA). There, every application is processed and approved, and recommendations for NGOs are then forwarded to the so-called Committee of NGOs. This body discusses every single case and makes recommendations to ECOSOC which makes the final decisions. About 80 per cent of all applications of NGOs for consultative status are accepted. Of those not approved, many simply had not completed the application process correctly (Interview UN-3).

One of the main hurdles for NGOs to be accredited today is that the system has reached its 'natural limits' (Interview UN-3). With the opening of the consultative status to national NGOs and increased awareness about participation within the framework of the UN, the number of applications for consultative status has mushroomed. More and more national NGOs seek consultative status, and those that had been associated with single UN agencies or had been accredited as consultants for a special occasion now apply for admission status also. As a result, the system of NGO accreditation 'imploded' (Interview NR-1). The number of NGO applications has risen from 300 to 400 a year, but the NGO Committee can only deal with around 100 applications at each annual session (Interview UN-3; UN Doc. E/1998/43). For this reason, NGOs now have to wait for several years for their application to be processed.

The following illustrates a sample of the work of the committee and the accreditation of NGOs: At one session in 2000, the Committee on NGOs considered 80 new applications for consultative status and another 37 applications deferred from its 1998 and 1999 sessions. Of those, the committee recommended that ECOSOC grant consultative status to 37 of those organizations, that five not be granted status at all, that two applications be resubmitted, and that one be closed. Eventually, 72 applications were deferred to the following session. In addition, one NGO was reclassified from special to general consultative, one NGO had to reapply as a new legal entity and two others had their status suspended for three years (UN Doc. E/2000/88 Part I).

Selection process of NGOs

The composition of the NGO Committee is an important aspect of NGO accreditation for consultative status. It consists of 19 members who are representatives of their governments at the UN, according to a geographic ratio which allows for the various regions of the world to be represented. The composition of the committee takes place informally, thus, each regional group decides among themselves which nations to place on the committee. The seats on the committee rotate; each country serves for a period of four years, but there is no limit to serving consecutive periods. Officially, the committee meets for two sessions of three weeks a year, but due to its increase in work, these sessions are usually extended another three weeks (Interview NR-1).

For some states, serving on the NGO Committee is of interest because of the power to deny certain NGOs access to the UN. As the committee discusses all NGO-related matters, some states are particularly cautious and make sure that any NGO which seeks to undermine the state's authority will not succeed with its application process. Thus, some countries are very keen on having a representative on the committee. China and Cuba, for example, have been members for decades, and successfully stopped the applications of many anti-Cuban and anti-Chinese NGOs. Thus, committee decisions can be highly political and depend on the political climate between the states involved. As Lagoni (1995: 907) points out, '[i]t is hardly surprising that the decision of the Council to make an arrangement with a particular non-governmental organization or to place it on the Roster or, on the other hand, to suspend or withdraw its status may be influenced by political considerations'. Because of this high politicization, the NGO Committee is one of the most debated in the UN and is regarded by many as the 'committee with the worst reputation' (Interview NR-1).

Membership on the NGO Committee is not only a useful way to block participation of certain NGOs, it may also be used to promote that of others and can be a tool to bring in 'government-friendly' ones. Although the opening of the consultative status for national NGOs was intended to create more diversity within the NGO community, single governments make use of the new accreditation options to promote national NGOs that support their policies or even create NGOs themselves only for having them associated with the UN. As an NGO representative reports (Petroula 2001: 53), 'looking closely at the reports of the Committee of NGOs since 1996, it can be seen that GONGOs [Government-Organized NGOs] from countries such as Cuba, Tunisia, China, Pakistan and India have obtained consultative status'. Some observers fear that these developments will undermine the whole system of NGO accreditation because it calls into question their credibility as independent societal actors (Interview Add. NGOs-1).

Withdrawal of consultative status as a threat

While consultative status offers advantages for accredited NGOs, it can also be used as a threat against NGOs. As Chiang (1981: 233) recognized early on,

> [t]here is a tendency for the UN to attempt to 'control the character and activities' of the NGOs by threatening to withdraw the consultative status of those whose activities outside the UN it does not approve, as well as those NGOs which criticize certain decisions or actions of the UN or those certain governments; and by threatening to reject those NGOs.

Consultative status can be withdrawn for various reasons, many of them concerning procedural aspects (Interview UN-2). For example, when an NGO does not complete the required quadrennial report about its activities with the UN or when it abuses its status for other purposes, it gives states ground for complaint. Activities contrary to the purposes and principles of the UN Charter, criminal activities like money laundering or illegal arms or drug trade, secret funding by governments, and not making any positive or effective contribution to the work of the UN also lead to a suspension or withdrawal of the consultative status (Interview NR-2).

Complaints about NGOs may be submitted to the NGO Committee at any time throughout the year. Often, single country delegates search for reasons to expel particular NGOs disliked by their government. In particular, some states intensely observe the behaviour of NGOs and statements made by them during the sessions of the Commission on Human Rights in order to suspend those that do not follow the procedural rules. Very alarming for NGOs is also the period when the quadrennial reports are due, as governments tend to use this occasion to report incidents and form coalitions against single NGOs; the committee then decides on the gravity of these complaints. Under exceptional circumstances the committee can also ask for a report from an individual organization outside the regular quadrennial due dates (Interview UN-3).

NGOs are examined much more critically since the 1996 review process (Interview UN-3). In fact, more NGOs than ever before have been under dispute or suspended from their consultative status since Resolution 1996/31 went into force. The exact number of suspensions, however, is difficult to estimate. The DESA provides some figures but these are not complete and only provide the reasons for withdrawal. For some observers, these developments show a change in the policy towards NGO access to the UN. In the human rights sector, NGO representatives have the impression that governments have become more hostile or restrictive to NGOs and suspension or withdrawal of consultative status has developed into a possible threat to them (Interviews FIDH-4, HRW-3, Add. NGOs-1, HRW-2, FIDH-2).

Moreover, there are some issue-areas in which accreditation is more difficult to obtain or to keep than in others. This particularly applies to NGOs which are active in specific issue-areas or geographical regions which concern the interest of a member of the NGO Committee. For example, NGOs engaging in issues surrounding Chechnya or Kashmir have difficulties being accredited, when Russia and India are members of the NGO Committee. Similarly, religious and minority organizations have problems receiving official status. On the whole, however, human rights NGOs are the most discussed group of organizations. NGO representatives estimate that out of ten applications discussed before the Committee, nine of them concern human rights NGOs (Interviews AI-2, HRW-2).[55]

In addition, human rights NGOs are the only group of NGOs whose UN interaction is specifically defined regarding the purposes of activities. As it is phrased in the 1996/31 resolution,

Organizations to be accorded special consultative status because of their interest in the field of human rights should pursue the goals of promotion and protection of human rights in accordance with the spirit of the Charter of the United Nations, the Universal Declaration of Human Rights and the Vienna Declaration and Programme of Action.

This special reference to human rights NGOs became part of the UN's regulation of NGO accreditation in 1968 when a revised resolution was approved.[56]

Consultative status – two sides of the same coin?

NGOs are interested in gaining consultative status at the UN because this status provides them with several opportunities to obtain information and to promote their own interests. ECOSOC status is like the hurdle which NGOs have to jump before starting activities with the UN. On a formal level consultative status at the UN facilitates access to the work of the regional and special committees and entitles NGOs to receive official documents. They may also be invited to attend conferences and meetings or to make statements on a particular issue. On an informal level, consultative status enables NGOs to promote their cause.

Representatives of NGOs with official status receive a pass and a badge which allows them to enter official UN buildings, thus granting them the chance to get in direct contact with governmental delegates and other representatives. This access is of highest importance, since it enables NGOs to keep themselves informed about current decisions and to lobby officials informally in corridors or cafeterias. In fact, these opportunities to meet are often more effective than the official proceedings. 'At any UN meeting the discussions in the coffee lounges and corridors are as important as, if not more important than, the official speeches' (Cook 1996: 187).

Consultative status is an 'official way' to participate in international policy making processes. Recognition by the UN implies acknowledgement of NGOs as international actors (Ritchie 1996: 180–1). It provides them with a 'label of international credibility' which allows other parts of the UN or other IGOs to have legitimate contact with NGOs (Bettati 1986: 12). However, consultative status does not only award rights and privileges; it also implies duties such as required submission of budget and funding data. Even when fulfilling all the criteria set by the UN, NGOs have no legal claim to be admitted to consultative status (Lagoni 1995: 907).

Although the consultative status opens doors for NGOs, it also raises negative responses. Major criticism accuses the selection procedures and composition of the NGO Committee of being biased by consisting of governmental representatives. Some observers have argued that NGOs must be in accordance with the 'ideological conformism' (Merle 1986: 164–5) to be recognized by the selecting body. In addition, consultative status puts pressure on NGOs: having attained consultative status, they must play by the rules of the game. In international-federative composed NGOs, for example, every affiliate or single representative has to abide by the instructions of the consultative status. Some authors have argued that as a result, NGOs lose their independence necessary for their work as 'critical observers' (Schulze 1994: 134), since they become too integrated into the system itself. Moreover, consultative status does not necessarily portray a representative sample of the NGO community. It has been argued that the selection procedure of consultative status is biased towards major international NGOs, such as large umbrella organizations, whereas smaller NGOs are left outside the integration framework (Schmidt and Take 1997: 19).

In brief, consultative status is characterized by ambivalences. On the one hand, NGOs seek consultative status at the UN because they gain access to buildings, delegates, meetings and so on, and obtain information; the consultative status also implies international recognition by governmental authorities. On the other hand, the integration of NGOs into intergovernmental bodies may have negative implications for the role of NGOs as independent observers. It is an imposed status on the NGOs which the UN defines and has the power to withdraw it, and admissions to consultative status may heavily depend on political considerations.

Single cases and their consultative status at the UN under examination

After having presented some general observations and broad features of the UN's consultation with NGOs, in the following section I explore consultative status for the four main case studies. With reference to the methodological approach, I take into account for each of the cases the type of status they maintain, the significance of having the status, and its meaning as a source of reputation. I also illustrate the historical development of their individual consultative status with any up- and down-gradings as well as threats to lose status. I then present briefly the other four NGOs and their perception of consultative status.

Amnesty International: consultative status as an entrance key

Amnesty International acquired consultative status with ECOSOC in 1964, three years after its founding. Because it is a human rights NGO specialized in political prisoners, the UN perceives AI as being concerned with a specific issue only. For this reason, it has always maintained the second highest status of relations with the UN, which is reserved for NGOs working in only a few ECOSOC areas. Under the new resolution of 1996, AI was again classified with 'specialized' consultative status. Since its accreditation almost four decades ago, it has never been up- or down-graded; nor has it been suspended from the status.

Dependency, significance and means of reputation

The spectrum of interaction between AI and the UN and its increase over recent years is explained only partially by its having formal status with the UN. Consultative status has primarily practical relevance for AI's work at the UN: the NGO sees the symbolical importance of status and considers it the 'entrance key' to the IGO (Interview AI-6). Being accredited to the UN through consultative status enables AI to access the UN in a variety of ways (Interview AI-10). On the one hand, status allows AI to receive all official documents and information material issued by the UN.

Official status puts AI on various distribution lists and keeps it informed about future and ongoing events at the UN. It enables AI representatives to enter UN buildings, to attend meetings and hearings, and to get together with other NGOs. Representatives can also meet informally with governmental delegates (for example in the UN building) in order to receive information from them about ongoing discussions and projects (Interviews AI-6, AI-5).

On the other hand, having status as a consulting NGO also makes it possible for AI to feed its own information into the UN machinery. It may actively participate in working groups and informal meetings, circulate documents and make interventions in ECOSOC meetings. Moreover, consultative status allows AI's representatives to give speeches at the Commission on Human Rights and its sub-commissions (Interview AI-8). As an NGO with special consultative status, AI is allowed to submit information to the ECOSOC, knowing that it will be distributed to all members (Interview AI-3). Most importantly, AI representatives can meet officially with delegates and lobby them for the objectives of the NGO (Interview AI-6).

In recent years, however, consultative status lost some significance for AI. Consultative status with ECOSOC is not an important requirement for activities with many UN bodies such as the Security Council, for example. These UN organs do not formally accredit NGOs themselves, and they interact with them based on their standing rather than because of their official UN recognition. Thus, significance of the consultative status shrinks to mere facilitation of physical access to the UN through badges.[57] Moreover, as a source of reputation consultative status with the UN does not play a role for AI either.

Though considered important in the early years when fewer organizations had obtained it, the status holds little significance today. Since AI's reputation is high in general, accreditation on the scheme of the consultative status does not add any extra value to its standing in the eyes of the general public. Therefore, AI does not put consultative status on its letterheads or its internet homepage. As a representative expressed it, AI has no need for using it as a source of reputation, especially since UN recognition is only one status among many it maintains with various IGOs (Interview AI-7).

Threats to its consultative status

Unlike many other human rights NGOs, AI does not fear the loss of its status at the UN. Despite its dependence on consultative status as a means to physically enter UN buildings, a withdrawal is no real threat for the NGO (Interview AI-6). As the major non-governmental organization for human rights, AI is simply 'too credible, too high profile, and has too good a reputation' (Interview AI-2) to be expelled from the UN in response to criticism by governments. As a representative expressed it, unlike many other human rights organization, AI has the 'luxury' of not having to fear a withdrawal of the consultative status and there have not been any real attempts over the last decade to withdraw AI's status (Interview AI-4).

Amnesty International's approach to consultative status and the unlikelihood of withdrawal, however, has changed over time. During its early days at the UN, there were various incidents when AI was threatened with a withdrawal. A major threat, for example, took place in 1978, when ECOSOC demanded the quadrennial reports, and the USSR and Argentine delegations sought actively to expel AI and some other human rights organizations from the UN (Interview AI-3). Argentina, angered by the criticism of certain human rights NGOs, insisted that the long neglected provision of the consultative arrangements in 1968 be implemented; these required NGOs in category I and II to submit quadrennial reports of their activities to the Committee on NGOs (Chiang 1981: 172). In this context, the USSR representative charged AI, the ILHR and the Anti-Slavery Society with abuse of status by engaging in political attacks on member states. The representative threatened the NGOs with the remark that the consultative status could be withdrawn if abused, urging the Council to investigate the activities of these NGOs to see whether they conform to the provisions of Resolution 1296 (Chiang 1981: 172).

Amnesty International, in response, worked both 'exhaustively and exhaustingly' (Interview AI-3) on this quadrennial report in order to fulfil all the requirements set out in the regulations on consultative status. The NGO prepared extensive documentation of its activities within the UN framework in order to prove its eligibility for consultative status. It even sent its secretary-general to the actual council meeting as it took this threat very seriously. However, in the end, the attack against AI had no consequences and the NGO kept its status.

After the 1978 attack, AI never again really feared a withdrawal of status, despite minor incidents where it had to clarify certain issues or subject matters. Although many countries with a record of human rights violations would prefer to see AI's accreditation withdrawn, the NGO is confident that these states do not dare to launch any accusations against it. Due to AI's good overall reputation, an attempt to remove its status at the UN would create media attention which could only be counterproductive for the country aiming to undermine AI's credibility.

Recently, some countries tried to question AI's standing at the UN by criticizing its limited focus on political prisoners. In the 1990s Cuba and other nations criticized that AI did not work on economic and social rights. As mentioned in a UN document: 'Some members of the Committee stated that the organization [Amnesty International] should consider expanding its activities in all areas relevant to human rights, including economic, social and cultural rights, within the framework of the Vienna Declaration adopted by the World Conference on Human Rights in 1993' (UN Doc. E/1996/17 §9). Amnesty International responded to this accusation quickly and settled the matter before official complaints occurred.

Although AI has no reason to fear a possible withdrawal of its accreditation at the UN, the NGO makes sure not to give states grounds upon which to suggest revoking status. That is to say, AI keeps to the procedural rules and makes sure to properly fulfil all the required formalities, such as writing the quadrennial report (Interview AI-6). In particular, the NGO is very careful not to accept any funding from governments regarding its UN activities as this could be interpreted as being accountable to official institutions (Interview AI-4). Also, unlike other human rights NGOs, AI does not provoke the UN by accrediting non-Amnesty members to speak on behalf of the NGO at the sessions of the Commission on Human Rights. As mentioned by a representative of the organization, AI is careful about how to use its consultative status and does not provoke complaints (Interview AI-5).

In sum, the consultative scheme has little impact on AI's spectrum of interaction at the UN level. Although it is significant for the NGO to have the status as it facilitates the entrance to the UN, enables the NGO to meet UN officials, and allows for the exchange of information, however, for many of its activities, the importance of the status does not go beyond its practical value. As an advocacy NGO, AI also had to cope in the past with threats to its status, but negative pressure of consultative status does not present a problem for the NGO anymore. Since AI has a high reputation and standing in the public, it maintains a privileged position at the UN. As a centralist NGO, AI does not view the status as source of reputation or special means to access the international sphere.

FIDH: dependence on formal status as mouthpiece

The FIDH received consultative status early on, being accredited to the UN in 1952. Typical for a human rights organization, it has always been registered on the second highest 'specialized' consultative status. Despite various attempts, the NGO has never been suspended nor has status been withdrawn during the last 50 years.

Dependency, significance and means of reputation

The FIDH's activities with the UN depend significantly on having formal status. Consultative status is an important source of reputation and symbolizes its acknowledgement as an important actor in the international human rights field. Since its members are usually only domestically active, the FIDH as a whole is not as well known as other NGOs, such as AI, and so it is in search of international recognition. Therefore, the status at the UN serves as a tool for the FIDH to show its credibility. Being accredited to the UN as a consultant makes it a respected player, and thus, distinguishes it from other human rights bodies. Moreover, such recognition functions as a means of prestige for the individual affiliates of the FIDH (Interview FIDH-3). Through the recognition of the international federation to which they belong they are also recognized as trustworthy, and their activities on the national level get acknowledged (Interview FIDH-2).

For this reason, the FIDH makes clear that it has maintained status at the UN for a long time. Unlike AI, the FIDH frequently refers to its consultative status at the UN on its websites and brochures. In fact, the activities with the UN on the basis of the consultative status are mentioned as part of one of its four major domains of action on its homepage and other information material (Fédération Internationale des Droits de l'Homme 1998, 2005a). The FIDH emphasizes that consultative status had much influence on the development and the activities of its international organization as a whole. 'As a non-governmental organisation accredited to the United Nations, the FIDH has significantly developed its activities during the last 50 years, multiplying its fact-finding missions and training workshop abroad, as well as its activities within international institutions' (Fédération Internationale des Droits de l'Homme 2005a).

Consultative status has practical value because it functions as a means for the FIDH's national NGOs to access the international sphere (Interview FIDH-2). Because their federative body maintains status, national affiliates are allowed to become active at the UN. Thus, the FIDH becomes a mouthpiece for the single members and enables them to 'make their voice heard' (Interview FIDH-4) outside their respective domestic arenas, where they otherwise operate exclusively. In fact, for many national member NGOs, consultative status of the FIDH is the only way to enter the UN (Interview FIDH-3). For example, national member NGOs are allowed to make a statement before the community of states only because of the status of the federation as a whole. That is to say, the Tunisian member NGO can take the floor and bring forward accusations against its government on human rights violations. These activities – although they may not have direct immediate impact – are intended to have long-term effects on various levels: on the international level the government is shamed before the international community of states and must justify domestic activities. On the national level, speeches of respective NGOs may have an impact as the media makes the public aware of these events and informs them about the activities of their national organization (Interview FIDH-3).

With the revision of the accreditation scheme in 1996, having consultative status as an international federative NGO has become even more valued. Although the new resolution allows national NGOs to apply for consultative status, their contributions are often not considered useful or trustworthy. This is due to the large number of single-state NGOs being accredited now that are significantly supported by 'their' home governments. Only international NGOs maintain a good standing before the international community of states and their contributions are considered significant. Paradoxically, national NGOs are now able to apply for consultative status themselves, but are more reliant than before on affiliation with an international body which enjoys credibility.[58]

Moreover, many affiliated NGOs of the FIDH are not able to receive consultative status at the UN individually despite the opening of the status to national NGOs because they heavily criticize their own governments, which then lobby against their accreditation (Interview FIDH-3). As a result, national NGOs continue to rely on a federation to be represented at the UN level. Similarly, many newly founded national human rights NGOs seeking consultative status face the same problem: they are blocked by their own governments and will not receive consultative status. For such new groups, international federative NGOs like the FIDH can be a means for access to the UN (Interview FIDH-2).

The FIDH provides such opportunities to 'piggy-back' national NGOs, for example for the organization Human Rights In China (HRIC). It became an affiliate to the FIDH in January 2001, because it was unable to obtain consultative status by itself. In fact, HRIC tried to receive accreditation to the UN but its application was never approved (Interview FIDH-6). Becoming an FIDH affiliate allowed it to participate in UN forums that would otherwise have been inaccessible. For example, HRIC was able to participate during the session of the Commission on Human

Rights in 2002, where it was accredited through the FIDH and represented by its director and another staff member. When being denied accreditation prior to joining the FIDH, HRIC experienced the typical obstacles faced by national NGOs. The original application for consultative status was sent to the UN in 1998. Administrative procedures took several months, as the NGO was asked to clarify various aspects of the application and had to send additional information. Finally, the full application was considered during the June 1999 session of the Committee on NGOs (Interview FIDH-6). Expecting to have a difficult time receiving the status, the NGO lobbied and met with delegation members during the weeks before the session. Some of these delegates, however, indicted beforehand that the Chinese were pressuring against approval of the application. One delegation even asked the NGO to withdraw the application (Interview FIDH-6). When on 4 June 1999, the session took place during which the application of the NGO was considered, the case of HRIC surpassed all expectations. Unlike the usual procedure in which an NGO is discussed for five to 30 minutes, its application took six hours. The session was well attended and some delegations sent more representatives than usual; for example, China was represented by five delegates instead of the usual two (Human Rights in China 2001).

During the discussions, the Chinese strategy was to prevent the HRIC representative from taking the floor, although it is part of the normal procedure that NGOs present their standpoint against allegations made by a country. Immediately after announcing that HRIC was up for review, the Chinese delegate stated that after having 'studied the case of this organization from many angles' the NGO would not qualify for any form of consultative status for various reasons (UN Doc. E/1999/109 §24–6). The NGO should not receive consultative status because members of the organization were living outside China without showing concern about the human rights situation in the country they are living in. Moreover, the majority of them have either never set foot on Chinese soil or have not gone back to China in recent years, and therefore do not know the situation in China (UN Doc. E/1999/109 §24–6).

He continued that the NGO had done nothing so far to improve the human rights situation in China: it did not support China when the country was hit by a great flood and suffered from economic losses in 1998 in which 20 million were affected nor did it react when the Chinese embassy in Yugoslavia was bombed in May 1998 and the diplomatic personnel suffered. Many of the HRIC's board members were criminals who had been punished for their acts, and the entire NGO was linked to secessionist groups in Tibet according to the Chinese delegate. After hour-long discussions and various debates, HRIC was not granted consultative status by 13 to three votes; only France, Ireland and the US voted in favour of granting (UN Doc. E/1999/109 §24–6).

Threats to the consultative status

Not only does the FIDH rely more on having the consultative status to express the views and concerns of its member leagues, it is also more vulnerable to *losing* this status. In particular, it depends on the compliance of every single member NGO with the requirements of consultative status. Since federative NGOs can exercise less authority over their affiliates than centralist NGOs over their sections, the NGO is only as strong as the weakest part in the chain; if one member NGO violates or breaks a rule, the whole NGO can lose consultative status. Thus, when status is under dispute (for instance when a government seeks to go against 'its' national member NGO), federative NGOs are particularly threatened.

It is also more challenging for federative NGOs like the FIDH to rely on their public reputation when their consultative status is questioned because federative NGOs are often not as well known as centralist NGOs. Because the bulk of their work is performed on the domestic level within the national branches, their reputation often does not go beyond national borders and rarely reaches an international public. The UN's NGO Committee itself is not always informed about the NGOs in question. The FIDH, for example, is a well-known and highly respected NGO in the community of human rights actors surrounding the High Commissioner in Geneva, but the Committee deciding on status questions, however is based out of New York and knows little about the FIDH's valued work in Geneva (Interview FIDH-4).

The FIDH has often come close to being suspended from consultative status in its history of relations with the UN when single affiliated members faced problems with their respective governments (Interview FIDH-4). For four years in a row at the turn of the century, the FIDH feared its status would be withdrawn, as single states confronted the NGO with complains about its appearance at the UN level. Often, the content of the NGO's UN contributions is not the issue of complaint, but rather countries claim it has violated procedural rules. In 1999, for example, the FIDH was accused of not having explained its policy and modalities on accreditation of representatives to the Commission on Human Rights (UN Doc. E/1999/109 §55).

In 2000, the NGO Committee discussed the status of the FIDH because the Algerian government accused a member of the NGO of having insulted and physically attacked a representative of the Algerian delegation. 'The Algerian ambassador was talking to an Algerian accredited by FIDH when two other Algerians came up and hostilely accosted the diplomat. The ambassador accused the FIDH representative of complicity in the incident' (Paul 1999). The issue was solved in an informal manner in January 2001 before an actual decision on the status of the FIDH could take place. The NGO lobbied other governments which convinced the Algerian ambassador to take back his accusations (Interview FIDH-3).

In 2001, the government of Bahrain accused the FIDH of having accredited people without properly checking their identity. During the session of the NGO Committee, a representative of Bahrain complained about an FIDH representative who had circulated materials 'detrimental to the Government of Bahrain'. He also accused this person of having insulted the government of Bahrain verbally. In the end, the issue was solved by appealing to the FIDH not to repeat such incidents 'for the sake of all non-governmental organizations working with the United Nations' (UN Doc. E/2001/8 §94–8). However, the governmental representative pointed out that these incidents signified a pattern of violations for which NGOs can be suspended from consultative status (UN Doc. E/2001/8 §94–8).

In recent years, such attacks against the FIDH have taken on a new dimension and challenged the organization's integrity. During the sessions of the Commission on Human Rights in 2002, the NGO was not only criticized for neglecting to comply with formal procedures, but also directly attacked by individual governments for its very existence. Whenever the FIDH took the floor on Algeria, for example, the Algerian government did not respond to the information submitted by the NGO, but instead attacked it as a whole, saying, for example that it should not sit in this forum because it spread false information, that it has a colonial structure and that its selection of countries and themes are inappropriate at the UN level (Interview FIDH-2). Such repeated attacks are worrisome for the FIDH as they always contain the same types of accusations, and thereby leave a negative impression on governmental representatives. The NGO cannot even defend itself, as it has no right to reply to such interventions (Interview FIDH-2).

In the past, there have also been several attempts to withdraw the status of the NGO. One incident, for example, took place in 1982, when a member of the Soviet delegation demanded that a representative of the FIDH represent the organization at the UN after it had reported on human rights violations in Russia (Bernheim 1983: 166–7). In his comments, the Soviet representative denied all violations in his country and stated that nothing in the report was true. He concluded that the information given by the FIDH on other countries was accordingly not true either since the NGO had been proven wrong in one case, and therefore its status should be withdrawn. Other countries, such as France, Costa Rica, the USA, and Sweden took the floor and defended the FIDH so that it was able to keep its status (Bernheim 1983: 167–8).[59]

In brief, consultative status is significant for the FIDH's activities with the UN. As a federative NGO, formal status with the UN is a tool of access that opens the doors for national affiliates to the intergovernmental sphere. Since the federation functions as the mouthpiece for its member NGOs, consultative status allows them to express their views and concerns above the domestic level in which they usually operate. Moreover, it is a 'quality label' by which the NGO gains recognition. Particularly in recent years, consultative status has become more significant and functions as a particular means of reputation. As an advocacy NGO, the FIDH is highly dependent on being officially recognized by the UN. It also had to cope with repeated threats to withdraw its status.

CARE International: consultative status as lowering bureaucratic hurdles

CARE belongs to the group of NGOs that received consultative status early on, as it has maintained the status since 1949. Despite being accredited for such a long time, the NGO rarely used its status. Even after being upgraded in the early 1990s, the status holds little significance in terms of the NGO's activities with the UN.

CARE's type of consultative status

Even though CARE International has undergone some change regarding its formal status at the UN, it explains only little of its extended spectrum of interaction. The NGO was one of the first to be accredited when consultative status was introduced in the 1940s. However, for most of the time the status pertained only to the US-American section of CARE International. Only recently did CARE International obtain recognized UN status as an international body. In the early 1990s, CARE Canada and CARE UK applied for consultative status, and the UN insisted that all CAREs apply as one international NGO (Interview CARE-2). The president of the ECOSOC at the time requested that CARE International ask for consultative status as one international NGO in order to avoid the repeated independent applications of each individual CARE section (Interview CARE-2).

As part of the new arrangement between CARE International and the UN, the NGO was 'upgraded' in its status with ECOSOC (Interview CARE-2). Until 1991, CARE USA only held 'specialized' consultative status, the second highest official UN affiliation. CARE International was upgraded to 'general' consultative status, officially extending its options for participation at the UN. Unlike CARE USA, CARE International is now allowed to make statements and propose agenda items before ECOSOC and its sub-commissions. However, CARE International has not used this privilege much yet; it rarely put items on the agenda of ECOSOC in the last decade.

Moreover, the NGO never feared losing consultative status at the UN. Neither CARE USA nor later CARE International were ever threatened with removal of status. Since the NGO and the UN are equally dependent on each other for the proliferation of services, CARE International is 'self-confident' enough not to fear a loss of its status. The upgrade issue was the only time CARE's status was ever significantly discussed (Interview CARE-2).

Significance of consultative status and means of reputation

For CARE International, the consultative status does not constitute a source of reputation, nor does it function as a means of recognition. As one NGO representative expressed it, it is 'a fact of life' (Interview CARE-6). The relationship between CARE International and the UN is one of 'mutual dependent partnership' of which the formal arrangement is unimportant for the NGO because the two organizations would cooperate, even without official status (Interview CARE-1). The UN needs organizations like CARE International as an implementing operator; NGOs like CARE International need the UN as security guarantor and for the provision of logistical facilities.

Thus, official recognition through consultative status is only a way for CARE International to reduce bureaucracy. It enables the NGO to access the UN without the burdens of entrance control, for example (Interview CARE-1). Since CARE International predominantly works with the UN and UN agencies on the ground, it 'just seemed to be natural' to discuss issues with the community of states also, but not because of the NGO's consultative status (Interview CARE-2). In addition, CARE International's representatives in Geneva are well known at the UN, since they were in contact with the UN in the field for several decades. They are perceived as credible persons and accepted as colleagues: getting in contact with UN representatives is easy for this reason, rather than because of CARE's consultative status (Interview CARE-4). As one former representative of

CARE International in Geneva expressed it, 'having consultative status within the ECOSOC is formally important in the sense that you are an accepted player in the broader humanitarian effort. From a pragmatic and practical point of view I never saw much value in CARE having consultative status. ... I never feared losing that status' (Interview CARE-5).

Consultative status has very little impact on CARE International's activities with the UN. Being a centralist NGO, the consultative status has little significance, nor is it a source of good reputation for this NGO. It simply allows interaction with the UN without bureaucratic hurdles. As a service NGO, the status puts no negative pressure on the NGO; throughout its 50-year history of involvement with the UN, CARE International never feared losing its status at the UN. Although it maintains the highest status given, the NGO does not exhaust the opportunities it offers.

Oxfam International: little significance of consultative status

Of all the NGOs explored in this study, Oxfam maintains the greatest number of official status with the UN. Oxfam International now maintains consultative status as an international body of all the Oxfams and, in addition, three single Oxfams are accredited for consultative status individually. Despite these quantities, Oxfam International's activities with the UN are little explicable by its formal status.

Oxfam International's type of consultative status with the UN

Oxfam International is formally accredited at the UN in four ways: Of the Oxfam affiliates which maintain official relations with the UN, the oldest of the Oxfams, Oxfam GB, was the first to be accredited to the UN and has had consultative status since 1973.[60] It was followed by Oxfam USA which holds consultative status since 1993 and by Novib/Oxfam Netherlands, which was accredited to the UN in 1995. As an international NGO, Oxfam is formally accredited on the consultative status since 2002 only, and at the same time, the three single Oxfams continued to individually maintain consultative status, too. Whereas the single Oxfams are accredited with 'special' consultative status, Oxfam International now holds 'general' consultative status.

Compared to other NGOs in this study, the federation of all the Oxfams did not see any need for applying as an international body to the UN for a long time. In 2001, in fact, Oxfam International discussed whether it needed to apply for consultative status as one international NGO, but decided that the current arrangement of having consultative status through the various Oxfam affiliates separately was still sufficient and

Oxfam International had no intention of applying as one common international federation. Instead, it had been decided that Oxfam International would carry on working through the current mechanism, as it had worked well so far and no other status was needed (Interview Oxfam-4).

Significance of the consultative status to
Oxfam and means of reputation

Consultative status is not considered by the NGO as a particularly significant tool of recognition. As a representative of Oxfam Great Britain expressed it, consultative status is 'no focus in our mind' and the organization 'does not give much attention' to it (Interview Oxfam-1). Oxfam has contacts with high-ranking UN officials, even with the Secretary-General of the UN, because of its size and impact, and not through its consultative status. As a staff member of the federation of the Oxfams rhetorically questioned, 'would we have any less access to the UN without the status?' (Interview Oxfam-1).

Thus, Oxfam International does not perceive its status at the UN as an additional source of reputation and therefore does not include it, for example, on letterheads (Interview Oxfam-4). However, having the status frees up information and leads to more exchange of data. The organization receives information about sessions and it is more likely to be invited to them formally (Interview Oxfam-4). It covers the 'mechanical aspects' like getting passes and badges for entering the UN more easily. Moreover, legally, it allows the NGO to feed information into the UN system, not only informally but also in a formal manner (Interview Oxfam-3). Other then that, consultative status is not a significant means for access, because 'the UN wants to include you as a group of players anyway' (Interview Oxfam-4).

However, for Novib/Oxfam Netherlands did consultative status make a difference in its range of activities with the UN. Before Novib/Oxfam Netherlands received its own formal status with the UN, it was represented through ICVA, a network of humanitarian and development NGOs, which – as a network – had consultative status with the UN. Novib/Oxfam Netherlands could only make statements through them and sent in its statements to ICVA whenever the network was planning to make a contribution at the UN. However, as Novib/Oxfam Netherlands was not able to make statements in its own name, or to enter the corridors and talk to people, it decided to apply for its 'own' status. Through its status, Novib/Oxfam Netherlands now receives more information about ongoing activities at the UN than before (Interview Oxfam-6).

Oxfam International never experienced any threats to UN status. As a service organization, the NGO never had any problems with the consultative status, nor did the single accredited Oxfam affiliates ever have to cope with any threats to its status.

Having consultative status cannot account for Oxfam International's activities with the UN. Unlike the FIDH, Oxfam International does not see consultative status as a channel to represent the different single national affiliated members at the international level, nor does status present a means of reputation. Rather, single Oxfam affiliates kept maintaining separate formal relations with the UN for most of the time, and the international body only recently applied as a federation for a common status. As a service NGO, Oxfam International mainly relies on consultative status because it facilitates administrative matters but puts no negative pressure on the NGO.

Other NGOs

In addition to the main set of NGOs presented above, I briefly explore the set of backup NGOs and the importance of consultative status to them. The perception of consultative status in the second set of NGOs is similar to that of the main cases: the degree of significance of and dependency on official accreditation by the UN varies according to their composition and function.

Human Rights Watch

Human Rights Watch expanded its activities at the UN in the 1990s when it acquired consultative status. The NGO did not even try to obtain status earlier because its leader's personal conviction was that the UN and its subsidiary bodies 'were more talk than action' (in Welch 2001: 110; similarly Korey 1998: 351). As the UN became a more prominent actor in international affairs after the end of the Cold War, however, HRW sought to establish relations. With new leadership of HRW, the NGO changed its perception of the UN and sought to apply for formal recognition (Schmitz 2001: 11).

Human Rights Watch first applied for consultative status in 1991, but its application was rejected on the grounds that the NGO would spread false information. Although it was the second largest human rights organization in the world, a group of states denied HRW status because the NGO had criticized their human rights records. The 'gang of six', as the New York Times called Cuba, Iraq, Syria, Liberia, Algeria, and Sudan, succeeded in stopping HRW's application (Korey 1998: 352). After waiting two years to reapply, the NGO received the status in 1993, as new dynamics in the committee had changed admission procedures. The then new Russian delegation agreed to grant HRW to consultative status, but more importantly the consensus rule was dropped so that the NGO could receive consultative status despite some countries' votes against it (Interview HRW-3). As a human rights NGO HRW, too, is considered an organization with a limited focus and received 'special' consultative status.

As with AI and CARE International, the consultative status is not regarded as a source of reputation, but seen as a means of access (Interviews HRW-1, HRW-2). It enables the NGO 'to get through the doors' of the UN and lobby delegates (Interview HRW-3). Moreover, through having its status, HRW maintains the right to address the UN and monitor meetings (Interview HRW-3). The NGO can supply information in decision-making processes inaccessible to those without the status (Interview HRW-1). Most importantly, it enables the NGO to enter UN buildings and speak and meet with governmental delegates. Like AI, HWR makes sure to keep to procedural rules so as not to give states grounds on which to argue for status withdrawal (Interview HRW-3).

The International League for Human Rights

Similar to the FIDH, the ILHR values consultative status, as it presents the channel for national affiliated members to express their views on the international stage. Most importantly, UN status facilitates the international work of its affiliates (Interview ILHR-1). Special consultative status gives the NGO more access than other forms of status, such as accreditation with the Department of Public Information. It also signifies a source of credibility (Interview ILHR-2). The ILHR also has consultative status for practical reasons like easy access and the opportunity to participate at major events. For example, the consultative status allows the NGO to submit written documents, and consult with rapporteurs or independent experts on treaty bodies (Interview ILHR-2).

The ILHR's consultative status has been threatened repeatedly. During the 1968 review, a Soviet delegate characterized the ILHR as 'consisting of a constellation of traitors expelled from their own countries who had formed a league to slander their former homelands' (in Chiang 1981: 178). Supported by Bulgaria and by representatives of Islamic countries, the USSR demanded to vote on the suspension of consultative status of the NGO's status, but was denied by a vote of three to 13 with seven abstentions (Chiang 1981: 178). During the 1970s, the possible loss of the consultative status had been a threat to the ILHR in several occasions, too. In May 1977, for example, the Soviet representative again publicly attacked the ILHR for having engaged in activities that 'poisoned detente and slandered the Socialist countries ... abuses of privileges would lead to cancellation of this consultative status' (in Korey 1998: 147). An ILHR representative notes that even today,

> a long list of states are always threatening, in speeches and privately, to get our status pulled. ... They have challenged our speakers' and affiliates' credentials, they have quizzed us intensively during the quadrennial review. But we have survived these sorts of attacks for 60 years and I think we'll go on surviving. However, the climate is definitely more hostile than any time since the cold war, when the Soviets kept out a lot of the human rights groups. (Interview ILHR-2)

Recently, Cuba tried to retract the status of the ILHR because it wanted to stop the activities of the NGO's Cuban affiliate (Interview ILHR-2).

Like the FIDH, the ILHR perceives the opening of the consultative status for national NGOs as a threat to its work because the whole system of NGO accreditation has imploded. As the representative of the ILHR at the UN emphasized, 'the atmosphere towards human rights NGOs in particular has grown increasingly restrictive and increasingly hostile, especially from the "violator countries" who are violating human rights massively. With thousands of NGOs now accredited to the UN, there has come to be a backlash' (Interview ILHR-2). Moreover, the new dynamics concerning human rights NGOs make the ILHR's work at the UN more difficult. Although the NGO is recognized as a special consultant, the status does not protect it from being suspended. 'In this climate, it is helpful to have "special consultative status" for reasons of access and cooperation. However, it is always in danger of being pulled due to the hostile actions of violator states' (Interview ILHR-2).

International Save the Children Alliance

Like CARE International, the ISCA has undergone some change in its consultative status at the UN. The ISCA was accredited as an internationally operating NGO in 1993 and since then maintains 'general' consultative status at the UN. However, like CARE, single sections of the NGO were involved with the UN independently before that and maintained consultative status separately. For example, the Swedish section of the ISCA (Rädda Barnen) has had consultative status independently since 1981.

The significance of the consultative status for the ISCA is the provision of access to the UN (Interviews ISCA-1, ISCA-2). Through the status, it receives badges and access passes which make it easier to enter UN buildings. Moreover, it facilitates the exchange of information. However, apart from such practical relevance for the NGO, status 'is a paper thing' as a staff member from the international secretariat mentioned (Interview ISCA-3). Accordingly, the consultative status is not perceived as a source of reputation. As service organizations are rarely turned down consultative status, the ISCA does not see any additional value of recognition in being officially accredited at the UN level (Interview ISCA-1).

Action Aid Alliance

The AAA's consultative status with the UN is typical of a loose federation. Similar to Oxfam International, single members maintain consultative status rather than the Alliance as a whole. In fact, only the largest member NGO, Action Aid UK, is accredited to the UN and maintains 'special' consultative status since 1991. Predominantly because status makes the flow of information easier, the significance of status lies in the fact that the organization receives more information about ongoing events and projects of the UN (Interview AAA-2). However, status is not perceived as an additional source of reputation, and AA UK does not, for example, mention on its letterhead. In fact, many staff members in the NGO are not aware of the UN status (Interview AAA-2).

Therefore, differences between the three statuses at the UN are not of relevance for the NGO and AAA has not considered applying for any higher status or seeking accreditation as an internationally operating NGO. During the years Action Aid has had UN status, there have been no threats to revoke it (Interview AAA-2). Some local partners, however, are aware of Action Aid's status and see it as a means to have more contact with the UN and a channel to get access. As the representative of Action Aid noted, 'they see us as a way to get involved' with the UN (Interview AAA-2).

Summary

NGOs today increasingly seek consultative status with the UN. They apply for status because it facilitates activities with the UN, presents a tool to gain access to information and people, and serves as a source of reputation. However, the analysis of examples of NGOs in consultative status with the UN reveals a mixed picture. For some, status increases possibilities for working with and through the UN, but at the same time puts them under pressure, as they may fear losing it. For others, consultative status only makes bureaucratic necessities easier. In short, depending on the function and on the composition of NGOs, some rely more on the status than others which do not see any particular value in it.

The status NGOs receive depends on their function. Advocacy NGOs are usually granted 'specialized' consultative status. Despite their large size and range of activity, the status of human rights NGOs, for example, is restricted. Although many human rights NGOs, such as AI, HRW or the FIDH and the ILHR, have members from many countries and operate globally, they receive 'specialized' status because their focus is considered limited on human rights only. In the service sector, instead, NGOs are easily 'upgraded' and receive the highest status, as evidenced by the cases of CARE International or the ISCA.

Rights and duties of the three different statuses do not make much difference in practice. Service NGOs could use their 'general' consultative status to, for instance, propose items to the agenda of the UN, but they do not make use of these options. Supporting this argument is the fact that Oxfam International could have possibly received a higher status without much difficulty being an international federation in the service sector, but did not intend to apply for a long time as no additional benefits from 'general' status were expected (see Table 5.3).

Table 5.3   NGOs and their consultative status

	Year	Status
AI	1964	SCS
HRW	1993	SCS
FIDH	1952	SCS
ILHR	1946	SCS
CARE International	1991	GCS
(CARE USA)	(1949)	(SCS)
ISCA	1993	GCS
(Rädda Barnen, Save the Children Sweden)	(1981)	(SCS)
Oxfam International	2002	GCS
(Oxfam USA)	(1993)	(SCS)
(Oxfam UK and Ireland – now Oxfam GB)	(1973)	(SCS)
(Novib/Oxfam Netherlands)	(1995)	(SCS)
Action Aid Alliance	–	–
(Action Aid UK)	(1991)	(SCS)

Notes: GCS – General Consultative Status; SCS – Special Consultative Status.
Source: UN Doc. E/2000/INF/4 and own research.

The danger of losing the status depends on the function of the respective NGO. While advocacy NGOs rely on consultative status because they need direct access to decision-makers, service NGOs use consultative status only for its administrative function as it facilitates access to UN buildings and offices. As explored in the empirical sections, advocacy NGOs consider the consultative status an 'entrance key' to the UN. Formal recognition enables them to do advocacy work on the international level. For them therefore, consultative status also contains a 'negative fear' of a possible loss. Advocacy NGOs must be careful not to provoke governments, giving them reason to withdraw status. Advocacy NGOs are specifically watched by certain states more than NGOs in other fields because some states try to find reasons to repeal status.

A threat to official status can be balanced with good reputation outside the UN context, so that single states have no interest in withdrawing status. The example of the centralist NGO AI showed that high public standing makes it difficult for human rights violating states to attempt to suspend it, as this would only attract more interest. The media attention attached to the first denial of status to HRW has shown how it can be counter-productive for states to seek the exclusion of well-known organizations. Thus, centralist advocacy NGOs, like AI and HRW, generally do not have to fear losing their consultative status. For service NGOs, instead, the consultative status is only a formality with limited practical advantages. The examples of humanitarian NGOs show that the consultative status does not play a significant role for service NGOs because they work with the UN regardless of any official recognition and are thus not worried about losing their formal status.

Federative advocacy NGOs are most interested in maintaining recognition at the UN. For them, the consultative status is considered highly important as it enables affiliated members access to the UN. The examples of the FIDH and the ILHR show how NGOs depend on consultative status as a channel for their national member NGOs. Despite the opening of the consultative status for national NGOs in 1996, accreditation at the UN as an international federation has not lost its importance. In fact, because of the opening, the national members of federative advocacy NGOs rather maintain a certain 'quality label' as part of a well-established and recognized international NGO. They are thus distinguished from newly founded national NGOs whose objectives and basis are often unclear.

In the service sector, by contrast, the federative element plays less of a role. Single member NGOs of a federation in the field of humanitarian relief can easily be granted consultative status individually. Formal

Table 5.4 Perceived value of consultative status today

	Practical relevance as tool for access	Value of consultative status as means of reputation	Threats to losing the consultative status
AI	High	Low	Low
HRW	High	Low	Low
FIDH	Very High	High	Very High
ILHR	Very High	High	Very High
CARE	Medium	Low	Low
ISCA	Medium	Low	Low
Oxfam GB (Novib/Oxfam	Medium	Low	Low
Netherlands)	(Medium)	(Medium)	(Low)
AAA	Medium	Low	Low

accreditation to consultative status is not necessary for activities between service NGOs and the UN in the field. Thus, the service function is more vital than the federative composition among single national member NGOs (see Table 5.4).

The perception of rules and regulations for NGO accreditation to the UN has generally decreased in significance over the 1990s. Although there are differences between single types of NGOs, overall consultative status plays a minor role in NGO–UN relations.

6
NGOs in the UN System and Beyond – Final Remarks

Non-governmental organizations have consolidated their role in international relations. Although their involvement in global affairs can be traced back for centuries, their activities have taken a new dimension over the course of the last decade. Intergovernmental organizations, such as the UN, increasingly provided for the participation of NGOs within their systems. Today, a greater number of NGOs have begun working with the UN, and NGOs that had already done so in the past have progressively intensified their UN relations.

My aim in this book was to explore the responses of NGOs to the increased possibility of interacting with the UN. By examining their relations with an intergovernmental organization from this angle, I intended to develop further the analysis of NGOs and identify their position in international affairs. The empirical data presented in this study has shown that as NGOs gained more and diverse possibilities for interaction, they adjusted their patterns of activity vis-à-vis the UN.

This concluding chapter summarizes the findings and presents them in three steps. First, I briefly review the conceptual frame I developed for studying NGO–UN relations. Second, I evaluate the propositions of the theoretical approach against the empirical data. And third, I assess the findings in light of their contribution to the study of NGOs and note areas of possible further research as resulting from my findings.

Conceptualization and theoretical frame

Current theoretical approaches provided the background for understanding NGOs and their relations with intergovernmental organizations. Transnational and transsocietal approaches explain the reasons and motives for NGOs to interact with IGOs. In transnational accounts, intergovernmental organizations serve as the mediator of NGO activity.

As shown in the 'boomerang pattern' or the 'spiral model', NGOs form alliances with IGOs in order to advance their aims and goals. Thus, from working with IGOs, nongovernmental organizations gain additional channels for activity on the international level. Transsocietal approaches emphasize that relations with IGOs are attractive to NGOs because an intergovernmental framework supports the emergence of a global civil society. By providing transnational opportunity structures, IGOs facilitate or constrain the amount and impact of NGO activity.

Such approaches explain why NGOs work with IGOs, but this study required a guiding theoretical account capturing the responses of NGOs given the chance to work more closely with IGOs. In order to examine NGO–IGO interactions from this perspective, I applied social movement theories to NGOs. These have been used to explore diverse facets of the relationship between societal actors and official institutions on the domestic level, particularly resource mobilization theory and the neo-institutionalist perspective of channelling mechanisms provided a framework for identifying facets worthy of deeper study. Both perspectives argue that societal actors increasingly institutionalize their relations with official institutions and subsequently adjust their pattern of activity, but the approaches give different reasons for this. On the one hand, changes in the spectrum of interaction vis-à-vis the UN are due to internal factors, like professionalization and bureaucratization. On the other hand, differences in the pattern of activity are due to external demands resulting from the perception of official rules and regulations for the relationship between both actors.

In order to measure the degree to which NGOs adjusted their patterns of activity, I categorized NGO activities related to the UN as *policy initiating activities* (agenda-setting, information provision, lobbying), *policy developing processes* (policy formulation, policy advice) or *policy implementing practices* (supplementing work, subcontracting). This classification allows comparison, and I was able to identify differences in the types of activities within the same NGO over time and in contrast to other NGOs. Following on from that, I adapted the two notions of institutionalization for the study of NGOs in the UN system. From the 'internal' perspective, I explored institutionalization through NGO representation and representatives at the UN level. From the 'external' perspective, I referred to institutionalization as the perception of the rules and regulations for NGO accreditation, and examined these as represented by ECOSOC status with the UN.

I used the categorization of NGOs to identify their significant characteristics. The category of 'transboundary composition' distinguishes international NGOs by the arrangement of their respective national units. Centralist NGOs have strong headquarters which guide the whole organization's policy, including that of its national sections, whereas federative NGOs are loosely connected by an international body which coordinates the affiliates' common projects and constitutes their representation at the international level. The category of 'NGO function' distinguishes two broad types of organizations which differ in their objectives. Advocacy NGOs typically seek to change the ideological context whereas service NGOs are primarily interested in providing their target groups with goods.

I chose four case studies based on this characterization – one for each combination of differing composition and function. I argued that these differences explain the variation in their degree to which groups institutionalize their relations to the UN. Amnesty International (centralist composition, advocacy function), Fédération Internationale des Droits de l'Homme (federative composition, advocacy function), CARE International (centralist composition, service function) and Oxfam International (federative composition, service function) provided the primary set of cases for deeper analysis as they fit well the two categories of 'NGO composition' and 'NGO functions'. In addition, I addressed four other NGOs briefly to see whether they generally confirm the findings of the first set.

Derived from the conceptualization of NGOs and the theoretical accounts, I developed propositions on how the characteristics of NGOs influence the institutionalization of their UN relations, which in turn account for the degree to which they adjust their patterns of activity toward the IGO. This work has depicted and described the change in interaction between the selected NGOs and the UN since the mid-1990s. It drew on dominant features of NGO–UN relations according to the academic literature, but the main analysis relied on expert interviews with staff members and representatives of NGOs, which were conducted over two years. It also drew on UN documents on NGOs and the NGO's own material.

Adjustments in NGO patterns of activity with the UN

Amnesty International has interacted with the UN for a long time. Early on, the NGO provided information to selected UN bodies in charge of human rights, seeking to shape the agenda of the IGO. In recent years, it shifted away from some of these activities and put more efforts into maintaining contacts with the operational bodies and agencies of the UN. As a result, it interacts with the UN system in a variety of ways today, including operational bodies in the field. In brief, AI broadened its spectrum of interaction with the UN in response to changed opportunities: until the early 1990s, it mainly interacted with the UN on policy initiating and developing activities, whereas since the mid-1990s, it has shifted some of its attention to policy implementing practices.

Until recently, CARE International's activities with the UN have been in the area of policy implementation. The NGO has long maintained connections to the operating UN bodies and had relations with the UN in a variety of ways in its field of activity. In recent years, however, CARE International expanded its spectrum of interaction by adding policy developing and policy initiating activities to its catalogue of activities. In addition to its contract work and implementing projects with operational bodies of the UN, CARE International has participated in forums such as the IASC and SCHR since the mid-1990s, playing a leading role.

In contrast to AI and CARE International the FIDH did not expand its activities beyond already established links. Though it intensified such activities in recent years, for instance by supplying more information to the Commission on Human Rights since the mid-1990s, it has not moved beyond this type of activity. Thus, it rather deepened its activities within its old frame by significantly increasing its policy initiating activities over the course of the last decade, such that today the NGO provides much more information to the UN.

Oxfam International only slightly expanded its activities with UN institutions. The operational Oxfams have led activities with a variety of UN bodies on a field level for a long time and continued to keep these throughout the 1990s. Other than on the operational level, however, the Oxfams only irregularly interact with the UN and occasionally function as advisor. Moreover, UN activities are less coordinated between different affiliates of the international body than in other NGOs. Thus, after the opening of the UN system, the NGO moved only slightly beyond its usual implementational connection to the UN.

In short, the NGOs examined in this study adjusted their patterns of activity to the UN differently over the course of the last decade. While some added new types of activities or set different priorities, others expanded them only to a limited degree. These varying adjustments in the pattern of activity between societal actors and official institutions needed more explanation than what was accounted for by the mere opening of the UN system to NGO contributions.

NGO representation and representatives

The degree to which NGOs have institutionalized their relations to the UN internally over time accounts to a large extent for the scope of

NGO adjustments in their patterns of activity vis-à-vis the IGO. In recent years, NGOs have both invested in and internally structured their UN representation. How and to what extent NGOs have institutionalized their relations with the UN depends on their type. Particularly, the composition of NGOs has an impact on the resources devoted to representation. In line with the theoretical model, centralist NGOs were able to dedicate more resources to their UN relations than federative NGOs. The centralist NGOs examined in this study invested more in their representation at the UN and developed organizational structures for it. They maintain permanent offices and professional representatives in major UN locations important for their issues of concern. They have also developed a system of division of labour among headquarters and the different UN offices.

The cases of AI and CARE International (as well as the ISCA and HRW) have shown how centralist NGOs dedicate resources to their UN representation. Amnesty International established elaborate organizational structures for its representation in all major UN locations and at headquarters level. Recently, it also increased the number of staff working on UN relations. Similarly, CARE International had the means to invest in more UN representation. The NGO established full-time posts in UN locations recently, and divided tasks and duties between the national sections and the international headquarters. Federative NGOs have comparatively few resources to dedicate to UN relations, as the cases of the FIDH and Oxfam International (or ILHR and AAA) demonstrate. The FIDH maintains representation only in one major UN location. Oxfam International, too, has long been represented on a voluntary basis only. Moreover, also within its international body, UN-related work is less structured, and not all representation goes through one representative.

NGO functions also have an impact on how the organizations recruit personnel for UN representation. As assumed in the theoretical model, the advocacy NGOs explored in this study recruit representatives on the basis of professional criteria and seek highly qualified people, whereas the examined service NGOs need representatives with local knowledge and experience within the organization. Advocacy NGOs seek highly skilled professionals trained in their issue area, and prior involvement with or long-term commitment to the NGO is of less importance. Amnesty International, for example, employs mainly human rights lawyers to conduct its UN relation, most of whom have experience with the UN, either academically or through working experience. The FIDH also recruits highly trained representatives, usually with a background in human rights law.

Service NGOs, on the other hand, recruit representatives from within their own organization. For the post of UN representative, service NGOs seek people who have been working for the NGO for a long time and are therefore familiar with the organization. Educational background and academic career do not play a particularly significant role, as shown by CARE International, ISCA, AAA and Oxfam International.

Rules and regulations for NGO accreditation at the UN level

External arrangements for NGO consultation at the UN level have had limited impact on NGO activities with the UN. The highest form of formal UN recognition for NGOs (consultative status) provides various rights, but rules and regulations have less influence than the theoretical model suggested. Although the UN's consultative status is important as a means of access, it is often perceived as a mere formality. For example, the composition of those NGOs examined in this study has an effect on their perception of provisions for accreditation for the consultative status, although only to some extent. Federative NGOs are more eager to maintain formal recognition from the UN than centralist NGOs, because they depend highly on the status. Consultative status functions as the mouthpiece for federative NGOs' affiliated members and serves as a means to express their views and concerns on a level above the domestic one on which they usually operate. Particularly since the revision of the consultative status in 1996, it is also a source of positive reputation as it awards NGOs the standing of internationally recognized actors.

As the examples of the FIDH and the ILHR illustrate, however, this is only true for federative advocacy NGOs. Federative *service* NGOs, in contrast, interact with the UN individually and are not dependent on their international body, as the analysis of Oxfam International and AAA has revealed. For centralist NGOs, such status is not a significant source of prestige or reputation: Amnesty International, HRW, CARE International and the ISCA do not see any particular value in being recognized by the UN through consultative status.

Functions NGOs take on also have some influence on the way the selected NGOs regard consultative status, however this is different from the assumed theoretical model. Although service NGOs receive consultative status more easily than advocacy NGOs, they do not exhaust its potential in terms of UN interaction. Advocacy NGOs rely more on their status than service NGOs, and are in danger of losing it. However, this does not hinder them from pursuing activities within the UN system. For service NGOs, the consultative status is simply a formality rather than a tool for UN interaction. It is not a threat to them either, as the UN would work with them regardless of their status. Moreover, as the examples of CARE International, the ISCA, Oxfam International and the AAA have shown, service NGOs do not use all possibilities for UN interaction that consultative status offers. They see the formal status only as a means to interact with the UN without bureaucratic hurdles.

For advocacy NGOs, instead, the formal recognition by the UN is an entrance key. It enables them to access UN buildings and to meet with officials and UN representatives. Advocacy NGOs, particularly federative ones, are frequently threatened with a withdrawal of their status. Despite attempts to remove their status, however, these NGOs continue to conduct their activities at the UN level. The examples of the FIDH and the ILHR have illustrated this perception of the consultative status as it pertains to them.

In sum, drawing from the empirical evidence collected for this study, the initial assumptions which guided this work can be refined and the significance of the various modes of influence can be determined more precisely. Figure 6.1 shows the causal paths and the relations between NGO characteristics, institutionalization of relations to the UN, and adjustments in NGO patterns of activity. Significant changes in the patterns of activity between NGOs and the UN are due to the form of NGO representation to the UN. A centralist composition in particular enables NGOs to institutionalize internally their UN relations. As a result, organizations with those characteristics have adjusted their patterns of activity with the UN most thoroughly. Rules and regulations for accreditation to

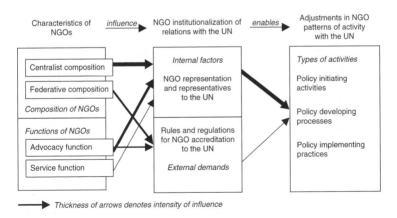

Figure 6.1   NGO institutionalization in the UN system – evaluated model

the UN, instead, affect the changes in NGO–UN interaction much less. Federative and advocacy characteristics shape the perception of rules and regulations to the UN to some degree, mainly in combination. Thus, except for federative advocacy NGOs, external institutionalization of relations with the UN affects the way NGOs adjust their pattern of activities less than the theoretical model suggested.

Contribution of this study and future prospects

This work on NGOs and their relationship with the UN contributes to the study of societal actors in global affairs in a variety of ways. Most significantly, this study presents genuine information about NGOs and their relationship with the UN that has not been analysed academically. Bringing together information from interviews with NGO representatives facilitated a comparison of several organizations and their relationship with the UN, both over time and in contrast to each other. Therefore this study can be regarded as a pilot project, providing future studies with data and material which has not been available previously.

The findings of this study show the path that societal actors take in becoming part of international life. NGOs have not only been recognized as participants in global affairs, but have been integrated into the UN framework. In response, NGOs have adapted to these increased opportunities by altering their patterns of activity over the course of the last decade. The UN is a model case for many IGOs in this respect; its relationship with NGOs has always attracted attention and it is one of the most sophisticated. Its scheme for integrating NGOs into its system has also become an example to many other IGOs which are currently interacting more intensely with NGOs.

This study suggests that professionalization plays a greater role for NGOs acting at the international level. It shows that professional UN representation impacts the spectrum of interaction of NGOs within the UN context. Those NGOs employing permanent professional staff with experience and training in their UN-related tasks are deeply and continuously involved in the political processes at the UN level. This implies that NGOs with less means and possibilities of having staff representing them at the UN have fewer abilities to work with the IGO. The majority of NGOs has very limited means at its disposal, so only the resourceful ones have a say in global affairs. As a consequence, poorer NGOs are left without much influence.[61] Thus, increased opportunities for activities with the UN and the correlating greater participation of NGOs does not necessarily lead to a more balanced representation of civil society in international affairs, as normative approaches often imply.

NGOs need the recognition of consultative status with the UN to enter into policy initiating and developing processes. While service providing NGOs may be able to develop relations with single operational UN bodies without formal status, relations beyond the project level require the 'entrance key' of formal recognition. On the whole, however, consultative status influences the relationship with the UN less than has frequently been assumed. NGOs must keep to procedural rules so as not to provide antagonistic states or officials with reasons to revoke their status. This is particularly true for advocacy NGOs.

This study has shown that theoretical approaches initially developed within the national frame are valid on the international level. Following previous studies which referred to social movement theory for analysis of societal actors operating on an international scale, this study applies such theoretical approaches to NGOs and their participation in global affairs. Thus, it may be valuable to use other approaches to societal activism on the international level as well, such as for example corporatist studies in their diverse variations. Although the corporatist approach has been mentioned as a possible model for analysis of societal activism in international affairs (Wahl 1997), only in recent years has it found some application to NGOs, with the UN and the EU as a point of reference (Hix 1999; Martens 2001b; Ottaway 2001).[62] Other approaches that may prove useful include those that take into account the increasing intertwining of business, societal actors, and official actors. Approaches to public–private partnerships (Osborne 2000; Vaillancourt 2000; Börzel and Risse 2005) are a step in this direction. Considering the significance of NGO characteristics, organizational theory as applied to international organizations (Gordenker and Saunders 1978; Ness and Brechin 1988; Scott 1994, 1995) could also be further developed and applied to NGOs.

What are some resulting future subjects of research? The case studies in this work are all representatives of their respective conceptual category. In addition, they are all well-known internationally operating players. Thus, they present model cases for other NGOs to whom they offer an example. Their relationship with the UN was chosen for analysis because it is the most developed between NGOs and IGOs. There are many possibilities for future research in this field building upon the analysis in this study:

First, as this study has clearly exposed, there is not enough knowledge about individual organizations. Although it is commonly accepted that the term NGOs encompasses a heterogeneous group of actors, many studies do not acknowledge their differences or they generalize having only a particular set of organizations in mind. How do the characteristics of NGOs affect and shape their scope of activity and their capability to react to a changing environment? This study has brought forward some first findings, and more comparative case studies guided by a theoretical approach could provide deeper insight about the factors which explain NGO involvement in international relations.

Second, as the UN's relationship to NGOs has been analysed more than that of other IGOs, future research could contrast NGOs' relations to the UN with other IGOs' schemes to incorporate societal actors. How are NGOs integrated into the frameworks of other intergovernmental organizations? What kinds of NGOs are interacting with what types of IGOs? Does their relationship show the same tendencies as the NGO–UN case? Comparative studies of various NGO–IGO relations (EU, OECD, NATO, ASEAN and others) would deliver more significant and broader knowledge about societal actors and their activities in global affairs.[63]

Third, with NGOs directly shaping the design of political processes, operationalization and implementation, questions of legitimacy should be given more attention. Although these issues have been part of the discussion (Najam 1996; Beisheim 1997; Schmidt and Take 1997), they are worth exploring further since NGO interaction with IGOs has reached a new dimension of intensity. To whom are NGOs accountable? Whom do they represent? And how is their representation internally organized? Future studies should draw attention to the legitimate role and the legitimizing function of NGOs as well.

The results of this study are embedded in the broader context of research on societal actors and international relations in general. This study has shown that NGOs and their relationships with IGOs change over time as the parameters evolve. However, it can only be a first step in the wider exploration of societal actors and their position in global affairs. The findings of this study will likely spur more in-depth qualitative and large-scale quantitative research in this area.

Notes

1   NGOs, International Relations and the UN System – Introductory Observations

1   Accordingly, the suggestions in this study are based on the assumption that relations between societal actors and official institutions at the national level are comparable to the relations between NGOs and intergovernmental organizations at the international level. Various scholars have drawn these parallels. For example, Rucht (1999: 219) has pointed out that the incorporation of transnationally operating organizations into UN structures of global governance is similar to the institutionalization of social movements at the national level and could lead to the same effects. He argues that formalization affects the structure of transnational social movement organizations and tends to make their demands more moderate. McCarthy (1997: 253), too, notes that 'similar homogenizing forces emanate from processes of formal organizational access at the national level, not unlike that of receiving formal UN status at the transnational level'.

2   NGO Institutionalization into the UN System – Theoretical Framework

2   Similarly to Tilly's (1984) argument about the shift of social activity from the local to the national level, in international studies the emergence and increasing importance of intergovernmental institutions has been seen as the shift of political processes from the national to the international level. Accordingly, the focal point for societal actors has also been shifted to the international level. Thus, NGOs extend their activity to the global world in which IGOs like the EU or the UN play a vital role as addressees of social activism (Marks and McAdam 1996: 251).
3   For an overview of the different applications of the concept of political opportunity structures in international studies, see Martens (2001a).
4   When applying approaches about social movements on NGOs, it is important to note the evolution of such accounts. Whereas the notion of 'NGOs' developed in order to define actors different from states, social movements as a concept developed to distinguish a particular type of societal actors from others, namely interest groups and political parties. However, in international studies, approaches to social movements have been taken into account because 'such work on organisations does provide important insights for scholars of organisations that transcend national borders' (Smith *et al.* 1994: 123). This is so because NGOs have been interpreted as part of the 'family of social movements' (Keck and Sikkink 1998b: 218). In fact, as Kaldor (1999: 202) argues, the connotation of the term 'social movements' has changed

over the last two decades. Whereas 'social movements' in the 1980s referred to agents of civil society – mainly to societal actors in Eastern Europe – in the 1990s, they became associated with 'non-governmental organizations'.

5 Social movement theory has coined various terms for this change in patterns of activity, such as 'consequences' (Brand 1999: 36; Kjellberg 1975: 2), 'effects' (Jiménez 1999: 150), 'dilemmas' (Rootes 1999: 2), 'transition' (Carmin 1999: 102), or 'transformation' (Zald and Ash 1987).

6 In social movement theory, the notion of 'institutionalization of societal actors' has been examined in diverse contexts, in which it has been treated as dependent variable, but also as independent variable. For an overview on the different research designs involving the applications of institutionalization, see Scott (1994).

7 Most accounts use these or similar terms in order to differentiate between divergent modes of interaction between social movement organizations and governmental institutions. Rootes (1999: 3), for example, distinguishes between 'conventional' and 'unconventional' forms of action; for Brand (1999: 51), interactions range from 'confrontational' to 'dialogical' strategies; Meyer and Tarrow (1998: 25) distinguish between 'disruptive' and 'conventional' activities and forms.

8 Young (1999), for example, differentiates between 'complementary', 'supplementary' or 'adversarial' roles between NGOs and the state. Similarly, Najam (2000) distinguished the relationship between NGOs and governments with the four C's of 'cooperation', 'cooptation', 'complementary' and 'confrontation'.

9 Gidron, Kramer and Salamon (1992: 11) also state, 'nonprofits have both service functions, social functions, and representational functions. ... It is therefore quite possible for third-sector organizations to have one set of relationships with government with respect to their service functions and another with respect to their representational or advocacy functions'.

10 The notions 'internal' and 'external' institutionalization follow the differentiation used by McCarthy, Britt and Wolfson (1991: 50). These scholars distinguish particularly well between both notions, asserting that challenges to societal activism have long been explained by focusing on 'internal factors' while 'external demands' have been ignored. See also, for example, Kjellberg (1975) who argues that institutionalization occurs in two dimensions. On the one hand, it is formed by the inner differentiation, particularly the establishment of internal structures; on the other hand, institutionalization is the process of incorporating smaller units (such as communities) into the society itself. Rootes (1999: 1) argues that institutionalization occurs in terms of professionalization of activists and regulation of access to policy making.

11 In accordance with Zald and Ash (1987: note 1), this study argues that, although Michels' iron law of oligarchy was originally employed for political parties of the left, it can be considered a general line of analysis in social movement research.

12 The workers' movement is often regarded as a prototypical example for the sequence of stages. Starting diffuse and scattered, workers groups slowly adopt an organizational form and finally end up as large institutions with bureaucratic structures (party, trade union, for example), which gain influence on the political scene but loose contact with the individual and give up their mobility for action (Raschke 1987: 377).

13 See also Kubik (1998) who analyses the institutionalization of rules for protest during the democratic consolidation of Central Europe. For him, external conditions include state-authorized procedures for recognizing societal actors and their activities.

14 In recent years, scholars have drawn more attention to this status and emphasized its significance for the NGO–UN relationship (Lagoni 1995; Hüfner 1996; Willetts 2000; Aston 2001).

15 In addition to ECOSOC consultative status, DPI and NGLS status, various UN agencies have their own procedures for NGO accreditation, which are usually modelled on ECOSOC status. For information about NGO relations with specific UN organizations, see UN Doc. A/53/170.

16 The composition or organizational structure across borders is a factor which has only sporadically been explored in studies on NGOs (Young 1991a; Thränhard 1992; Lindenberg and Bryant 2001). Social movement research, on the other hand, has long acknowledged the significance of movement structure (Freeman 1979: 182).

17 I use the term 'international' in the context of federative NGOs to express that domestic factors matter in the way NGOs are set up (inter-national, between-nations), whereas I employ 'transnational' with centralist NGOs to emphasize that in their composition, national factors are of minor significance (trans-national, across-nations).

18 To express the differences in the linkages between national units and the international organization, I use 'sections' when referring to national units of transnational-centralist NGOs to convey their close relation with the mother organization, whereas I employ 'affiliates' for national units of an international-federative NGO to express their loose linkages with the international secretariat.

19 Where national concerns play a great role, such as among cultural organizations, many NGOs conform to the international-federative type rather than following the transnational-centralist model (Thränhardt 1992: 226).

20 Because of their singular approach on the global level, Thränhardt (1992: 226) refers to this type of NGO as a 'corporate identity' NGO.

21 As indicator for institutionalization, Rucht and Roose (1999: 78) refer to office space and division of labour. Similarly, Diani and Donati (1999: 19) measure the establishment of units and departments. Dalton, Kuechler and Bürklin (1990: 15) give the counter-example of an environmental group which did not relocate the offices in order to avoid too close contact with government.

22 For Meyer and Tarrow (1998: 16), professionalization involves that part-time activists become full-time movement professionals. Raschke (1993: 465, 630) talks about 'Verberuflichung'.

23 Social movement scholars have examined the perception of formal rules and regulations given by official institutions as indicators for external recognition. Jiménez (1999: 159) refers to 'contractual forms', meaning that social movement organizations have received public recognition. McCarthy, Britt and Wolfson (1991: 47–8) studied documents for evidence of the extent to which NGO activities conform with state regulations. Rucht and Roose (1999: 78) perceive the legal status of organizations as an indicator for institutionalization.

24 Although many NGOs in one way or the other accomplish both functions (or can be positioned somewhere in-between), this characteristic will be

treated as dichotomous to reduce complexity. 'The analytic distinction between advocacy and service organizations loses much of its neatness when we apply it to the empirical world. Service organizations can, of course, contribute to placing an environmental issue on the political agenda; advocacy organizations, on the other hand, may also provide services to states and international organizations, but this is rather the exception' (Breitmeier and Rittberger 1998).

25 In research on social movement organizations, this aspect is referred to as the degree of qualification needed for the position (Raschke 1993: 465, 630; Nullmeier 1989: 14). In their 'institutionalization index', Rucht and Roose (1999: 78), for example, refer to professionalization as 'members with special training relevant to their role in the group'; Brand (1999: 40, 47) refers to expertise such as subject knowledge, academic training and so on. For Diani and Donati (1999: 20), it means training in specific fields relevant to their work. In environmental organizations, for example, this includes training such as communication and journalism, but also a background in science and law.

26 The term NGO applies to a broad variety of organizations. For this reason, NGOs differ according to factors like size, cultural background, historical establishment, ideological orientation, and many more. In order to reduce complexity, the NGOs selected in this study are all very similar in these respects. They are all large internationally operating NGOs with a comparatively long history; they are all of Western background and do not intend to spread any ideology or (religious) belief as is the case for many humanitarian NGOs with Christian background, such as Caritas or World Vision. Thus, the selection of cases limits – as far as possible – variance introduced by factors other than the explanatory independent variables (Przeworski and Teune 1970: 33; King *et al.* 1994: 129).

27 An exception is Amnesty International. A few case studies have been conducted on this NGO and its relationship with the UN. See for example Ennals (1982), Cook (1986) and Thakur (1997).

28 For one of the latest and most comprehensive accounts on the history of AI, see Power (2001: 119–64).

29 Compare also with AI's statute: 'Responsibility for *Amnesty International* work on violations of human rights in any country or territory, including the collection and evaluation of information, and the sending of delegations, lies with the international governing bodies of the organization, and not with the sections, groups or members in the country or territory concerned' (Amnesty International 1999b).

30 The changed goals of CARE are reflected in its name: originally CARE stood for 'Cooperative for American Remittances to Europe'; now it is registered as 'Cooperative for Assistance and Relief Everywhere'.

31 The ILHR was issued in 1942 under New York State Law with the name 'International League for the Rights of Man and for the New Democracy', but the annex 'New Democracy' was dropped in the early 1950s, and in 1976 the name was changed to International League for Human Rights (Clark 1981: 102, note 2).

32 There was a Save the Children International Union established in 1920 but the connections between the organizations were disrupted by the Second World War (Penrose and Seaman 1996: 242).

33 Since 2004 the Action Aid Alliance has been restructuring its international federation, establishing a common office in South Africa and changing its name to Action Aid International.

3 Activities in the UN Context – Changing Patterns of Interaction

34 My analysis in this section concentrates on the policy fields of human rights and humanitarian intervention, since I explore NGOs and their interaction with the UN in these two issue areas.
35 Such information from NGOs is necessary to make the system of human rights protection reliable, as it is often the only non-governmental source of information. 'If they [UN officials] were unable to obtain the relevant information from independent sources (and UN backup facilities are often unable to produce an in-depth analysis), committee members would have to take government reports at their face value and would be hard pressed to challenge them' (Weschler 1998: 144).
36 According to the information provided on the origins of the Arria Formula by Global Policy Forum, the formula is named after the Venezuelan Ambassador to the UN, Diego Arria, who devised it in 1993. During the crisis in Yugoslavia at that time, a Bosnian priest came to New York and asked various Security Council members to meet informally. Only the Ambassador Arria agreed to meet with him, and was so impressed by the information provided by the priest that he felt that all members of the Security Council should hear about it. Since there were no official proceedings to invite an individual like a priest, Arria simply invited Security Council members to gather over coffee in the delegates' lounge (Paul 2003).
37 Drawing from her own experience, Picken observed that 'because they are not trained in human rights, "diplomats are usually less and less competent" as the details of human rights norms become more complex' (in A. Clark 2001: 35). Similarly, Weschler (1998: 153) describes this misplacement as follows: 'Very often young diplomats represent their countries at the Commission and in the UN General Assembly's Third Committee. For them this is a start of their career. As a result, they lack experience and rotate their jobs very frequently. Sometimes, there is a lack of continuity between a particular government's human rights work in Geneva (where the Commission meets) and its activities at the Third Committee of the General Assembly, whose sessions are held in New York, due to the fact that the work is handled by different individuals who do not always communicate effectively with one another.'
38 Clapham supposes that experts in the treaty bodies, for example, are usually in full time employment with other tasks and arrive for a meeting straight from their regular work. They often do not have the time or the incentives to study cases and reports sent to them carefully enough prior to the examination during the sessions of the treaty bodies. In addition, they receive insufficient support from the secretariat in the preparation of questions and scanning of information material. Their expertise, however, is neither questioned nor examined (Clapham 2000: 188).

39 For a detailed account on the dependency of NGOs on the UN for security matters, see Harris and Dombrowski (2002).

40 See Hamm (2001) for the extended perception of human rights using the example of UNDP.

41 Cook (1996: 209) summarizes the diverse challenges arising from intense interaction through such activities at the UN level: 'These tensions between quiet diplomacy and public campaigning are not easy for an NGO to resolve. Some argue that working at the United Nations calls for too many compromises and brings NGOs too close to governments. Others insist that, to be effective, NGOs have to function within the system and play by its rules. This conflict continues to be the subject of intense debate within the Amnesty movement. What is perhaps most important for Amnesty is always to maintain its independence and never to compromise its *capacity* to criticize and to insist on the highest standards of human rights protection at the UN' [italics in the original].

42 In the past, AI instead often assisted informally during drafting procedures. Since such processes sometimes took place in private, Amnesty members participated in working groups during the preparation phases. They not only provided background information or explained in informal discussion with government delegation what they believed should be included in the respective documents, but were also often asked directly for their expertise on specific wording or technical issues, for example. Occasionally, in fact, Amnesty informally prepared a draft and provided governments with it, sometimes even on their request. For example, in the 1980s, Amnesty assisted in preparing a draft on extra-juridical execution asked for by Austria and subsequently proposed by Norway. Leary (1979: 203) also reports that an AI representative participated in an informal working group during the Geneva Congress which eventually led to the declaration against torture. Amnesty members may have also participated in drafting committees as independent advisor; for example when they were on a sabbatical from their position at the NGO, they attended such committees as private persons or representing other institutions (Interviews AI-3, AI-7, AI-5).

43 Building upon the EU Association experience and the collaboration of a single section of AI with the ICC, AI seeks sub-contracting arrangements whereby, for example, a section is mandated to take direct responsibilities for a designated body of work and could include IGO work on women's human rights, work on the World Bank, or WTO.

44 For example, the organization produced a report on peacekeeping and human rights with 15 recommendations and wrote training documents for the UN on coaching civilian police in monitoring (Amnesty International 1996: 35). Moreover, it made recommendations on the work of the Human Rights Unit of the Angola Verification Mission (Amnesty International 1998: 52). In 1997, together with other Geneva based NGOs, it produced a manual for Refugees on how to use international human rights mechanisms (Amnesty International 1999a: 67).

45 In the report, the FIDH drew attention to illegal procedures to cover up significant violations of the maximum period of pre-trial custody (UN Doc. CAT/C/SR.358 §26). In response, a Tunisian delegate felt obliged to answer questions raised by to the FIDH's report (CAT/C/SR.359 §28–9).

4 Representation and Representatives to the UN – Institutionalization as an Internal Factor

46 However – as Chiang (1981: 244) recognized – an increased professionaliza-tion of NGO representatives may, in fact, change the low reputation of NGO representatives and have an impact on the amount and quality of activities between NGOs and the UN. 'NGO relations undoubtedly will improve to the extent the quality of NGO representatives at the UN rises. Upgrading their quality will necessarily involve a search for representatives with expertise and sophistication, but also with a knowledge both of the organization they present, its history, purpose, and politics, and of the purpose and functions of NGOs, historically, politically, and philosophically, vis-à-vis the govern-ments and IGOs such as the UN. Coupled with an understanding of the changes occurring daily in the world, in international politics and at the UN, such NGO representatives may well serve their role as initiators and partici-pants in a continuing dialogue involving the various communities of the world, both within and outside the UN.'

47 Intra-organizational provisions also created tension between headquarters and AI's UN offices. The New York office was meant to become a part of the legal office, but staff members in New York wanted to be directly responsible to the secretary-general of AI. For years, an argument went on between the represen-tatives in New York and the international secretariat in London and the situa-tion remained undefined for some time. When the Geneva office was set up, in fact, headquarters made clear that it forms part of the legal division of Amnesty. This decision catalysed the confrontation regarding the New York office, and the office there then became subordinated to the legal office as well.

48 For example, one UN representative in Geneva did several years of letter-writ-ing and fund-raising work at the local level (Interview AI-4).

49 An exception are the temporary AI representatives in New York who took over to represent the organization during the recruitment process of a third representative. They were sent by headquarters.

50 As a former head of Legal Office expressed it: 'It was recognised early on that there was enormous potential for greater involvement in UN work by Amnesty members. As the membership grew, educational materials and lob-bying and campaigning techniques were gradually developed to encourage this. Today, an extensive UN programme is carried out by the joint efforts of professional staff in the Secretariat's Legal and International Organizations Programme, including its New York and Geneva offices and its volunteer representatives to the UN in Vienna' (Cook 1996: 186).

51 For the position in New York, CARE decided to hire a person with a media or diplomatic background, so experience in journalism was favoured. The person should know the media and have connections to bring issues and information to the public. Alternatively, a former diplomat was considered appropriate as he or she would have personal connections and a lot of credibility due to the prior status (Interview CARE-2).

52 As the NGO is moving away from a federative to a more centralist type of structure, activities between the single Oxfams are 'harmonized' (Interview Oxfam-1) and its representation at the UN is becoming increasingly coordi-nated. As a result Oxfam International considered to substitute the volunteer

representative and to create a common full-time position for its UN representation by sending someone permanently to New York. The recruit's duties are to coordinate UN representation and develop more clearly defined goals and objectives for the NGO's presence at the UN level (Interview Oxfam-4). Unfortunately the person who started on this position did not reply to several inquiries for an interview.

53 Due to its location in New York City, the ILHR had always envisioned activities with the UN. For this reason, the ILHR always had a 'representative' for UN relations. In a document from the 1950s, a former League of Nations official is mentioned to be the representative for the ILHR before the UN (International League for Human Rights 195?: 8) whose main purpose was to follow UN meetings.

54 However, this lawyers' committee broke away from the ILHR in 1987 and became an NGO of its own (Korey 1998: 157).

5 Accreditation to the UN through Rules and Regulations – Institutionalization as an External Demand

55 Examples of human rights NGOs whose status has been under discussion recently are: Freedom House, Christian Solidarity International, or Transnational Radical Party, see for example UN Doc. E/2000/88 (Part II) §70–124 and UN Doc. E/2001/8; for a good analysis of some of these cases, see Aston (2001).

56 The previous resolution on NGO accreditation stated that human rights NGOs 'should have a general international concern with this matter, not be restricted to the interests of a particular group of States' (UN Resolution 1296 XLIV §17).

57 As a former head of legal office summarized, '[i]n formal terms consultative status gives the organization international standing and enables it to attend relevant UN meetings, to submit documents and to make statements. However, the way in which NGO access and participation have developed in practice had given Amnesty much greater scope for formal and informal participation at the UN than is suggested by the wording of ECOSOC Resolution 1296 (XLIV) [the previous resolution on NGO accreditation from 1968] which now governs such status. Consultative status opened the door for Amnesty to undertake a whole range of vigorous political campaigning initiatives at the UN' (Cook 1996: 184–5).

58 Petroula (2001: 52), a former representative of FIDH noted in a report how this development is perceived by the NGO: '[f]ive years after this reform of consultative status, the FIDH noted with concern that, while resolution 1996/31 aimed to increase participation by all NGOs, it appears today that States display the highest degree of reluctance when it comes to independent human rights NGOs. Some of the provisions in resolution 1996/31 are used in an abusive way by some governments, either to block certain national human rights NGOs that are independent, credible and efficient from making use of consultative status, or to favour access by national pro-government NGOs.'

59 Also during the 1978 review, the Argentine representative cited the FIDH and other NGOs as having attacked certain governments during the Commission on Human Rights in 1977 and in some sub-commissions, either in statements or by circulating material (Chiang 1981: 188). The FIDH was specifically accused of having accredited as members terrorists: an Argentine stated that the NGO had accredited a leader of the women's branch of the Montonero terrorist movement and other terrorist groups from Latin America. These had formed the Revolutionary Coordination Committee in Paris and directed of organized international terrorism in various countries in Latin America (in Chiang 1981: 194–5).

60 In 1998, Oxfam UK split up, and Oxfam Ireland became a separate organization. Oxfam Great Britain 'inherited' the consultative status at the UN.

6 NGOs in the UN System and Beyond – Final Remarks

61 Such developments have already been observed in the environmental sector. Chatterjee and Finger (1994: 68) talk about the 'big 10', referring to those environmental NGOs which are resourceful, and hence have a say in political processes and dominate the scene.

62 In the past, the concept of corporatism has been applied only sporadically in international relations. Glagow and Schimank (1983), for example, developed a model for 'corporatist administration' in order to explain administrative structures of aid politics between official institutions and NGOs.

63 For some first results comparing NGO access and interaction in relation to different IGOs, see Nanz and Steffek (2005).

References

64 Interviews were conducted with current and former NGO representatives to the UN of the selected eight organizations as well as with representatives at headquarters who deal with the organization's UN matters. Moreover, some other relevant NGO representatives, UN officials and national representatives of a permanent mission to the UN were interviewed for this study. The interviews were coded by a random scheme. Codes show the institutional affiliation of the interviewee: AI (Amnesty International representatives), FIDH (representative of the Fédération Internationale des Droits de l'Homme), CARE (CARE International representative), Oxfam (Oxfam International representative), HRW (Human Rights Watch representative), ILHR (representative of the International League for Human Rights), ISCA (representative of the International Save the Children Alliance), AAA (representative of the Action Aid Alliance), NR (national representative to the UN), Add. NGOs (additional NGO representatives), UN (UN officials and staff members).

References

Published sources

Action Aid Alliance (no date), *Principles and common objectives* (Brussels: Action Aid Alliance)

Amnesty International (1995), *Report 1994* (London: Amnesty International)

Amnesty International (1996), *Report 1995* (London: Amnesty International)

Amnesty International (1997), *Report 1996* (London: Amnesty International)

Amnesty International (1998), *Report 1997* (London: Amnesty International)

Amnesty International (1999a), *Report 1998* (London: Amnesty International)

Amnesty International (1999b), *Statute of Amnesty International* (as amended by the 23rd International Council Meeting, 12–19 December 1997, updated 28 May 1999)

Amnesty International (2001a), *Report 2000* (London: Amnesty International)

Amnesty International (2001b), *Statute of Amnesty International* (as amended by the 25th International Council in Dakar, Senegal, 17–25 August 2001)

Amnesty International (2002), *Report 2001* (London: Amnesty International)

Amnesty International (2004a), 'Justice and the Rule of Law: The Role of the United Nations' [*available online at*: http://www.globalpolicy.org/security/mtgsetc/040930ai.htm (accessed 31 January 2005), paper dated 30 September 2004]

Amnesty International (2004b), 'Statement to the UN Security Council about Its Visit to West Africa, 20 to 29 June 2004' [*available online at*: http://www.globalpolicy.org/security/mtgsetc/040616ai.htm (accessed 31 January 2005), paper dated 16 June 2004]

Amnesty International (2005), 'About Amnesty International' [*available online at*: http://web.amnesty.org/pages/aboutai-index-eng (accessed 28 January 2005)]

Andretta, Massimiliano, della Porta, Donatella, Mosca, Lorenzo and Reiter, Herbert (2003), *No Global – New Global. Identität und Strategien der Antiglobalisierungsbewegung* (Frankfurt: Campus)

Anheier, Helmut and Kendall, Jeremy, eds, (2001), *Third Sector Policy at the Crossroads: An International Nonprofit Analysis* (London: Routledge)

Anheier, Helmut, Glasius, Marlies and Kaldor, Mary (2001), 'Introducing Global Civil Society', in Anheier, Helmut, Glasius, Marlies and Kaldor, Mary, eds, *Global Civil Society* (Oxford: Oxford University Press), pp. 3–22

Archer, Angus (1983), 'Methods of Multilateral Management: The Interrelationship of International Organizations and NGOs', in Trister Gati, Toby, ed., *The US, the UN and the Management of Global Change* (New York: UNA-USA), pp. 303–26

Aston, Jurij (2001), 'The United Nations Committee on Non-Governmental Organizations: Guarding the Entrance to a Politically Divided House', *European Journal of International Law* 12:5, pp. 943–62

Atwood, David C. (1997), 'Mobilizing Around the United Nations Special Sessions on Disarmament', in Smith, Jackie, Chatfield, Charles and Pagnucco,

Ron, eds, *Transnational Social Movements and Global Politics. Solidarity Beyond the State* (Syracuse, NY: Syracuse University Publication), pp. 141–74

Azzam, Fateh (1993), 'Non-Governmental Organizations and the UN World Conference on Human Rights', *The Review* (International Commission of Jurists) 50, pp. 89–100

Beigbeder, Yves (1991), *The Role and Status of International Humanitarian Volunteers and Organizations: The Right and Duty to Humanitarian Assistance* (Dordrecht: Nijhoff)

Beisheim, Marianne (1997), 'Nichtregierungsorganisationen und ihre Legitimität', *Aus Politik und Zeitgeschichte* B43/1997, pp. 21–9

Bennett, A. LeRoy and Oliver, James K. (2002), *International Organizations. Principles and Issues*, 7th edition (Englewood Cliffs, NJ: Prentice Hall)

Bernheim, Jean-Claude (1983), *Rompre le silence. Fédération internationale des droits de l'Homme* (Montreal: Boréal Express)

Bettati, Mario (1986), 'La Contribution des Organisations Non Gouvernementales à la Formation et l'Application du Droit International', in Bettati, Mario and Dupuy, Pierre-Marie, eds, *Les O.N.G. et le Droit International* (Paris: Economia), pp. 1–21

Black, Maggie (1992), *A Cause for Our Times. Oxfam – the first 50 years* (Oxford: Oxford University Press)

Bock, Edwin A. (1955), *Representation of Non-Governmental Organizations and the United Nations* (Public Administration Clearing House)

Bogner, Alexander, Littig, Beate and Menz, Wolfgang, eds, (2002), *Das Experteninterview – Theorie, Methode, Anwendung* (Opladen: Leske and Budrich)

Boli, John and Thomas, George M., eds (1999a), *Constructing World Culture: INGOs Since 1875* (Stanford, CA: Stanford University Press)

Boli, John and Thomas, George M. (1999b), 'INGOs and Organization of World Culture', in Boli, John and Thomas, George M., eds, *Constructing World Culture: INGOs Since 1875* (Stanford, CA: Stanford University Press), pp. 13–49

Börzel, Tanja and Risse, Thomas (2005, forthcoming), 'Public-Private Partnerships: Effective and Legitimate Tools of International Governance?', in Grande, Edgar and Pauly, Louis W., eds, *Complex Sovereignty: On the Reconstitution of Political Authority in the 21st Century* (Toronto: University of Toronto Press)

Brand, Karl-Werner (1999), 'Dialectics of Institutionalisation: The Transformation of the Environmental Movement in Germany', *Environmental Politics, Special Issue: Environmental Movements – Local, National and Global* 8:1, pp. 35–58

Brand, Ulrich, Brunnengräber, Achim, Schrader, Lutz, Stock, Christian and Wahl, Peter (2000), *Global Governance. Alternative zur neoliberalen Globalisierung?* (Münster: Westfälisches Dampfboot)

Breitmeier, Helmut and Rittberger, Volker (1998), 'Environmental NGOs in an Emerging Global Civil Society', *Tübinger Arbeitspapiere zur Internationalen Politik und Friedensforschung* 32 [available online at: http://www.uni-tuebingen.de/uni/spi/taps/tap32.htm (accessed 30 March 2001)]

Brett, Rachel (1995), 'The Role and Limits of Human Rights NGOs at the United Nations', *Political Studies, Special Issue: Politics and Human Rights* 43, pp. 96–110

Broadhurst, Arlene I. and Ledgerwood, Grant (1998), 'Environmental Diplomacy Corporations and Non-Governmental Organizations: The Worldwide Web of Influence', *International Relations* 14:2, pp. 1–19

Burnham, Peter, Gilland, Karin, Grant, Wyn and Layton-Henry, Zig (2004), *Research Methods in Politics* (Basingstoke: Palgrave MacMillan)

Campbell, Wallace J. (1990), *The History of CARE – A Personal Account* (London: Praeger)

CARE International (2000a), 'Structure' [*available online at*: http://www.care-international.org/structure.htm (accessed 18 September 2000)]

CARE International (2000b), 'Member Countries' [*available online at*: http://www.care-international.org/member.htm (accessed 18 September 2000)]

CARE International (2001), *Priority Strategy Direction 1* (Brussels: CARE International)

CARE International (2004), 'Address to the Security Council on the Role of Civil Society in Post-Conflict Peace Building' [*available online at*: http://www.globalpolicy.org/security/mtgsetc/040622care.htm (accessed 31 January 2005), paper dated 22 June 2004]

CARE International (2005), 'Our Vision – Our Mission' [*available online at*: http://www.care-international.org/about%20care.htm (accessed 28 January 2005)]

Carmin, JoAnn (1999), 'Voluntary Associations, Professional Organisations and the Environmental Movement in the United States', *Environmental Politics, Special Issue: Environmental Movements – Local, National and Global* 8:1, pp. 101–21

Centre for the Study of Global Governance (2004), *Global Civil Society 2004/5* (London: Sage)

Chandler, David (2001), 'The Road to Military Humanitarianism: How the Human Rights NGOs Shaped A New Humanitarian Agenda', *Human Rights Quarterly* 23:3, pp. 678–700

Charnovitz, Steve (1997), 'Two Centuries of Participation: NGOs and International Governance', *Michigan Journal of International Law* 18:2, pp. 183–286

Chatterjee, Pratap and Finger, Matthias (1994), *The Earth Brokers. Power, Politics and World Development* (London: Routledge)

Chiang, Pei-heng (1981), *Non-Governmental Organizations at the United Nations. Identity, Role and Functions* (New York: Praeger)

Clapham, A. (1994), 'Creating the High Commissioner for Human Rights. The Outside Story', *European Journal of International Law* 5:4, pp. 556–68

Clapham, Andrew (2000), 'UN Human Rights Reporting Procedures: An NGO Perspective', in Alston, Philip and Crawford, James, eds, *The Future of UN Human Rights Treaty Monitoring* (Cambridge: Cambridge University Press), pp. 175–98

Clark, Ann Marie (2001), *Diplomacy of Conscience. Amnesty International and Changing Human Rights Norms* (Princeton, NJ: Princeton University Press)

Clark, Ann Marie, Friedman, Elisabeth and Hochstetler, Kathryn (1998), 'The Sovereign Limits of Global Civil Society: A Comparison of NGO Participation in UN World Conferences on the Environment, Human Rights, and Women', *World Politics* 51:1, pp. 1–35

Clark, John (2001), 'Trans-national Civil Society: Issues of Governance and Organisation' (paper prepared for presentation at a seminar, June 1–2, London School of Economics and Political Science)

Clark, Roger S. (1981), 'The International League for Human Rights and South West Africa 1947–1957: The Human Rights NGOs as Catalyst in the International Legal Process', *Human Rights Quarterly* 3:4, pp. 101–36

Coate, Roger A., Alger, Chadwick F. and Lipschutz, Ronnie D. (1996), 'The United Nations and Civil Society: Creative Partnership for Sustainable Development', *Alternatives* 21:1, pp. 93–122

Cook, Helena (1996), 'Amnesty International at the United Nations', in Willetts, Peter, ed., *'The Conscience of the World'. The Influence of Non-Governmental Organisations in the UN System* (London: Hurst), pp. 181–213

Coston, Jennifer M. (1998), 'A Model and Typology of Government–NGO Relationship', *Nonprofit and Voluntary Sector Quarterly* 27:3, pp. 358–82

Dalton, Russell J., Kuechler, Manfred and Bürklin, Wilhelm (1990), 'The Challenge of New Movements', in Dalton, Russell J. and Kuechler, Manfred, eds, *Challenging the Political Order. New Social and Political Movements in Western Democracies* (Oxford: Polity Press), pp. 3–22

Dawson, Carl A. and Gettys, Warner E. (1935), *Introduction to Sociology* (New York: Ronald Press)

della Porta, Donatella and Kriesi, Hanspeter (1999), 'Social Movements in a Globalizing World: an Introduction', in della Porta, Donatella, Kriesi, Hanspeter and Rucht, Dieter, eds, *Social Movements in a Globalizing World* (Chippenham: St. Martin's), pp. 3–22

della Porta, Donatella, Kriesi, Hanspeter and Rucht, Dieter, eds (1999), *Social Movements in a Globalizing World* (Chippenham: St. Martin's)

Department of Economic and Social Affairs (2005), 'NGOs in Consultative status with ECOSOC' [*available online at*: http://www.un.org/esa/coordination/ngo/about.htm (accessed 28 June 2005)]

Diani, Mario and Donati, Paolo R. (1999), 'Organisational Change in Western European Environmental Groups: A Framework for Analysis', *Environmental Politics, Special Issue: Environmental Movements – Local, National and Global* 8:1, pp. 13–34

DiMaggio, Paul J., and Powell, Walter W. (1983), 'The Iron Cage Revisited: Institutional Isomorphism and Collective Rationality in Organizational Fields', *American Sociological Review* 48, pp. 147–60

DiMaggio, Paul J., and Powell, Walter W. (1991), 'Introduction', in Powell, Walter W. and DiMaggio, Paul, J., eds, *The New Institutionalism in Organizational Analysis* (Chicago, IL: University of Chicago Press), pp. 1–39

Ennals, Martin (1982), 'Amnesty International and Human Rights', in Willetts, Peter, ed., *Pressure Groups in the Global System. The Transnational Relations of Issue-Orientated Non-Governmental Organizations* (London: Frances Pinter), pp. 63–83

Fédération Internationale des Droits de l'Homme (1998), *Report of Activities 95–97* (Paris: FIDH)

Fédération Internationale des Droits de l'Homme (2005a), 'FIDH-History' [*available online at*: http://www.fidh.org/fidh-en/uhistory.htm (accessed 28 January 2005)]

Fédération Internationale des Droits de l'Homme (2005b), 'FIDH-Observing, Alerting' [*available online at*: http://www.fidh.org/fidh-en/observe.htm (accessed 28 January 2005)]

Fédération Internationale des Droits de l'Homme (2005c), 'ONU' [*available online at*: http://www.fidh.org/intgouv/onu/index.htm (accessed 28 January 2005)]

Finger, Matthias (1994a), 'NGOs and Transformation: Beyond Social Movement Theory', in Princen, Thomas and Finger. Matthias, eds, *Environmental NGOs in World Politics. Linking the Local and the Global* (London: Routledge), pp. 48–67

Finger, Matthias (1994b), 'Environmental NGOs in the UNCED Process', in Princen, Thomas and Finger, Matthias, eds, *Environmental NGOs in World Politics. Linking the Local and the Global* (London: Routledge), pp. 186–216

Finnemore, Martha (1996), 'Norms, Culture, and World Politics: Insights from Sociology's Institutionalism', *International Organization* 50:2, pp. 325–47

Fitzduff, Mari and Church, Cheyanne (2004), *NGOs at the Table. Strategies for Influencing Policies in Areas of Conflict* (Lanham: Rowman and Littlefield)

Freeman, Jo (1979), 'Resource Mobilization and Strategy: A Model for Analyzing Social Movement Organization Actions', in Zald, Mayer N. and McCarthy, John, eds, *The Dynamics of Social Movements: Resource Mobilization, Social Control and Tactics* (Cambridge: Winthrop), pp. 167–89

Freeman, Kathleen (1965), *If Any Man Build. The History of the Save the Children Fund* (London: Hodder and Stoughton)

French, Hilary (1996), 'The Role of Non-state Actors', in Werksman, Jacob, ed., *Greening International Institutions* (London: Earthscan Publications), pp. 251–8

Gaer, Felice (1996), 'Reality Check: Human Rights Nongovernmental Organisations confront Governments at the United Nations', in Weiss, Thomas G. and Gordenker, Leon, eds, *NGOs, the UN, and Global Governance* (Boulder, CO: Lynne Rienner), pp. 51–66

Gidron, Benjamin, Kramer, Ralph M. and Salamon, Lester M. (1992), 'Government and the Third Sector in Comparative Perspective: Allies or Adversaries?', in Gidron, Benjamin, Kramer, Ralph M. and Salamon, Lester M., eds, *Government and the Third Sector: Emerging Relationships in Welfare States* (San Francisco, CA: Jossey-Bass), pp. 1–30

Glagow, Manfred and Schimank, Uwe (1983), 'Korporatistische Verwaltung: Das Beispiel Entwicklungspolitik', *Politische Vierteljahresschrift* 24:3, pp. 253–74

Global Policy Forum (2000a), 'CARE to Brief U.N. Security Council Members on the Protection of Civilians in Armed Conflict' (CARE Press Release, April 11, 2000) [*available online at*: http://www.igc.org/globalpolicy/security/security/issues/general/carearms.htm (accessed 10 March 2001)]

Global Policy Forum (2000b), 'NGO Working Group on the Security Council – Information Statement' [*available online at*: http://www.globalpolicy.org/security/ngowkrp/statements/current.htm (accessed 16 February 2001), paper dated December 2000]

Global Policy Forum (2001a), 'A Short History of the NGO Working Group on the Security Council' [*available online at*: http://www.globalpolicy.org/security/ngowkrp/history.htm (accessed 28 January 2005), paper dated April 2001]

Global Policy Forum (2001b), 'Amnesty Leader Pierre Sané Briefs Council in Historic Step – Broadening NGO Consultation' [*available online at*: http://www.igc.org/globalpolicy/security/mtgsect/sane.htm (accessed 10 March 2001)]

Global Policy Forum (2001c), 'Security Council Consultation with Humanitarian NGOs' [*available online at*: http://www.igc.org/globalpolicy/security/mtgsect/somavint.htm (accessed 10 March 2001)]

Global Policy Forum (2002), 'Presentation to the Arria Formula Briefing of the Security Council on Angola' [*available online at*: http://www.globalpolicy.org/security/mtgsetc/oxfamliberia.htm (accessed 28 January 2005), paper dated 5 March 2002]

Global Policy Forum (2003), 'NGO Working Group on the Security Council – List of Members' [*available online at*: http://www.globalpolicy.org/security/ngowkgrp/members.htm (accessed 28 January 2005), list dated November 2003]

Global Policy Forum (2005a), 'Arria and other Special Meetings between NGOs and the Security Council Members' [*available online at*: http://www.globalpolicy.org/security/mtgsetc/brieindx.htm (accessed 28 January 2005)]

Global Policy Forum (2005b), 'Summary Data on the NGO Working Group on the Security Council' [*available online at*: http://www.globalpolicy.org/security/ngowkgrp/data.htm (accessed 28 January 2005)]

Gordenker, Leon and Saunders, Paul R. (1978), 'Organisation Theory and International Organisation', in Taylor, Paul, ed., *International Organisation. A Conceptual Approach* (London: Frances Pinter), pp. 84–110

Gordenker, Leon and Weiss, Thomas G. (1996), 'Pluralising Global Governance: Analytical Approaches and Dimensions', in Weiss, Thomas G. and Gordenker, Leon, eds, *NGOs, the UN, and Global Governance* (Boulder, CO: Lynne Rienner), pp. 17–50

Gordenker, Leon and Weiss, Thomas G. (1998), 'Devolving Responsibilities: a Framework for Analysing NGOs and Services', in Weiss, Thomas G., ed., *Beyond UN Subcontracting. Task-Sharing with Regional Security Arrangements and Service-Providing NGOs* (London: MacMillan), pp. 30–48

Guillet, Sara (1995), '*Nous, peuples des Nations Unies*'. *L'action des Organisations non Gouvernementales dans le système international de protection des droits de l'homme* (Paris: Montchrestien)

Hall, Peter A. and Taylor, Rosemary C. (1996), 'Political Science and the Three New Institutionalisms', *Political Studies* 43:5, pp. 936–57

Hamm, Brigitte (2001), 'A Human Rights Approach to Development', *Human Rights Quarterly* 23:4, pp. 1005–31

Harris, Andrew and Dombrowski, Peter (2002), 'Military Collaboration with Humanitarian Organizations in Complex Emergencies', *Global Governance* 8:2, pp. 155–78

Hix, Simon (1999), *The Political System of the European Union* (New York: St. Martin's)

Hüfner, Klaus (1991), 'Nichtstaatliche Organisationen', in Wolfrum, Rüdiger, ed., *Handbuch Vereinte Nationen*, 2nd edition (München: Beck), pp. 624–31

Hüfner, Klaus (1995), 'The Role of NGOs vis-à-vis International Organizations and National Governments', in Schramm, Jürgen, ed., *The Role of Non-Governmental Organizations in the New European Order* (Baden-Baden: Nomos), pp. 13–24

Hüfner, Klaus (1996), 'Non-Governmental Organizations (NGOs) im System der Vereinten Nationen', *Die Friedenswarte. Blätter für internationale Verständigung und zwischenstaatliche Organisation* 71:2, pp. 115–23

Human Rights in China (2001), 'Maligned & Excluded in a Politicized Process: HRIC Denied Consultative Status' [*available online at*: http://www.hrichina.org/crf/english/99fall/e14_excluded.html (accessed 7 May 2001)]

Human Rights Watch (2004a), 'Debate on Justice and Rule of Law' [*available online at*: http://www.globalpolicy.org/security/mtgsetc/040930hrw.htm (accessed 31 January 2005), paper dated 30 September 2004]

Human Rights Watch (2004b), 'Addressing Crimes against Humanity and "ethnic cleansing" in Darfur, Sudan' [*available online at*: http://www.globalpolicy.org/security/mtgsetc/0424darfur_hrw.pdf (accessed 31 January 2005), paper dated 24 May 2004]

Inter-Agency Standing Committee Secretariat (1998), *Concise Terms of Reference and Action Procedures* (Geneva: Inter-Agency Standing Committee Secretariat)

International League for Human Rights [International League for the Rights of Man] 1949, *no title* (New York: International League for Human Rights) [*available at*: New York Public Library]

International League for Human Rights 195? [exact date unclear], *La ligue internationale des droits de l'homme ... organisation non gouvernementale ayant de l'Organisation des nations unies statut consultatif, catégorie "B"* (New York: International League for Human Rights)

International Save the Children Alliance (2002), 'Who We Are' [*available online at*: http://www.savethechildren.net/stc/publicsite/editor/readnew.asp?id = 138 (accessed 2 February 2002)]

Jaeger, Gilbert (1982), 'Participation of Non-Governmental Organizations in the Activities of the United Nations High Commissioner for Refugees', in Willetts, Peter, ed., *Pressure Groups in the Global System. The Transnational Relations of Issue-Orientated Non-Governmental Organizations* (London: Frances Pinter), pp. 171–8

Jenkins, Craig J. (1983), 'Resource Mobilization Theory and the Study of Social Movements', *Annual Review of Sociology 9*, pp. 527–53

Jiménez, Manuel (1999), 'Consolidation Through Institutionalisation? Dilemmas of the Spanish Environmental Movement in the 1990s', *Environmental Politics, Special Issue: Environmental Movements – Local, National and Global* 8:1, pp. 149–71

Joachim, Jutta (2003), 'Framing, Issues and Seizing Opportunities: Women's Rights and the UN', *International Studies Quarterly* 47:2, pp. 247–74

Kaldor, Mary (1999), 'Transnational Civil Society', in Dunne, Tim and Wheeler, Nickolas J., eds, *Human Rights in Global Politics* (Cambridge: Cambridge University Press), pp. 195–213

Keck, Margaret E. and Sikkink, Kathryn (1998a), *Activists Beyond Borders* (Ithaca, NY: Cornell University Press)

Keck, Margaret E. and Sikkink, Kathryn (1998b), 'Transnational Advocacy Networks in the Movement Society', in Meyer, David S. and Tarrow, Sidney, eds, *The Social Movement Society* (Lanham, MD: Rowman and Littlefield), pp. 217–38

Keidel, Hannemor and Koch, Roland (1996), 'Die Rolle von NGOs bei humanitären Hilfseinsätzen im Rahmen der UN-Friedenssicherung', *Die Friedenswarte. Blätter für internationale Verständigung und zwischenstaatliche Organisation* 71:2, pp. 124–40

Khagram, Sanjeev, Riker, James V. and Sikkink, Kathryn, eds (2002), *Restructuring World Politics: The Power of Transnational Social Movements, Networks and Norms* (Minneapolis: University of Minnesota Press)

Kim, Young S. (1999), 'Constructing a Global Identity: The Role of Esperanto', in Boli, John and Thomas, George M., eds, *Constructing World Culture: INGOs Since 1875* (Stanford, CA: Stanford University Press), pp. 127–48

King, Gary, Keohane, Robert and Verba, Sidney (1994), *Designing Social Inquiry. Scientific Inference in Qualitative Research* (Princeton, NJ: Princeton University Press)

Kjellberg, Francesco (1975), *Political Institutionalization* (London: Wiley)

Korey, William (1998), *NGOs and the Universal Declaration of Human Rights* (New York: St. Martin's)

Kubik, Jan (1998), 'Institutionalization of Protest during Democratic Consolidation in Central Europe', in Meyer, David S. and Tarrow, Sidney, eds, *The Social Movement Society* (Lanham, MD: Rowman and Littlefield), pp. 131–52

Lagoni, Rainer (1995), 'Article 71', in Simma, Bruno, ed., *The Charter of the United Nations. A Commentary* (Oxford: Oxford University Press), pp. 902–15

Larsen, Egon (1978), *A Flame In Barbed Wire. The Story of Amnesty International* (London: Frederick Muller)

Leary, Virginia (1979), 'A New Role for Non-governmental Organizations: A Case Study of Non-Governmental Participation in the Development of International Norms on Torture', in Cassese, Antonio, ed., *U.N. Law/Fundamental Rights – Two Topics in International Law* (Rockville: Sijthoff and Nordhoff), pp. 197–210

Liang, Yuen-Li (1954), 'The Question of Access to the United Nations Headquarters of the Representatives of non-Governmental Organizations in Consultative Status', *American Journal of International Law* 48:3, pp. 434–50

Lindenberg, Marc and Bryant, Coralie (2001), *Going Global: Transforming Relief and Development NGOs* (Bloomsfield, CT: Kumarian Press)

Lipschutz, Ronnie (1992), 'Reconstructing World Politics: The Emergence of Global Civil Society', *Millennium* 21:3, pp. 389–420

Marks, Gary and McAdam, Doug (1996), 'Social Movements and Changing Structures of Political Opportunity in the European Community', *West European Politics* 19:2, pp. 249–78

Martens, Kerstin (2001a), 'Applying the Concept of "Political Opportunity Structures" in European and International Studies', *Transnational Associations* 1:2001, pp. 2–9

Martens, Kerstin (2001b), 'Non-governmental Organisations as Corporatist Mediator? An Analysis of NGOs in the UNESCO System', *Global Society* 15:4, pp. 387–404

Martens, Kerstin (2002), 'Mission Impossible? Defining Nongovernmental Organizations', *Voluntas* 13:3, pp. 271–85

Mathews, Jessica (1997), 'Power Shift', *Foreign Affairs* 76:1, pp. 50–66

McCarthy, John (1997), 'The Globalization of Social Movement Theory', in Smith, Jackie, Chatfield, Charles and Pagnucco, Ron, eds, *Transnational Social Movements and Global Politics. Solidarity Beyond the State* (Syracuse, NY: Syracuse University Publication), pp. 243–59

McCarthy, John and McPhail, Clark (1998), 'The Institutionalization of Protest in the United States', in Meyer, David S. and Tarrow, Sidney, eds, *The Social Movement Society* (Lanham, MD: Rowman and Littlefield), pp. 83–110

McCarthy, John and Zald, Mayer N. (1987) [1977], 'Resource Mobilization and Social Movements: A Partial Theory', in Zald, Mayer N. and McCarthy, John, eds, *Social Movements in an Organizational Society* (New Brunswick, NJ: Transaction), pp. 15–42

McCarthy, John, Britt, David W. and Wolfson, Mark (1991), 'The Institutional Channelling of Social Movements by the State in the United States', *Research in Social Movements, Conflict and Change* 13:1, pp. 45–76

Merle, Marcel (1986), *Les Acteurs dans les Relations Internationales* (Paris: Economia)

Merton, Robert K. and Kendall, Patricia L. (1979), 'Das fokussierte Interview', in Hopf, Christel and Weingarten, Elmar, eds, *Qualitative Sozialforschung* (Stuttgart: Klett-Cotta), pp. 171–204

Messner, Dirk and Nuscheler, Franz (1996), 'Die Weltkonferenzen der 90er Jahre. Eine "Gipfelei" ohne neue Perspektiven?', in Messner, Dirk and Nuscheler, Franz, eds, *Weltkonferenzen und Weltberichte. Ein Wegweiser durch die Internationale Diskussion* (Bonn: Institut für Entwicklung und Frieden), pp. 160–74

Meuser, Michael and Nagel, Ulrike (1991), 'ExpertInneninterviews – vielfach erprobt, wenig bedacht. Ein Beitrag zur qualitativen Methodendiskussion', in

Garz, Detlef and Kraimer, Klaus, eds, *Qualitativ-empirische Sozialforschung: Konzepte, Methoden, Analysen* (Opladen: Westdeutscher Verlag), pp. 441–71

Meyer, David S. and Tarrow, Sidney (1998), 'A Movement Society: Contentious Politics for a New Century', in Meyer, David S. and Tarrow, Sidney, eds, *The Social Movement Society* (Lanham, MD: Rowman and Littlefield), pp. 1–28

Meyer, John W. and Rowan, Brian (1991) [1977], 'Institutionalised Organizations: Formal Structure as Myth and Ceremony', in Powell, Walter W. and DiMaggio, Paul, J., eds, *The New Institutionalism in Organizational Analysis* (Chicago, IL: University of Chicago Press), pp. 41–62

Michels, Robert (1970) [1911], *Zur Soziologie des Parteiwesens in der modernen Demokratie. Untersuchungen über die oligarchischen Tendenzen des Gruppenlebens* (Stuttgart: Kröner)

Najam, Adil (1996), 'NGO Accountability: A Conceptual Framework', *Development Policy Review* 14:4, pp. 339–53

Najam, Adil (2000), 'The Four C's of Third Sector-Government Relations. Cooperation, Confrontation, Complementarity, and Co-optation', *Nonprofit Management & Leadership* 10:4, pp. 375–96

Nanz, Patrizia and Steffek, Jens (2005, forthcoming), 'Assessing the Democratic Quality of Deliberation – Criteria and Research Strategies', *Acta Politica, Special Issue: Deliberative Approaches to Empirical Politics* 40:3

Natsios, Andrew S. (1996), 'NGOs and the UN System in Complex Humanitarian Emergencies: Conflict or Cooperation?', in Weiss, Thomas G. and Gordenker, Leon, eds, *NGOs, the UN, and Global Governance* (Boulder, CO: Lynne Rienner), pp. 67–82

Ness, Gayl and Brechin, Steven R. (1988), 'Bridging the Gap: International Organizations as Organizations', *International Organization* 42:2, pp. 245–73

Nullmeier, Frank (1989), 'Bewegung in der Institutionalisierungsdebatte?', *Forschungsjournal Neue Soziale Bewegungen* 2:3–4, pp. 8–19

Olson, Mancur (2000) [1965], *The Logic of Collective Action. Public Goods and the Theory of Groups* (Cambridge, MA: Harvard University Press)

Osborne, Stephen P., ed. (2000), *Public–Private Partnerships. Theory and Practice in International Perspective* (New York: Routledge)

Ottaway, Marina (2001), 'Corporatism Goes Global: International Organizations, Nongovernmental Organizations Networks, and Transnational Business', *Global Governance* 7:3, pp. 265–92

Otto, Dianne (1996), 'Nongovernmental Organizations in the United Nations System: The Emerging Role of International Civil Society', *Human Rights Quarterly* 18:1, pp. 107–41

Oxfam International (2000a), *Towards Global Equity. Strategic Plan 2001–2004. A summary of Oxfam International's strategic plan for volunteers and staff* (Oxford: Oxfam International)

Oxfam International (2000b), '1998 Annual Report' [*available online at*: http://www.oxfam.org/a_report/default98.htm (accessed 12 September 2000)]

Oxfam International (2000c), 'Why Oxfams Work together' [*available online at*: http://www.oxfam.org/about/why.htm (accessed 12 September 2000)]

Oxfam International (2001), 'International' [*available online at*: http://www.oxfam.ca/about/international.htm (accessed 6 July 2001)]

Oxfam International (2002), 'Who We Are: The Structure of Oxfam International' [*available online at*: http://www.oxfaminternational.org/what_is_OI/whoweare.htm (28 June 2002)]

Oxfam International (2003), 'Presentation for Arria Formula Meeting on Liberia' [*available online at*: http://www.globalpolicy.org/security/mtgsetc/030909oxfam.htm (accessed 31 January 2005), paper dated 9 September 2003]

Oxfam International (2005), 'About Us' [*available online at*: http://www.oxfam.org/eng/about/.htm (accessed 28 January 2005)]

Passy, Florence (1999), 'Supranational Political Opportunities as a Channel of Globalization of Political Conflicts. The Case of the Rights of Indigenous Peoples', in della Porta, Donatella, Kriesi, Hanspeter and Rucht, Dieter, eds, *Social Movements in a Globalizing World* (Chippenham: St. Martin's), pp. 148–69

Paul, James (1999), 'NGO Access at the UN' [*available online at*: http://www.globalpolicy.org/ngos/analysis/jap-accs.htm (accessed 31 January 2005), paper dated July 1999]

Paul, James (2003), 'The Arria Formula' [*available online at*: http://www.globalpolicy.org/security/mtgsetc/arria.htm (accessed 30 January 2005), paper dated October 2003]

Penrose, Angela and Seaman, John (1996), 'The Save the Children Fund and Nutrition for Refugees', in Willetts, Peter, ed., *'The Conscience of the World'. The Influence of Non-Governmental Organisations in the UN System* (London: Hurst), pp. 241–69

Petroula, Eleni (2001), 'The United Nations Opens the Door to GONGOs', in The Observatory for the Protection of Human Rights, ed., *Human Rights Defenders on the Front Line – Annual Report 2000* (The Observatory for the Protection of Human Rights), pp. 52–3

Pole, Christopher and Lampard, Richard (2002), *Practical Social Investigation. Qualitative and Quantitative Methods in Social Research* (Harlow: Prentice Hall)

Power, Jonathan (2001), *Like Water on Stone: The Story of Amnesty International* (London: Allen Lane)

Price, Richard (1998), 'Reversing the Gun Sights: Transnational Civil Society Targets Land Mines', *International Organization* 52:3, pp. 613–64

Priller, Eckhard and Zimmer, Annette, eds (2001), *Der Dritte Sektor international. Mehr Markt – weniger Staat* (Berlin: Sigma)

Princen, Thomas and Finger, Matthias, eds (1994a), *Environmental NGOs in World Politics. Linking the Local and the Global* (London: Routledge)

Princen, Thomas and Finger, Matthias (1994b), 'Introduction', in Princen, Thomas and Finger, Matthias, eds, *Environmental NGOs in World Politics. Linking the Local and the Global* (London: Routledge), pp. 1–28

Przeworski, Adam and Teune, Henry (1970), *The Logic of Comparative Social Inquiry* (New York: Wiley)

Raschke, Joachim (1987), *Soziale Bewegungen. Ein historisch-systematischer Grundriß* (Frankfurt: Campus)

Raschke, Joachim (1993), *Die Grünen* (Köln: Bund-Verlag)

Risse, Thomas and Sikkink, Kathryn (1999), 'The Socialization of International Human Rights Norms into Domestic Practices: Introduction', in Risse, Thomas, Ropp, Stephen C. and Sikkink, Kathryn, eds, *The Power of Human Rights. International Norms and Domestic Change* (Cambridge: Cambridge University Press), pp. 1–39

Risse, Thomas, Ropp, Stephen C. and Sikkink, Kathryn, eds (1999), *The Power of Human Rights. International Norms and Domestic Change* (Cambridge: Cambridge University Press)

Risse-Kappen, Thomas, ed. (1995a), *Bringing Transnational Relations Back In: Non-State Actors, Domestic Structures and International Institutions* (Cambridge: Cambridge University Press)

Risse-Kappen, Thomas (1995b), 'Bringing Transnational Relations Back In: Introduction', in Risse-Kappen, Thomas, ed., *Bringing Transnational Relations Back In: Non-State Actors, Domestic Structures and International Institutions* (Cambridge: Cambridge University Press), pp. 3–36

Ritchie, Cyril (1996), 'Coordinate? Cooperate? Harmonise? NGO Policy and Operational Coalitions', in Weiss, Thomas G. and Gordenker, Leon, eds, *NGOs, the UN, and Global Governance* (Boulder, CO: Lynne Rienner), pp. 177–88

Rittberger, Volker and Zangl, Bernhard (2003), *Internationale Organisationen – Politik und Geschichte*. *Europäische und weltweite internationale Zusammenschlüsse*, 3rd edition (Opladen: Leske and Budrich)

Rittberger, Volker and Boekle, Henning (1996), 'Das Internationale Olympische Komitee – eine Weltregierung des Sports?', *Die Friedenswarte. Blätter für internationale Verständigung und zwischenstaatliche Organisation* 71:2, pp. 155–88

Rittberger, Volker, Schrade, Christina and Schwarzer, Daniela (1999), 'Introduction', in Alagappa, Muthiah and Inoguchi, Takashi, eds, *International Security Management and the United Nations* (New York: United Nations University Press), pp. 107–38

Robins, Dorothy (1960), *United States Non-Governmental Organizations and the Educational Campaign from Dumbarton Oaks, 1944 Through the San Francisco Conference, 1945* (New York: New York University)

Rodley, Nigel (1986), 'Le rôle d'une O.N.G. comme Amnesty International au sein des organisations intergouvernementales', in Bettati, Mario and Dupuy, Pierre-Marie, eds, *Les O.N.G. et le Droit International* (Paris: Economia), pp. 127–52

Rootes, Christopher (1999), 'Environmental Movements: From the Local to the Global', *Environmental Politics, Special Issue: Environmental Movements – Local, National and Global* 8:1, pp. 1–13

Rucht, Dieter (1999), 'The Transnationalization of Social Movements: Trends, Causes, Problems', in della Porta, Donatella, Kriesi, Hanspeter and Rucht, Dieter, eds, *Social Movements in a Globalizing World* (Chippenham: St. Martin's), pp. 206–22

Rucht, Dieter, Blattert, Barbara and Rink, Dieter (1997), *Soziale Bewegungen auf dem Weg zur Institutionalisierung. Zum Strukturwandel 'alternativer' Gruppen in beiden Teilen Deutschlands* (Frankfurt: Campus)

Rucht, Dieter and Roose, Jochen (1999), 'The German Environmental Movement at a Crossroad?', *Environmental Politics, Special Issue: Environmental Movements – Local, National and Global* 8:1, pp. 59–80

Rutherford, Kenneth R. (2000), 'The Evolving Arms Control Agenda: Implications of the Role of NGOs in Banning Antipersonnel Landmines', *World Politics* 53:1, pp. 74–114

Salamon, Lester M. (1994), 'The Rise of the Nonprofit Sector', *Foreign Affairs* 73:4, pp. 109–22

Salamon, Lester M., Anheier, Helmut K., Toepler, Stefan, Sokolowski, S. Wojciech and associates, eds (1999), *Global Civil Society: Dimensions of the Nonprofit Sector* (Baltimore, MD: Center for Civil Society Studies)

Schechter, Michael, ed. (2001), *United Nations-Sponsored World Conferences. Focus on Impact and Follow-up* (United Nations University Press)

Schmidt, Hilmar and Take, Ingo (1997), 'Demokratischer und besser? Der Beitrag von Nichtregierungsorganisationen zur Demokratisierung internationaler Politik und zur Lösung globaler Probleme', *Aus Politik und Zeitgeschichte* B43/1997, pp. 12–20

Schmitter, Philippe C. (1979), 'Still the Century of Corporatism?', in Schmitter, Philippe C. and Lehmbruch, Gerhard, eds, *Trends Towards Corporatist Intermediation* (London: SAGE), pp. 7–51

Schmitter, Philippe C. and Streek W. (1991), 'From National Corporatism to Transnational Pluralism', *Politics and Society* 19:2, pp. 133–64

Schmitz, Hans Peter (1997), 'Nichtregierungsorganisationen und internationale Menschenrechtspolitik', *Comparativ* 7:4, pp. 27–67

Schmitz, Hans Peter (2001), 'Menschenrechtswächter: partielle Midlife-crisis', *Vereinte Nationen* 1, pp. 7–12

Schoener, Wendy (1997), 'Non-governmental Organizations and Global Activism: Legal and Informal Approaches', *Global Legal Studies Journal* 4:2, pp. 537–69

Schulze, Peter M. (1994), 'Nicht-Regierungsorganisationen und die Demokratisierung des VN-Systems', in Hüfner, Klaus, ed., *Die Reform der Vereinten Nationen. Die Weltorganisation zwischen Krise und Erneuerung* (Opladen: Leske and Budrich), pp. 119–40

Scott, John (1990), *A Matter of Record. Documentary Sources in Social Research* (Cambridge: Polity Press)

Scott, W. Richard (1994), 'Institutional Analysis: Variance and Process Theory Approaches', in Scott, W. Richard, and Meyer, John W., eds, *Institutional Environments and Organizations* (London: SAGE), pp. 81–112

Scott, W. Richard (1995), 'Introduction: Institutional Theory and Organizations', in Scott, W. Richard and Christensen, Soren, eds, *The Institutional Construction of Organizations. International and Longitudinal Studies* (London: SAGE), pp. xi–xxiii

Skjelsbaek, Kjell (1975), 'A Survey of International Nongovernmental Organisations', in Galtung, Johan, ed., *Essays in Peace Research* (Copenhagen: Ejlers), Volume 4: Peace and World Structure, pp. 418–36

Smith, Jackie (1995), 'Transnational Political Processes and the Human Rights Movement', *Research in Social Movements, Conflict and Change* 18, pp. 185–219

Smith, Jackie (1997), 'Characteristics of the Modern Transnational Social Movement Sector', in Smith, Jackie, Chatfield, Charles and Pagnucco, Ron, eds, *Transnational Social Movements and Global Politics. Solidarity Beyond the State* (Syracuse, NY: Syracuse University Publication), pp. 42–58

Smith, Jackie (1998), 'Global Civil Society? Transnational Social Movement Organizations and Social Capital', *American Behavioral Scientist* 42:1, pp. 93–107

Smith, Jackie and Johnston, Hank, eds (2002), *Globalization and Resistance: Transnational Dimensions of Social Movements* (Lanham, MD: Rowman and Littlefield)

Smith, Jackie, Chatfield, Charles and Pagnucco, Ron, eds (1997), *Transnational Social Movements and Global Politics. Solidarity Beyond the State* (Syracuse, NY: Syracuse University Publication)

Smith, Jackie, Pagnucco, Ron and Chatfield, Charles (1997), 'Social Movements and World Politics: A Theoretical Framework', in Smith, Jackie, Chatfield, Charles and Pagnucco, Ron, eds, *Transnational Social Movements and Global Politics. Solidarity Beyond the State* (Syracuse, NY: Syracuse University Publication), pp. 59–80

Smith, Jackie, Pagnucco, Ron and Lopez, George A. (1998), 'Globalizing Human Rights: The Work of Transnational Human Rights NGOs in the 1990s', *Human Rights Quarterly* 20:2, pp. 379–412

Smith, Jackie, Pagnucco, Ron and Romeril, Winnie (1994), 'Transnational Social Movement Organisations in the Global Political Arena', *Voluntas* 5:2, pp. 121–54

Sphere Project (2000), *Humanitarian Charter and Minimum Standards in Disaster Response* (Geneva: The Sphere Project)

Staggenborg, Suzanne (1997) [1988], 'The Consequences of Professionalization and Formalization in the Pro-Choice Movement', in McAdam, Doug and Snow, David A., eds, *Social Movements: Readings on their Emergence, Mobilization, and Dynamics* (Los Angeles, CA: Roxbury), pp. 421–39

Stamp, Elizabeth (1982), 'Oxfam and Development', in Willetts, Peter, ed., *Pressure Groups in the Global System. The Transnational Relations of Issue-Orientated Non-Governmental Organizations* (London: Frances Pinter), pp. 84–104

Steering Committee for Humanitarian Response (2000), *SCHR* (Geneva: Steering Committee for Humanitarian Response)

Stephenson, Carolyn M. (2000), 'NGOs and the Principal Organs of the United Nations', in Taylor, Paul and Groom, A.J.R., eds, *The United Nations at the Millennium: the Principal Organs* (London: Continuum), pp. 271–94

Stosic, Borko D. (1964), *Les Organisations Non Gouvernementales et les Nations Unies* (Paris: Droz)

Tarrow, Sidney (1998), *Power in Movement. Social Movements and Contentious Politics*, 2nd edition (Cambridge: Cambridge University Press)

Taylor, Paul (1995), 'Options for the Reform of the International System for Humanitarian Assistance', in Harriss, John, ed., *The Politics of Humanitarian Intervention* (London: Pinter), pp. 91–143

Taylor, Paul, Daws, Sam and Adamczick-Gerteis, Ute (1997), *Documents on Reform of the United Nations* (Dartmouth: Aldershot)

Taylor, Rupert, ed. (2004), *Creating a Better World: Interpreting Global Civil Society* (Bloomfield, CT: Kumarian Press)

Thakur, Ramesh (1997), 'Human Rights: Amnesty International and the United Nations', in Diehl, Paul F., ed., *The Politics of Global Governance. International Organizations in an Interdependent World* (Boulder, CO: Lynne Rienner), pp. 247–68

Thränhardt, Dietrich (1992), 'Globale Probleme, globale Normen, neue globale Akteure', *Politische Vierteljahresschrift* 33:2, pp. 219–34

Tilly, Charles (1984), 'Social Movements and National Politics', in Bright, Charles and Harding, Susan, eds, *Statemaking and Social Movements: Essays in History and Theory* (Ann Arbor, MI: University of Michigan Press), pp. 297–317

Tocqueville, Alexis de (1997) [1835], *Über die Demokratie in Amerika* (Stuttgart: Reclam)

Truman, David B. (1971) [1951], *The Governmental Process. Political Interests and Public Opinion*, 2nd edition (New York: Knopf)

Turner, Scott (1998), 'Global Civil Society. Anarchy and Governance: Assessing an Emerging Paradigm', *Journal of Research* 35:1, pp. 25–42

Union of International Associations (2004), *Yearbook of International Organisations* (Brussels: UIA), Volume 40

Uvin, Peter and Weiss, Thomas G. (1998), 'The United Nations and NGOs: Global Civil Society and Institutional Change', in Glassner, Martin Ira, ed., *The United Nations at Work* (Westport, CT: Praeger), pp. 213–38

Vaillancourt Rosenau, Pauline, ed. (2000), *Public–Private Policy Partnerships* (Cambridge, MA: MIT Press)

van Rooy, Alison (2004), The Global Legitimacy Game: Civil Society, Globalization and Protest (Basingstoke: Palgrave Macmillan)

Wahl, Peter (1997), 'Mythos und Realität internationaler Zivilgesellschaft. Zu den Perspektiven globaler Vernetzung von Nicht-Regierungs-Organisationen', in Altvater, Elmar, Brunnengräber, Achim, Haake, Markus and Walk, Heike, eds, *Vernetzt und verstrickt: Nicht-Regierungs-Organisationen als gesellschaftliche Produktivkraft* (Münster: Westfälisches Dampfboot), pp. 293–314

Wapner, Paul (1995), 'Politics beyond the State: Environmental Activism and World Civic Politics', *World Politics* 43:3, pp. 311–40

Wapner, Paul (1997), 'Governance in Global Civil Society', in Young, Oran R., ed., *Global Governance: Drawing Insights from the Environmental Experience* (Cambridge, MA: MIT Press), pp. 65–84

Weiss, Thomas G., ed. (1998), *Beyond UN Subcontracting. Task-Sharing with Regional Security Arrangements and Service-Providing NGOs* (London: MacMillan)

Weiss, Thomas G. and Gordenker, Leon, eds (1996), *NGOs, the UN, and Global Governance* (Boulder, CO: Lynne Rienner)

Welch, Claude E. (2001), 'Amnesty International and Human Rights Watch: A Comparison', in Welch, Claude E., ed., *NGOs and Human Rights. Promise and Performance* (Philadelphia, PA: University of Pennsylvania Press), pp. 85–118

Weschler, Joanna (1998), 'Non-Governmental Human Rights Organizations', *Polish Quarterly of International Affairs* 7:3, pp. 137–54

White, Lyman C. (1933), *The Structure of Private International Organizations* (New Brunswick, NJ: Rutgers University Press)

Willetts, Peter, ed. (1996a), *'The Conscience of the World'. The Influence of Non-Governmental Organisations in the UN System* (London: Hurst)

Willetts, Peter (1996b), 'Introduction', Willetts, Peter, ed., *'The Conscience of the World'. The Influence of Non-Governmental Organisations in the UN System* (London: Hurst), pp. 1–14

Willetts, Peter (1996c), 'Consultative Status for NGOs at the United Nations', in Willetts, Peter, ed., *'The Conscience of the World'. The Influence of Non-Governmental Organisations in the UN System* (London: Hurst), pp. 31–62

Willetts, Peter (1996d), 'From Stockholm to Rio and beyond: the Impact of the Environment Movement on the United Nations Consultative Arrangements for NGOs', *Review of International Studies* 22:1, pp. 57–80

Willetts, Peter (2000), 'From "Consultative Arrangements" to "Partnership": The Changing Status of NGOs in Diplomacy at the UN', *Global Governance* 6:2, pp. 191–212

Winston, Morton E. (2001), 'Assessing the Effectiveness of International Human Rights: Amnesty International', in Welch, Claude E., ed., *NGOs and Human Rights. Promise and Performance* (Philadelphia, PA: University of Pennsylvania Press), pp. 25–54

Wiseberg, Laurie S. and Scoble, Harry M. (1977), 'The International League for Human Rights: The Strategy of a Human Rights NGO', *Georgia Journal of International and Comparative Law* 7, pp. 289–313

Young, Dennis R. (1999), 'Complementary, Supplementary, or Adversarial? A Theoretical and Historical Examination of Nonprofit-Government Relations in the United States', in Boris, Elizabeth T. and Steuerle, C. Eugene, eds, *Nonprofits* and Government. *Collaboration and Conflict* (Washington, DC: The Urban Institute Press), pp. 31–67

Young, Dennis R. (1991a), 'The Structural Imperatives of International Advocacy Associations', *Human Relations* 44:9, pp. 921–41

Young, Dennis R. (1991b), 'Organising Principles for International Advocacy Associations', *Voluntas* 3:1 pp. 1–28

Zald, Mayer N. and Ash, Roberta Garner (1987) [1966], 'Social Movement Organisations: Growth, Decay, and Change', in Zald, Mayer N. and McCarthy, John, eds, *Social Movements in an Organizational Society* (New Brunswick, NJ: Transaction), pp. 121–42

Ziegler, Julie (1998), *Die Beteiligung von Nichtregierungsorganisationen (NGOs) am Menschenrechtsschutzsystem der Vereinten Nationen* (München: Akademischer Verlag)

UN documents

UN Charter, *We the Peoples of the United Nations ... United for a Better World*, (26 June 1945)

UN Doc. A/35/372, 'Torture and other cruel, inhuman or degrading treatment or punishment', (16 September 1980)

UN Doc. A/39/480, 'Torture and other cruel, inhuman or degrading treatment or punishment', (11 September 1984)

UN Doc. A/39/505, 'Importance of the Universal Realization of the Right of People to Self-Determination and of the speedy Granting of Independence to Colonial Countries and Peoples for the effective Guarantee and Observance of Human Rights', (28 September 1984)

UN Doc. A/51/950, 'Renewing the United Nations: A Programme for Reform', (14 July 1997)

UN Doc. A/53/170, 'Arrangement and practices for the interaction of non-governmental organizations in all activities of the United Nations system', (10 July 1998)

UN Doc. A/54/2000, 'We the peoples: the role of the United Nations in the twenty-first century', (27 March 2000) ['Millennium Report']

UN Doc. A/54/942-S/2000/707, 'Letter dated 17 July 2000 from the Chargé d'affaires a.i. of the Permanent Mission of Canada to the United Nations addressed to the Secretary-General', (19 July 2000)

UN Doc. A/57/387, 'Strengthening of the United Nations: an agenda for further change', (9 September 2002)

UN Doc. A/58/817, 'We the peoples: civil society, the United Nations and global governance', (11 June 2004)

UN Doc. A/CONF.183/SR.9, 'United Nations Diplomatic Conference of Plenipotentiaries on the Establishment of the International Criminal Court. Summary Record of the 9th Plenary Meeting', (25 January 1999)

UN Doc. A/CONF.191/13, 'Report of the Third United Nations Conference on the Least Developed Countries', (20 September 2001)

UN Doc. CAT/C/SR.264, 'Second periodical report of the Russian Federation', (18 November 1996)

UN Doc. CAT/C/SR.358, 'Second periodical report of Tunisia', (20 November 1998)

UN Doc. CAT/C/SR.359, 'Second periodical report of Croatia, second periodical report of Tunisia', (15 October 1999)

UN Doc. E/1996/17, 'Report of the Committee on Non-Governmental Organizations on its resumed 1995 session', (26 April 1996)

UN Doc. E/1998/43, 'Work of the Non-Governmental Organizations Section of the Secretariat', (8 May 1998)

UN Doc. E/1999/109, 'Report of the Committee on Non-Governmental Organizations on its 1999 Session', (15 July 1999)

UN Doc. E/2000/88 (Part I), 'Report of the Committee on Non-Governmental Organizations on its resumed 2000 Session', (5 July 2001)

UN Doc. E/2000/88 (Part II), 'Report of the Committee on Non-Governmental Organizations on its resumed 2000 Session', (13 July 2001)

UN Doc. E/2000/INF/4, 'List of the non-governmental organizations in consultative status with the Economic and Social Council as at 31 October 2000', (9 November 2000)

UN Doc. E/2001/8, 'Report of the Committee on Non-Governmental Organizations on its resumed 2000 regular session', (22 February 2001)

UN Doc. E/43/Rev.1, 'Consideration of the revised Report of the Committee on Arrangements for consultation with non-governmental organisations', (21 June 1946)

UN Doc. E/C.2/1982/2/Add.1, 'Quadrennial report on the activities of non-governmental organizations in categories I and II consultative status with the Economic and Social Council. Quadrennial reports 1978–1981', Addendum 1, (5 February 1982)

UN Doc. E/C.2/1982/2/Add.2, 'Quadrennial report on the activities of non-governmental organizations in categories I and II consultative status with the Economic and Social Council. Quadrennial reports 1978–1981', Addendum 2, (9 February 1982)

UN Doc. E/C.2/1982/2/Add.3, 'Quadrennial report on the activities of non-governmental organizations in categories I and II consultative status with the Economic and Social Council. Quadrennial reports 1978–1981', Addendum 3, (16 February 1982)

UN Doc. E/C.2/1982/2/Add.4, 'Quadrennial report on the activities of non-governmental organizations in categories I and II consultative status with the Economic and Social Council. Quadrennial reports 1978–1981', Addendum 4, (16 February 1982)

UN Doc. E/C.2/1987/2, 'Quadrennial report on the activities of non-governmental organizations in categories I and II consultative status with the Economic and Social Council. Quadrennial reports 1981–1985', (16 October 1986)

UN Doc. E/C.2/1987/2/Add.1, 'Quadrennial report on the activities of non-governmental organizations in categories I and II consultative status with the Economic and Social Council. Quadrennial reports 1981–1985', Addendum 1, (16 October 1986)

UN Doc. E/C.2/1991/2, 'Quadrennial report on the activities of non-governmental organizations in categories I and II consultative status with the Economic and Social Council. Quadrennial reports 1986–1989', (23 July 1990)

UN Doc. E/C.2/1991/2/Add.1, 'Quadrennial report on the activities of non-governmental organizations in categories I and II consultative status with the Economic and Social Council. Quadrennial reports 1986–1989', Addendum 1, (7 September 1990)

UN Doc. E/C.2/1991/2/Add.2, 'Quadrennial report on the activities of non-governmental organizations in categories I and II consultative status with the Economic and Social Council. Quadrennial reports 1986–1989', Addendum 2, (7 September 1990)

UN Doc. E/C.2/1993/2, 'Quadrennial report on the activities of non-governmental organizations in categories I and II consultative status with the Economic and Social Council. Quadrennial reports 1988–1991', (4 December 1992)

UN Doc. E/C.2/1995/2, 'Quadrennial reports on the activities of non-governmental organizations in consultative status with the Economic and Social Council, categories I and II, Quadrennial Reports, 1990–1993', (16 December 1994)

UN Doc. E/C.2/1995/2/Add.1, 'Quadrennial reports on the activities of non-governmental organizations in consultative status with the Economic and Social Council, categories I and II, Quadrennial Reports, 1990–1993', Addendum 1, (18 November 1994)

UN Doc. E/C.2/1997/2/Add.1, 'Quadrennial report, 1992–1995 submitted through the Secretary-General pursuant to Economic and Social Council resolution 1996/31', Addendum 1, (15 December 1997)

UN Doc. E/C.2/1997/2/Add.2, 'Quadrennial report, 1992–1995 submitted through the Secretary-General pursuant to Economic and Social Council resolution 1996/31', Addendum 2, (6 March 1997)

UN Doc. E/C.2/1999/2/Add.10, 'Quadrennial report, 1995–1998 submitted through the Secretary-General pursuant to Economic and Social Council resolution 1996/31', Addendum 10, (10 February 1999)

UN Doc. E/C.2/1999/2/Add.14, 'Quadrennial report, 1995–1998 submitted through the Secretary-General pursuant to Economic and Social Council resolution 1996/31', Addendum 14, (19 March 1999)

UN Doc. E/C.2/1999/2/Add.7, 'Quadrennial report, 1995–1998 submitted through the Secretary-General pursuant to Economic and Social Council resolution 1996/31', Addendum 7, (10 February 1999)

UN Doc. E/C.2/2000/2/Add.1, 'Quadrennial reports, 1994–1997/1995–1998 submitted through the Secretary-General pursuant to Economic and Social Council resolution 1996/31', Addendum 1, (16 May 2000)

UN Doc. E/C.2/2001/2/Add.13, 'Quadrennial report, 1996–1999, submitted through the Secretary-General pursuant to Economic and Social Council resolution 1996/31', Addendum 13, (15 December 2000)

UN Doc. E/C.2/2001/2/Add.19, 'Quadrennial report, 1997–2001 submitted through the Secretary-General pursuant to Economic and Social Council resolution 1996/31', Addendum 19, (13 April 2001)

UN Doc. E/C.2/2001/2/Add.3, 'Quadrennial report, 1995–1998 submitted through the Secretary-General pursuant to Economic and Social Council resolution 1996/31', Addendum 3, (10 November 2000)

UN Doc. E/C.2/23, 'Activities undertaken by non-governmental organizations up to 1 June 1949 in connection with their consultative status', (25 November 1949)

UN Doc. E/CN.4/1998/24, 'Question of the Realization in all Countries of the Economic, Social and Cultural Rights Contained in the Universal Declaration of Human Rights and in the International Covenant on Economic, Social and Cultural Rights, and Study of Special Problems which the Developing Countries Face in their Efforts to Achieve these Human Rights', (5 January 1998)

UN Doc. S/2001/1298, 'Letter dated 21 December 2001 from the Permanent Representative of Ireland to the United Nations addressed to the President of the Security Council', (31 December 2001)

UN Resolution 1296 (XLIV), 'Arrangement for consultation with non-governmental organizations', (23 May 1968)

UN Resolution 1996/31, 'Consultative relationship between the United Nations and non-governmental organizations', (25 July 1996)

UN Resolution 288(X), 'Review of consultative arrangements with non-governmental organizations', (27 February 1950)

Interviews[64]

Amnesty International representatives

Martin Macpherson, AI Head of Legal Office, interviewed in London, 21 June 2001

Nigel Rodley, former Staff Member and AI Head of Legal Office (1973–1990), interviewed in New York, 21 March 2001

Nicholas Howen, former Staff Member of AI International Secretariat (1991–1998), interviewed in London, 30 November 2001

Melinda Ching, AI Representative in Geneva, interviewed in Geneva, 4 December 2000

Isabelle Scherer, former AI Representative in Geneva (1992–2000), interviewed by correspondence, 10 May 2001

Mariette Grange, former AI Representative in Geneva (1988–1992), interviewed in Geneva, 29 May 2002

Yvonne Terling, AI Representative in New York, interviewed in New York, 20 March 2002

Anne Burke, temporary AI Representative in New York (2000–2001), interviewed in New York, 8 February 2001

Iain Levine, former AI Representative in New York (1997–2000), interviewed in New York, 16 February 2001

Andrew Clapham, former AI Representative in New York (1991–1997), interviewed by correspondence, 3 May 2001

Federation Internationale des Droits de l'Homme representatives

Antoine Madelin, FIDH Representative in Geneva, interviewed in Geneva, 28 May 2002

Eleni Petroula, former FIDH Representative in Geneva (1998–2001), interviewed in Geneva, 5 December 2000

Sara Guillet, former FIDH Representative in Geneva (1994–1998), interviewed in Paris, 14 June 2001

James Paul, Director of Global Policy Forum and former FIDH Representative in New York (1995–1999), interviewed in New York, 14 February 2001

Béatrice Laroche, UN Liaison Person of Human Rights In China (member of the FIDH), interviewed in Paris, 13 June 2001

Brigitta Pöhler, Staff member of the Liga für Menschenrechte (German member of the FIDH), interviewed by correspondence, 28 July 2001

CARE International representatives

Graham Miller, CARE International Representative in Geneva, interviewed in Geneva, 4 December 2000

Ralph Hazelton, former CARE International Representative in Geneva (1997–1998), interviewed by correspondence, 3 April 2001

Sandra Tully, CARE International Representative in New York, interviewed in New York, 7 March 2001

Kate Hunt, CARE International Representative in New York, interviewed in New York, 19 March 2002

Tom Hurley, Assistant Secretary-General of CARE International, interviewed in Brussels, 12 June 2001

Howard Bell, Assistant Secretary-General of CARE International, interviewed in Brussels, 11 June 2001

Carsten Völz, Staff member of CARE Deutschland, interviewed in Bonn, 13 August 2001

Oxfam International representatives

Peter Davies, Oxfam Representative in New York, interviewed in New York, 14 March 2001

Celine Charveriat, Head of Advocacy Office of Oxfam International in Geneva, interviewed in Geneva, 29 May 2002

Paul Bendix, Director of Oxfam Germany, interviewed in Berlin, 25 July 2001.

Caroline Wildeman, Contact Person for the UN and Policy Adviser of Novib/Oxfam Netherlands, interviewed in The Hague, 12 June 2001

Mario Weima, Policy Adviser of Novib/Oxfam Netherlands, interviewed in The Hague, 12 June 2001

Ambereene Hussain, Financial and Administrative Manager of Oxfam International, interviewed in Oxford, 19 June 2001

Ed Cairns, Senior Policy Adviser of Oxfam Great Britain, interviewed in Oxford, 19 June 2001

Jörn Kalinski, Communications and Projects, Oxfam Germany, interviewed in Berlin, 25 July 2001

Nick Roseveare, Humanitarian Deputy Director of Oxfam Great Britain, interviewed in Oxford, 25 February 2002

Human Rights Watch representatives

Joanna Weschler, HRW Representative in New York, interviewed in New York, 27 February 2001

Wilder Taylor, HRW Legal and Policy Director, London Office, interviewed in London, 4 December 2001

Loubna Freih, HRW Representative in Geneva, interviewed in Geneva, 30 May 2002

International League for Human Rights representatives

Alexei Korotayev, ILHR Representative in Geneva, interviewed in Geneva, 7 December 2000

Catherine Fitzpatrick, ILHR Representative in New York, interviewed by correspondence, 21 June 2001

International Save the Children Alliance representatives

Dan Seymour, ISCA Representative in New York, interviewed in New York, 28 February 2001

Helena Gezelius, ISCA Representative in Geneva, interviewed in Geneva, 30 May 2002

Simon Williamson, Staff member of the ISCA, interviewed in London, 21 June 2001

Action Aid Alliance representatives

Laura Kelly, Action Aid Representative and Food Trade Analyst, interviewed in London, 20 June 2001

Kate Farmer, Administrator, Action Aid Alliance, interviewed by correspondence 2 July 2001

Additional NGO representatives

Eylah Kadjar-Hamouda, IFTDH Representative in Geneva, interviewed in Geneva, 7 December 2000

Catherine Harper, MSF Representative in New York, interviewed in New York, 18 April 2001

Robert Muller, MSF Representative in Geneva, interviewed in Geneva, 6 December 2000

Nadja Houben, Staff member of the International Commission of Jurists, interviewed in Geneva, 6 December 2000

Archibald Puddington, Vice President of Freedom House, interviewed in New York, 12 April 2001

Lars Blackmore, Staff member of the International Rescue Committee, interviewed in New York, 17 April 2001

Carl Schieren, Conference of Non-Governmental Organizations in New York, interviewed in New York, 20 March 2001

Joel Macclellan, Steering Committee for Humanitarian Response, interviewed in Geneva, 30 May 2002

Ed Schenkenberg, International Council of Voluntary Associations, interviewed in Geneva, 8 December 2000

Kay Greene, NGO Representative, Department of Public Information/Non-Governmental Organization, interviewed in New York, 29 March 2001

UN officials and staff members

Bradley Foerster, UN Office for the Coordination of Humanitarian Affairs in New York, interviewed in New York, 20 April 2001

Elsa Stamatopoulou, Deputy to the Director of the New York Office of the High Commissioner for Human Rights in New York, interviewed in New York, 20 March 2001

Oleg Dzioubinski, UN Department of Public Information, interviewed in New York, 2 March 2001

Paul Hoeffel, UN Department of Public Information, interviewed in New York, 2 March 2001

Raymonde Martineau, UN NGO Liaison Office in Geneva, interviewed in Geneva, 4 December 2000

Stella Arthur, UN NGO Liaison Service in New York, interviewed in New York, 2 March 2001

Staff member (anonymous), UN Department of Economic and Social Affairs in New York, interviewed in New York, 18 April 2001

National representatives

Philip Ackermann, Permanent Mission of the Federal Republic of Germany to the UN, Member of the UN NGO Committee, interviewed in New York, 6 April 2001

Ilham Ibrahim Mohamed Ahmed, Permanent Mission of the Republic of the Sudan to the United Nations, Member of the UN NGO Committee, interviewed in New York, 17 April 2001

Index

Page numbers in italics indicate tables.

Action Aid Alliance (AAA)
  consultative status, 151, 161
  functions, 43
  history, 43
  relationship with UN, 89–90
  representation to the UN, 121, 159–60
  structure, 43
Amnesty International (AI)
  campaign against torture, 61–2
  functions, 35–6
  history, 34–5
  implementation, 63, 66–8
  information provision to UN, 57–60
  interaction with Security Council, 60–1
  lobbying of the UN, 64
  methods of interaction with UN, 56–7
  offices for UN representation, 100–2
  organizational structures for UN representation, 102–3
  qualifications of representatives, 103–6
  relationship with IGOs in general, 55
  representatives to the UN, 99–100, 158–9
  role as policy advisor to the UN, 65–6, 170
  significance of consultative status, 135–6, 160–1
  significance of interaction with UN, 56, 157–8
  standard setting in UN context, 61–3
  structure, 35
  threats to consultative status, 136–8
Anheier, Helmut, 4, 6
Annan, Kofi, 4
anti-globalization movement, 3
Arria Formula, 48–9, 54, 61, 73, 78–9, 84, 86, 91, 92, 169
Ash, Roberta Garner, 7, 21, 22, 166

Benenson, Peter, 34
Boli, John, 3, 5
boomerang model, 5, 14, 156
bureaucratization, see resource mobilization

Cardoso, Ernesto, see Panel of Eminent Persons on United Nations–Civil Society Relations
CARE (Cooperative for Assistance and Relief Everywhere)
  functions, 39
  history, 38
  information provision to UN, 78
  interaction with Security Council, 78–9
  organizational structures for UN representation, 113–14
  policy advisor to the UN, 76–8
  project implementation in cooperation with UN, 74–6
  qualifications of representatives, 114–15
  relationship with IGOs, 73
  representatives to the UN, 112–13, 158–60
  significance of consultative status, 145–6, 160–1
  significance of UN relations, 73–4, 158
  structure, 38–9
  threats to consultative status, 145–6
  type of consultative status, 144–5
Charnovitz, Steve, 3, 4
Chatfield, Charles, 6, 16
Chiang, Pei-heng, 5, 96, 132, 137, 149, 171, 173
Clapham, Andrew, 60, 62, 67, 169
Commission on Human Rights, 46, 59, 71, 72, 84, 86, 87, 93, 100, 102, 108–9, 118, 132, 136, 138, 142, 143, 158, 173

Committee Against Torture (CAT), 60,
  71, 101, 170
Committee on the Elimination of
  Racial Discrimination (CERD),
  60, 71
consultative status, *see* NGO
  relationship with the UN; *also
  under individual NGOs*
Cook, Helena, 55–6, 58, 61, 65, 66, 68,
  101, 104, 105, 134, 170, 171, 172
corporatism, 6, 163, 173
Council of Europe, 4, 55, 87

Declaration of Human Rights, 36, 56,
  61, 133
della Porta, Donatella, 6, 16
Department of Economic and Social
  Affairs (DESA), *see* NGO Section of
  the Department of Economic and
  Social Affairs
Department of Humanitarian Affairs
  (DHA), *see* Office for the
  Coordination of Humanitarian
  Affairs
Department of Public Information
  (DPI), 25, 149, 167
DiMaggio, Paul J., 7, 23, 24
Doctors without Borders, *see* Médecins
  sans Frontières

expert interviews, 2, 9, 34, 157, 162,
  173

Fédération Internationale des Droits
  de l'Homme (FIDH)
functions, 37–8
history, 36
information provision to the UN,
  70–1, 158
methods and aims, 69–70
offices for UN representation, 108
organizational structures for UN
  representation, 108
policy advisor to UN, 72–3
qualifications of representatives,
  110–11
relationship with IGOs, 69
representatives to the UN, 107–8,
  158–9

significance of consultative status,
  139–42, 160–1
structure, 36–7
threats to consultative status, 142–4
Finger, Matthias, 3, 6, 15, 173
Finnemore, Martha, 23
Food and Agriculture Organization
  (FAO), 75, 76, 81, 100
Friends of the Earth International,
  3, 27

global civil society, 6, 15, 156
Global Policy Forum, 49, 52, 61, 66,
  78, 79, 84, 85, 169
GONGO (Government-Organized
  Non-governmental Organization),
  131, 183
Gordenker, Leon, 5, 18, 19, 26, 31, 32,
  53, 163

High Commissioner for Human Rights
  (HCHR), 62–3, 65–6, 72, 86, 142,
  176
Hüfner, Klaus, 3, 9, 126, 127, 167
Human Rights Committee (CCPR), 57,
  60, 71
Human Rights in China (HRIC), 140–2
Human Rights Watch (HRW)
consultative status, 148–9, 160–1
functions, 42
history, 41
interaction with UN, 85–7
representation to the UN, 118–19,
  158–9
structure, 41–2

institutional channelling, 7–8, 24–5,
  156
institutionalization, 7–8, 10, 17, 20,
  165–6
Inter-Agency Standing Committee
  (IASC), 47–8, 84, 89, *92*, 158
interest group, 6, 9, 165; *see also*
  corporatism
intergovernmental organizations
  (IGOs), 10
growth of, 2
types of, *10*
Intermon, *see* Oxfam International

International Bank for Reconstruction and Development (IBRD), 75
International Committee of the Red Cross (ICRC), 81
International Council of Voluntary Associations (ICVA), 83, 147
International Covenant on Civil and Political Rights, 57
International Covenant on Economic, Social and Cultural Rights, 57
International Criminal Court (ICC), 63, 104, 170
International Federation Terre des Hommes (IFTDH), 27
International Labour Organization (ILO), 55, 69, 73
International League for Human Rights (ILHR)
  consultative status, 149–50, 160–1
  functions, 42
  history, 42
  interaction with UN, 87–8
  representation to the UN, 119–20, 158–9
  structure, 42
international organizations, *see* intergovernmental organizations; nongovernmental organizations
International Save the Children Alliance (ISCA)
  consultative status, 150–1, 160–1
  functions, 43
  history, 42–3
  interaction with UN, 88–9
  representation to the UN, 120–1, 159–60
  structure, 42–3
iron law of oligarchy, 7; *see also* Michels, Robert
isomorphism; *see* neo-instiutionalism

Jenkins, Craig J., 25, 28

Kaldor, Mary, 165
Keck, Margaret, 3, 5, 14, 30, 165
King, Gary, 168
Korey, William, 42, 57, 58, 59, 61, 62, 86, 148, 150, 172
Kriesi, Hanspeter, 16

Lagoni, Rainer, 131, 134, 167
Lipschutz, Ronnie D., 6, 15
logic of collective action, 6

Marks, Gary, 165
Martens, Kerstin, 9, 163, 165
McAdam, Doug, 165
McCarthy, John, 7, 21, 23, 24, 25, 29, 165, 166, 167
McPhail, Clark, 24
Médecins sans Frontières (MSF), 61, 78
Meyer, David S., 166, 167
Meyer, John W., 23, 24
Michels, Robert, 7, 20, 21, 166

Najam, Adil, 164, 166
neo-institutionalism, 23–5
NGO activities, types of, *19*
  policy developing processes, 18
  policy implementing practices, 19
  policy initiating activities, 18
NGO relationship with the UN
  application process for consultative status, 130–1
  criteria for consultative status, 127–8, 167
  information provision, 46–8
  lobbying, 49
  numbers of NGOs with consultative status, 128–9
  policy advisor, 49–52
  policy implementing, 52–4
  representatives to the UN, 95–9, 171
  resolutions concerning consultative status, 126–7
  value of consultative status, *154*
  withdrawal of consultative status, 132–3
NGO Section of the Department of Economic and Social Affairs (DESA), 130, 132
Non-Governmental Liaison Service (NGLS), 25, 83, 167
nongovernmental organizations (NGOs), 9
  advocacy function of, 30–1, 158–60, 160–2
  centralist structure of, 27–8, 158–60, 160–2

nongovernmental organizations
(NGOs) – *continued*
  composition of, 25–8, 158–60, 160–2
  federative structure of, 26–7,
    158–60, 160–2
  functions of, 30–1, 158–60, 160–2
  growth of, 2
  legitimacy of, 164
  participation at UN world
    conferences, 3, 9, 50
  relations to IGOs in general, 3–4
  relations to the League of Nations, 3
  service function of, 31, 158–60,
    160–2
North Atlantic Treaty Organization
  (NATO), 10, 164
Novib, *see* Oxfam International
Nullmeier, Frank, 22, 168

Office for the Coordination of
  Humanitarian Affairs (OCHA), 53,
  54, 67, 76, 82, 84, 86
Olson, Mancur, 6
Organization for Security and
  Cooperation in Europe (OSCE), 4,
  69, 87
Organization of American States
  (OAS), 55, 69
Oxfam International
  functions, 41
  history, 39
  interaction with Security Council,
    84–5
  organizational structures for UN
    representation, 116–17
  policy advisor to the UN, 82–4
  project implementation in
    cooperation with UN, 81–2
  qualifications of representatives,
    117–18
  relationship with IGOs, 79
  relationship with UN, 80–1, 158
  representatives to the UN, 115–16,
    158–60
  significance of consultative status,
    147, 160–1
  structure, 40–1
  threats to consultative status, 148
  type of consultative status, 146–7

Oxford Committee for Famine Relief,
  40; *see also* Oxfam International

Pagnucco, Ron, 6, 16, 35, 40
Panel of Eminent Persons on United
  Nations–Civil Society Relations, 4
Passy, Florence, 15, 16
Paul, James, 49, 143, 169
political opportunity structures (POS),
  15–16, 156, 165
Powell, Walter W., 7, 23, 24
professionalization, *see* resource
  mobilization
Przeworski, Adam, 168

Raschke, Joachim, 166, 167, 168
representation of NGOs to the UN, *see*
  under NGO relationship with the
  UN; *also under individual NGOs*
Resolution 1996/31, 127–8, 132, 172
resource mobilization, 7–8, 21–2, 156
Risse, Thomas, 5, 13, 14, 163
Rittberger, Volker, 3, 10, 30, 31, 32,
  168
Rodley, Nigel, 56, 61
Rowan, Brian, 23, 24
Rucht, Dieter, 15, 20, 22, 165, 167, 168

Salamon, Lester M., 2, 6, 166
Schmitter, Philippe C., 6
Schmitz, Hans Peter, 28, 50, 101, 148
Scoble, Harry M., 26, 36, 119
Scott, W. Richard, 9, 24, 163, 166
Sikkink, Kathryn, 3, 5, 14, 30, 165
Skjelsbaek, Kjell, 96
Smith, Jackie, 3, 4, 6, 15, 16, 27, 28,
  35, 36, 40, 165
social movement organization, 6, 7, 9,
  10, 12, 14, 20–24, 165–8
social movements, *see* social
  movement organization
social movement theory, 7, 17, 163,
  166; *see also* social movement
  organization
Somavia Formula, *see* Arria Formula
Sphere Project, 51
spiral model, 14, 156
Staggenborg, Suzanne, 22
Stamp, Elizabeth, 81, 82, 83

Steering Committee for Humanitarian Response (SCHR), 50–1, 77, 84, 89, 90, *92*, 113, 158

Tarrow, Sidney, 16, 166, 167
Taylor, Paul, 4, 26
Teune, Henry, 168
third sector, 6, 18, 166
Tilly, Charles, 165
Tocqueville, Alexis de, 6
transnational social movement organization, 6, 165; *see also* social movement organization

Union of International Associations (UIA), 2
United Nations Children's Fund (UNICEF), 67, 75, 76, 78, 81, 82, 84, 86, 88–90, *92*
United Nations Development Programme (UNDP), 67, 75, 76, 78, 82, 84, 86, 88, 89, 90, 170
United Nations Educational, Scientific and Cultural Organization (UNESCO), 55, 62, 67, 69
United Nations Fund for Population Activities (UNFPA), 74, 76
United Nations High Commissioner for Refugees (UNHCR), 50, 52, 53, 67, 75, 76, 78, 80–2, 86, 88, 89, *92*, 105, 112
United Nations Relief and Work Agency (UNRWA), 81, 89

UN Secretary-General, *see under* Annan, Kofi

van Rooy, Alison, 3

Wahl, Peter, 163
Wapner, Paul, 6, 15
Weiss, Thomas G., 5, 6, 18, 19, 26, 31, 32, 53
Weschler, Joanna, 46, 50, 54, 56, 87, 97, 169
White, Lyman C., 26
Willetts, Peter, 5, 9, 10, 18, 19, 30, 31, 127, 167
Wiseberg, Laurie S., 26, 36, 119
Working Group on the Security Council (WGSC), 51–2, 54, 66, 72, 84, 86, 88, 89, 90, *91*, *92*
World Food Programme (WFP), 75, 76, 78, 82, 89, 112
World Health Organization (WHO), 67, 81, 89
World Trade Union Congress (WTUC), 126

Young, Dennis R., 18, 19, 25, 26, 166, 167, 169

Zald, Mayer N., 7, 21, 22, 25, 29, 166
Zimmer, Annette, 6